The Ethical Gourmet

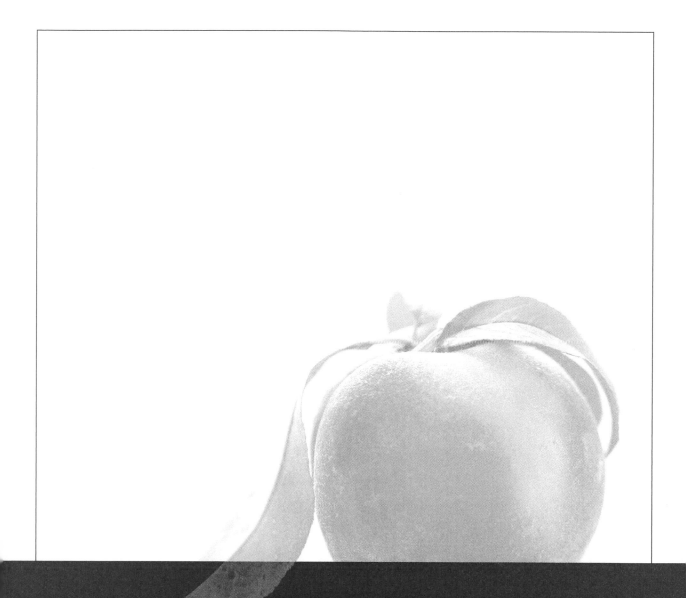

The Ethical Gourmet

Jay Weinstein

BROADWAY BOOKS NEW YORK

PRINTED IN THE UNITED STATES OF AMERICA

BROADWAY BOOKS and its logo, a letter B bisected on the diagonal, are trademarks of Random House, Inc.

Visit our Web site at www.broadwaybooks.com

Book design by Vertigo Design / NYC

Library of Congress Cataloging-in-Publication Data
Weinstein, Jay, 1965–
The ethical gourmet / Jay Weinstein.—1st ed.
p. cm.
Includes index.
1. Cookery (Natural foods) 2. Natural foods. I. Title.
TX741.W43 2006
641.5′63—dc22
2005053630

ISBN 0-7679-1834-7

10   9   8   7   6   5   4   3   2

First Edition

THIS BOOK IS DEDICATED, WITH LOVE AND RESPECT, TO MY PARENTS.

Contents

Acknowledgments

Thanks to my father, Seymour Weinstein, whose support, advice, research, and encouragement were indispensable in the writing of this book. Special thanks to my partner, Tuan Pu Wang, for keeping me focused on the task at hand and smoothing the rough places in the road. Thanks to Jacques de Spoelberch, a true gentleman, without whom this book would never have seen the light of day. Thanks to Jennifer Josephy, whose thoughtful guidance helped me refine rough concepts into finished thoughts. Thanks to Lucy Cohen, for her help with my research.

Chefs at the Culinary Institute of America and elsewhere, including Hinnerk von Bargen, Anna and David Kasabian, David Kamen, Kathryn Matthews, and Veronica Arcoraci, worked hard in the kitchen, testing and refining the recipes contained here. Thanks to my friends John Carroll and Mary Palermo, Josh Martin, James Moses, Rebecca Freedman, Douglas Clark, Momo Attaoui, Kevin Mulcahy, and Eric Svenson and to my sister, Naomi Dreeben, for their contributions, including hundreds of essential news clippings.

Numerous great chefs, especially Jasper White, instilled in me a respect for ingredients with integrity, for which I am eternally grateful. Thanks to Tim Cole and Diane Muhlfeld for giving me the latitude to work on this project. And thanks to the scientists, environmentalists, culinarians, and ethical consumers who are making the world a better place through their actions.

The Ethical Gourmet

Introduction

We're at a turning point in the history of American food production, when a reborn ethic—that we're responsible for the way we treat the land and its bounty—is changing what we see on our supermarket shelves and dinner plates.

Flavor, freshness, and overall quality of food are rising. It's easier than ever to buy ingredients that don't despoil the environment, exploit endangered wildlife, or create undue suffering in the world.

We have all heard of the rain forests that are continually disappearing, the rivers that are being polluted, and the acid rain that is harming our very being. But most of us are so overwhelmed by the magnitude of the problems that we just throw up our hands when it comes to trying to help solve them. This book is written in the belief that if each of us does his or her part we can make a difference, and the world will be a better place for it.

These pages feature more than a hundred recipes that showcase mainstream organic fruits and vegetables and ethically raised products. A combination lifestyle guide, shopper's resource, and cookbook, this book brings together the concepts, sources, and methods for enjoying today's conscientiously raised harvest.

The age of the industrial organic farm has arrived. While bad news for some small organic farmers, it's a boon for the ethical gourmet. Agribusiness, armed with the Food and Drug Administration's new organic labeling law, is undercutting mom and pop in the pesticide-free, naturally fertilized food market. Quality organic and environmentally sensitive food products are going mainstream—available in supermarkets and other food stores throughout the United States and abroad.

The vast majority of Americans identify themselves as environmentalists. If they had a choice, they would choose fish from nonendangered stocks, produce whose growth doesn't pollute the land and waterways, and pork from pigs that led a good life. Every recipe in this book is based on that assumption: People do the right thing if all else is equal. Here's a way to put beliefs into practice.

Whole grains used to be hard to find. They can replace meat's nutritional role if you can find them. Now, supermarkets carry wheat berries and quinoa. Even if yours doesn't, this book will tell you where to get them easily. You'll learn to recognize brand names of humanely raised meat and poultry you can trust, names of endangered fish and game species you'll want to avoid (even though they're cheap and widely available), and produce you know is grown right, even if it's from a factory farm.

With the endangered status of wild edibles constantly in flux, it's more important than ever to know the causes of species loss and the types of harvesting that wound the ecosystem. With the help of this book, savvy consumers will be able to assess for themselves the impact they make with each purchase.

No matter what the organic moralists tell you, there's no credible evidence that organic foods are any more nutritious than nonorganic foods. But there are good reasons to choose them. Their pesticide-free production causes much less pollution and degradation to the land and water that nourish them. They're free from dangerous residues. They also usually taste better. Ditto for humanely raised livestock. This book allows responsible stewards of the Earth to enjoy delicious foods. You can open any page of this cookbook and find recipes that will not make you feel guilty about what you're doing to the sea, air, or land. At the same time, you'll be making an unintentionally healthy choice by moving powerful pesticides out of your diet and giving meat an exalted place, rather than an overbearing one, on your menu, as a complement to wholesome grains, vegetables, and legumes.

The recipes come from my years of fine-dining restaurant experience and the Culinary Institute of America (CIA) training built into my repertoire, tempered by my lifelong commitment to the environment, understanding of our food system, and my respect for living things. My independent insight, earned from years of professional buying and cooking, is not driven by producers, but by knowledge, research, and principle.

In the 1980s, my chef and mentor at a New American restaurant in Boston's North End, Jasper White, engaged in the kind of ingredient sourcing that was sweeping the nation, from Alice Waters's Chez Panisse in Berkeley and Mark Miller's Coyote Café in Santa Fe to Paul Prudhomme's K-Paul's in New Orleans and Larry Forgione's American Place in New York. They were rejecting the consolidated food suppliers that had arisen in the last half-century, and going back to buying directly from producers. Jasper sourced ingredients from between sixty and seventy companies, large and small, while other, larger restaurants were buying from only six or seven megadistributors. Of course, we had accounts with giant suppliers like Sexton and Sysco, who sold virtually everything from daikon radishes to dish detergent. But Jasper White and his colleagues across America knew that the principles of buying locally, direct from producers, had tangible benefits that were being undermined by the consolidated food distribution system our country had developed since the end of World War II. That concept—consciously choosing where to buy ingredients rather than always going to the most convenient seller—makes as much sense for the individual as it does for the restaurateur.

We all care about preserving natural beauty, eliminating the suffering of the underprivileged, and treating animals humanely. But to put our money where our mouths are, we have to look beyond the convenience of supermarkets and "big box" stores some of the time. As the New American restaurant chefs know, there is a place for the big players in food sourcing. But there's also a place for producers who sell direct to the consumer. To know when to buy at Costco and when to buy from a family farm stand, or when to pick up meat at the supermarket versus when to order it over the Internet, read the pages ahead.

When you're the only one of your friends paying extra for organic milk or boycotting Atlantic cod, it's easy to think that your efforts are for naught, but what you're doing does matter. Instead of seeing yourself as filling the ocean with a teaspoon, think of eating ethically in the same way you view giving money to a grossly underfunded charity to, say, free African children from the threat of malaria. You won't be able to cure malaria by yourself. Perhaps even all of the current efforts to solve the problem aren't enough to end the scourge. But if your contribution buys one mosquito net that prevents one child from contracting the disease, then your effort has meaning.

The Politics of Food

Pork is more than just the other white meat. Political pork is the driving force behind needless overproduction in agricultural states where congressional representatives bring home federal farm subsidies.

The lion's share of these subsidies go not to the mythical "family farmer" so often evoked by politicians on both sides of the aisle, but to giant agribusinesses looking to fatten their bottom line. While factory farming isn't all bad (it may even be the route to affordable organic foods for the masses), paying off corporations for political support is undemocratic, and it undermines our natural environment. Protectionist tariffs, like those recently imposed on farmed catfish from Vietnam, undermine a proven ecologically responsible industry in a sensitive region to coddle a domestic niche in politically valuable Southern states. Cheese connoisseurs in the United States have lamented for years that fine, artisanal European cheeses are disingenuously prohibited because of so-called health protections. Obviously, the French, Italians, and Spanish aren't dropping like flies with every bite of raw-milk Morbier, Taleggio, and Cabrales. Could lobbyists for America's hormone-crazed dairy industry be behind the ban? Food quality and prices are more closely linked to government policy than many people know.

Agricultural Doublespeak

We love our cheap food in this country as much as we love our cheap gasoline. Most Americans think that farm subsidies are keeping food affordable. But agricultural subsidies hide the real cost of our foods, by artifically depressing prices of domestically produced goods with money paid by taxpayers. It's like giving the ice cream man a couple of hundred bucks every summer in return for a promise that he'll keep the price of a cone at one dollar. Sugar is the most egregious example, but wheat, soy, rice, and corn (the most heavily subsidized crop) also have hidden costs. Soy, mostly used as livestock feed in the meat industry, seldom reaches our plates in the healthy form of soy protein. Instead, it shows up as inexpensive (read: subsidized) oil and margarine, staples of processed foods. Both sugar and corn contribute to the massive oversweetening of the American diet that many nutritionists believe has led to the obesity epidemic in the U.S. I personally believe the roots of our country's weight problem lie mostly with excessive portion sizes and unwise individual choices, but one could argue that these are fueled by cheap food, too. In any case, this is less a book about health and good looks than a discussion of how what's beneficial for us in the short run can wreck our land in the long run.

Subsidies on food production give domestic producers a leg up on foreign competitors. I guess that was the original intention of most of these expensive programs. But while we encourage other peoples to adopt our economic system and values, we demand that they live up to standards we don't expect of ourselves. America encouraged impoverished Vietnamese farmers to convert their rice paddies into catfish farms so that they could produce a more lucrative crop and lift themselves out of economic stagnation (presumably so they could buy more American goods). But when they proved highly successful at raising catfish and began to export them, the U.S. put up trade barriers to protect domestic catfish farmers.

The farm bill signed in May 2002 by President George W. Bush represented nearly $200 billion in agricultural subsidies, mostly going to large corporate farms. The result is a vast oversupply and lower prices, which will inevitably lead to calls for more subsidies. I wish I could say that just one political party was the party of big subsidies, and the other was the one to vote for if you're concerned about destructive and wasteful farm policies. But on this issue, both major parties have shameful histories.

If farm subsidies are so counterproductive, enriching megafarm corporations far more than the much-glorified family farmer and supporting destructive encroachment of farming into ecologically sensitive areas, why hasn't the process been eliminated yet? The answer is simple: politics. Leaders of farm states need subsidy-supported farmers' votes, so they use all of their leverage, on both sides of the political aisle, to maintain the status quo. It's the most brazen example of buying votes in the country.

SCIENCE TAKES ITS LUMPS No administration has manipulated science to suit its own agenda as much as the administration of George W. Bush. From its endless "wait and see" approach to looming crises like global warming to the promotion of mineral and oil exploration in sensitive ecological areas, the Bush administration has chosen industry giveaways over science every time. Food policy reflects this approach. For example, the administration's policy makers redefined the term "wild" so that hatchery fish are counted in with threatened wild steelhead trout species. This enables them to fill Western rivers with genetically different hatchery spawn so they can circumvent protections that regulate irrigation diversions—a giveaway to corporate farmers looking for more free water. Similarly, the administration has made rule changes that will count hatchery salmon in with wild, so that much larger counts will be used to assess whether to remove fifteen species of salmon from federal threatened and endangered species lists.

FIDDLING WHILE ROME BURNS: REGULATORY GAMES Our employer-employee relationship with our elected representatives is an odd one. We hire them to enact our interests into law, but we can't exactly give them direct orders. Once they're hired, they can pretty much do as they please, at least until the next election comes around. Lately, many of the people we've hired to represent us in Congress have approached their jobs as though by doing nothing, they'll offend no one.

As industrial fishing operations strip-mine the oceans of large fish (wiping out 90 percent of them over the last thirty years), three initiatives to protect oceans and estuaries languish. Our leaders instead choose to debate the wording of the Pledge of Allegiance. While millions of gallons of fuel are burned flying foreign foods to our shores, consumers remain uninformed about the origins of most of their foods. A provision of the otherwise-egregious 2002 Farm Bill mandating country-of-origin labeling lies idle, while our representatives refine the definition of marriage. While consumers unknowingly buy severely depleted wild fish, legislation that would require stores to label fish as farmed or wild sits in limbo. Our elected officials are busy enacting additional tax cuts that will incur debts for future generations. Unfortunately, endangered birds, fish, forests, flora, and fauna have no voice—no representatives. But from the looks of our latest congressional sessions, it wouldn't do them much good anyway.

The White House has become much stronger because of Congress's inaction. Under the administration of George W. Bush, environmental regulations have been weakened, ecologically sensitive areas have been exploited for mineral wealth, polluters have been given massive breaks, and environmentalists have been maligned as nuisances at best, traitors at worst. In his drive to link every part of his agenda with the terror attacks of September 11 and the all-encompassing war on terror, the president has implied that opponents of his oil-drilling initiatives in the Arctic National Wildlife Refuge support continued dependence on oil from despotic Middle Eastern states. In rejecting the Kyoto global warming treaty, he severed U.S. environmental policy from that of the rest of the civilized world. A former head of the Environmental Protection Agency (EPA) for two Republican presidents called President Bush's record a "polluter protection" policy, saying he's weakened the Clean Air Act, among other things. The administration's disastrous policies, combined with Congress's inaction, have set America on a downhill slide that may take years to reverse. Food policy, strongly tied to land and ocean management policies, needs major attention from our politicians. Only a few are taking action.

The tug-of-war between the interests of the food industry and the concerns of voters sometimes forces politicians to choose between corporate and public benefit. Crop subsidies, drinking water protection, origin labeling, and organic certification are some issues where congressmen must grapple with their two constituencies: big donors and individual voters. The big donors fuel campaigns that draw more individual voters, so the choice is often money driven. That may be what decided the awful Farm Bill of 2002.

That single piece of legislation, originally intended by senators Tom Harkin (D-Iowa) and Richard Lugar (R-Indiana) as an ecologically constructive way to give small farmers a hand while ending huge agricultural subsidies, morphed into the most destructive policy the administration had undertaken until the Iraq invasion. It ended up costing taxpayers $248 billion—representing an increase of more than 80 percent over the 1996 Farm Bill. Since the aid focuses its cash largesse mainly on eight "program" crops (cotton, wheat, corn, soybeans, rice, barley, oats, and sorghum), it predominantly benefits breadbasket states, which happen to be electoral swing states.

During the run-up to the 2004 presidential election, the Food and Drug Administration did the beef and feed industries a huge favor: It slowed down. Following revelations about a case of mad cow disease in Washington State in 2003, the federal regulators had promised to swiftly reform practices in the meat industry that foment disease. But, in an effort to placate corporate sponsors of the Bush administration, the agency took steps to delay the most significant changes involving what could and could not be included in animal feed. Breaking with years of nonpartisan tradition, in 2004 the National Cattlemen's Association endorsed President Bush for reelection immediately after the delays were announced. It's common for agencies to go into semihibernation around election time, a process known as "slow rolling" to ensure that no controversial decisions upset the reelection campaign. But with the health of the American people and the welfare of tens of millions of animals at stake, this case of government inaction is particularly egregious.

We who care deeply about the Earth and other living things need to take back our policy-making role in this country. That means choosing candidates who stand up for the environment. To review ratings for all senators and congressional representatives, look at environmental scorecards and environmental group endorsements on the following Web sites: www.lcv.org and www.sierraclub.org.

HOLY ROLLING: WHEN RELIGION STEAMROLLS THE ENVIRONMENT

Environmental destruction is insignificant to anyone who believes that all must be destroyed for the coming of the Messiah. Today, belief in what is called the rapture, a global apocalypse preceding the salvation of all believers, is a fundamental belief of our most powerful elected leaders. From the White House to the houses of Congress, nearly half of our leadership receives between 80 and 100 percent endorsement from the three main proponents of that theory—the country's most powerful Christian right organizations.

The belief that the Day of Judgment requires the annihilation of nature is driving environmental policy in our time, with the White House and its congressional allies (including Senate Majority Leader Bill Frist, Assistant Majority Leader Mitch McConnell, Conference Chair Rick Santorum of Pennsylvania, House Speaker Dennis Hastert, and Majority Leader Roy Blunt) taking aim at the pillars of our nation's environmental protections, including land management policies on food production.

Along with the well-publicized agenda of oil and gas exploration of the Arctic National Wildlife Refuge and Padre Island National Seashore (the last pristine stretch of the great wild seashores that once hugged our perimeter); downward revisions of the Clean Water Act, Clean Air Act, and Endangered Species Act; and relaxations of emission standards for cars, SUVs, and heavy equipment (including farm machinery), the administration has set its sights on endangered species protections from pesticides, and it wants to waive environmental review for grazing permits on public lands. The free-for-all for polluters can easily be shrugged off by anyone who believes, as one-third of Americans do, according to a 2004 Gallup poll, that environmental degradation is part of God's divine plan.

It's against this backdrop that the not-for-profit caretakers of the last parcels of sensitive wilderness—groups like World Wildlife Federation, Sierra Club, and The Nature Conservancy—fret over the likely repercussions of the 2004 elections. What Vice President Dick Cheney describes as a mandate is viewed by many in the environmental movement as a death sentence to the most vulnerable creatures, lands, and waters in America. The irony that disdain for environmental safeguards is being practiced in the name of religion, which praises God for creation, is undeniable.

In a speech upon receiving the Global Environment Citizen Award from Harvard Medical School's Center for Health and the Global Environment, journalist Bill Moyers, an ordained Baptist minister, spoke about the wave of adherence to a doomsday belief sweeping the nation under the title, "The Godly Must Be Crazy." He pointed out that the bestselling books in the country are the twelve volumes of the "Left Behind" series by right-wing fundamentalist zealot Timothy LaHaye, who cites what Moyers calls "a fantastical theology concocted in the nineteenth century by a couple of immigrant preachers who took disparate passages from the Bible and wove them into a narrative that has captivated the imagination of millions of Americans." His succinct synopsis of the movement's viewpoint is chilling:

> Its outline is rather simple, if bizarre (the British writer George Monbiot recently did a brilliant dissection of it and I am indebted to him for adding to my own understanding): Once Israel has occupied the rest of its "biblical lands," legions of the anti-Christ will attack it, triggering a final showdown in the valley of Armageddon. As the Jews who have not been converted are burned, the Messiah will return for the rapture. True believers will be lifted out of their clothes and transported to heaven, where, seated next to the right hand of God, they will watch their political and religious opponents suffer plagues of boils, sores, locusts, and frogs during the several years of tribulation that follow.
>
> So what does this mean for public policy and the environment? Go to Grist [www.grist.org] to read a remarkable work of reporting by the journalist

Glenn Scherer—"the road to environmental apocalypse." Read it and you will see how millions of Christian fundamentalists may believe that environmental destruction is not only to be disregarded but actually welcomed—even hastened—as a sign of the coming apocalypse.

I read Moyers's words with horror but not surprise. It explained a lot about what was happening in our country, and how a toxic mixture of theology and ideology was taking us back to the future. We who believe in the value of nature, and try to protect it, are being swept back, along with the rest of the country, to an antiscience, anti-free-thought Dark Age, where fatalism and profligacy go hand in hand. We must swim against the tide if we hope to preserve what's left of our natural environment, and get back on the path toward making the world a cleaner place, with better quality of life for future generations of humans and our wild cohabitants on this planet.

"What would Jesus drive?" was the question posed by a responsible evangelical group, the Evangelical Environmental Network, which cites scripture in support of environmental protection. Noting that pollution causes suffering and disease, the group's Web site, www.whatwouldjesusdrive.org, cites the most famous proverb, "Do unto others as you would have them do unto you." Evoking Christianity's values of peace and goodwill, the group says that "dependence on foreign oil from unstable regions heightens the potential for armed conflict . . . working against the Prince of Peace."

The group's message about the real threats of global warming cites declines in agricultural output in poorer countries as one of the serious consequences the phenomenon may bring. By addressing the possibility that 80 to 90 million poor people could be at risk of hunger and malnutrition later in the twenty-first century, the group is sending out the message that I had thought religions generally taught: Help the poor first. The approach they're taking is "Protect and improve the things we share: air, water, and earth."

How Green Are the Golden Arches? If someone had told me a few years ago that McDonald's was insisting on humane practices from its chicken suppliers (mainly Tyson), phasing out growth-promoting antibiotics in its

meat supply, and touting organic salad dressings, I'd have thought he or she had mad cow disease. But the company *is* bowing to consumer concerns and making some changes. Premium producers like Ben & Jerry's ice cream, Starbucks coffee, and Sara Lee cakes have also made some (but not all) important decisions based on fair labor practices in foreign countries, sustainable practices from suppliers, and environmental protection. No major corporations are yet wholly dedicated to comprehensive ethical decision making, but efforts of those who are heading in the right direction should be reinforced with consumer support.

If McDonald's PR machine is to be believed, the company is not only benign, but a force for global good, cutting down on consumers' waste, helping reform the most inhumane practices of the meat industry, stemming the tide of rain forest destruction, and more. And if the animal rights groups, environmental organizations, and antiglobalization forces are to be believed, the company is bringing on the apocalypse, with utter disregard for animal welfare, massive pollution, decent standards of living for the underprivileged, and dwindling biodiversity. The truth lies somewhere in the middle.

WHAT CAME FIRST: THE CHICKEN McNUGGET OR THE EGG POLICY?

In a classic case of creating a problem and then taking credit for solving it, McDonald's is taking steps to end the trend of excessive antibiotic use in animal agriculture. Of course, the company's gargantuan demand for cheap meat products was one of the key forces that led to the egregious practices that have become commonplace in America's factory-farm meat-production system. Conditions caused by the speeding up of production, such as overcrowding and stacking of animals in dangerous forms of confinement, led to the higher rate of injury and infections that producers say necessitated preventive antibiotics applications. And the company's demand for massive amounts of chicken also led to the administering of antibiotics for the sole purpose of promoting faster growth in the birds.

Starting in the late 1990s, McDonald's began routinely auditing production facilities of its suppliers for adherence to humane treatment standards the company had developed with respected animal behaviorist Temple Grandin. The standards affected the living conditions and slaughter practices for cattle and pigs, as well as confinement criteria for egg-laying hens. Again, the company was addressing problems created, at least in part, by its own demands for cheap, plentiful products. Conditions had gotten so bad for animals by the 1980s that consumers were beginning to heed the alarms being raised by animal rights groups like People for the Ethical Treatment of Animals (PETA), who had been saying for years that meat industry practices were tantamount to torture. The bad publicity forced the company's hand. McDonald's now pays a little more for its eggs.

The company's humane standards are not yet equal to those that will be mandated by European Union (EU) animal welfare guidelines, scheduled to take effect in 2012, but are in line with humane standards set in place by United Egg Producers (UEP), an industry group that raised the bar in 1999. Those guidelines increased the minimum space allotted to each hen from between 48 and 54 square inches to between 67 and 84 square inches. At 48 square inches (about half the size of a sheet of copier paper), the hens had become so violent that they routinely pecked and scratched at each other through the cages, leading producers to cut off toes and beaks.

The European standards will prohibit "battery cages," where rows and tiers of wire cages confine the animals on sloped grades. The EU standards will also increase minimum cage size to one-third larger than the U.S. standard, and require that hens have a perch (which is comfortable for the hens, and promotes good leg bone health) and a litter-lined nest box to retreat to for laying eggs and natural dust-bathing activity. No word on when, if ever, McDonald's will adopt the stricter European standards, but the company does set trends. Burger King adopted the UEP standards shortly after McDonald's did. Now it's estimated that 80 percent of eggs produced in the United States are produced according to those standards. For consumers who wish to buy eggs that meet or exceed the coming EU regulations, Humane Farm Animal Care, an animal rights group, has instituted a certification program for beef, pigs, dairy cattle, laying hens, and broiler chickens. The label "Certified Humane Raised & Handled" indicates that the group audited eggs/meat/milk production and found it to be in compliance with its strict standards, posted at www.certifiedhumane.com.

WHERE'S THE BEEF? Although McDonald's has claimed for years that it never utilized beef grazed on land cleared from Amazon rain forest, witnesses have taken the stand in trials against the company in Britain, alleging they personally saw Brazilian rain forest slashed and burned to create land from which McDonald's currently sources beef. That said, the widespread belief that McDonald's is a major force behind the destruction of rain forests is untrue. Its American and Canadian outlets use only domestically produced beef, and European outlets use almost exclusively European beef.

McDonald's claim that it is eliminating growth-promoting antibiotic use in its meat is overblown (yes, antibiotics promote accelerated growth, just as hormones do). First of all, it merely *encourages* producers of beef, pork, and dairy to comply. Second, the directive applies only to firms that produce the meat *specifically* for McDonald's. That leaves a full 30 percent not even being "encouraged." Yes, lip service is better than nothing, and may yield some improvements, but for listings of eateries, markets, and producers near you that really do prohibit antibiotic-fattened meat, go to the search engine at www.eatwellguide.org, a service of the agro-environmentalist organization Institute for Agriculture and Trade Policy (www.iatp.org).

Shamefully, McDonald's, by its never-ending expansion into new markets, is promoting an ever-increasing worldwide demand for meat, which is indirectly responsible for 60 percent of the pesticides sprayed in the United States alone (in the form of treatments for corn and soybeans raised as feed). It is estimated that 70 percent of all water consumed in the U.S. is used to grow feed and provide drinking water for livestock (much of it in the drought-plagued West). McDonald's alone isn't responsible for the worldwide trend away from vegetable-based diets and toward meat-based diets. But it's a force, and is unapologetic about that.

THE VALUE OF WORK The fast-food industry possesses considerable political clout, and has used its influence to depress wages and worker protections. Industry lobbyists fight fiercely to prevent increases in the minimum wage, which is now worth only 40 percent of what it was in 1970, in inflation-adjusted dollars. Although the meatpacking industry, of which McDonald's is the world's biggest customer, has the highest incidence of workplace injuries in the country (exceeding even coal mining and firefighting), lobbyists, along with their mostly Republican allies in Congress and the White House, have ensured that safety oversight is minimal. Favorable legislation allows meatpackers in Texas to exempt their employees from workers' compensation. Instead, the company provides its own "compensation" on its own terms.

One form of worker exploitation that's become more common is intimidation.

Workers in slaughterhouses and meatpacking plants are told to hush up about injuries, so that the industry, facing public criticism about abusive work conditions, can claim that injuries are going down, rather than up. The workers, many of them illegal aliens, are cowed in submission, in fear of losing much-needed jobs.

Most fast-food employees earn the minimum wage, and the industry, the fastest-growing employer in the country, pursues mainly teenagers and immigrant labor to staff its stores. The McDonald's Corporation doesn't set wages paid at its franchisees' restaurants, but it sets conditions, such as food prices, that depress wages. A cycle of teens working at fast-food outlets, falling behind in school, and becoming trapped in a low-wage life track is widening the gap between rich and poor.

Farmworkers, mostly undocumented immigrants, are the nation's poorest group of workers. Migrant pickers of tomatoes and other agricultural products earn less than $8,000 a year, and the companies for whom they work often charge them for food, housing, transportation, and sometimes the fees paid to "wolves" who smuggle them across the border. In early 2005, boycotts and public outcry over the abuses of these modern-day slaves reached critical mass in Florida, where Yum Brands, owner of Taco Bell, KFC, Pizza Hut, and other fast-food brands, agreed to a stricter set of standards for farms that supply the millions of pounds of tomatoes Taco Bell uses every week. Their commitment amounts to a penny-per-pound increase in what they pay for tomatoes, but should roughly double the wages of many workers on their suppliers' farms. It seems that if we're unable to foment meaningful change through the government, pressure on corporate citizens is a good second line of attack for those who wish to end the exploitation of workers in our own country.

Fair Is Fair Trade

Buying locally supports our communities and reduces pollution. But some foods will never be local. Coffee, tea, and cocoa require tropical growing conditions that most of the United States doesn't have. However, half of Americans are regular coffee drinkers, and almost everyone eats chocolate. Raw materials for these beloved foods come from some of the poorest places on earth. When worldwide coffee prices collapsed in 2002, average prices for double lattes in

America, the world's largest importer of coffee, hardly budged. But millions of small-farmers who depend on coffee growing for their livelihood fell into abject poverty and debt. Only those producers who were guaranteed a fair price for their product, regardless of market fluctuations, were able to avoid the suffering. Those farmers were supported by buyers of Fair Trade–certified coffee. Fair Trade is a nongovernmental organization that certifies products produced according to its standards. The organization's American branch is called TransFair USA (www.transfairusa.org).

In exchange for conducting their farming in sustainable ways, these farmers received a livable rate of income, technological support, and help with their children's education.

More than 80 percent of Fair Trade coffee in the United States is certified organic. Fair Trade coffee is mostly grown under various fruit and shade trees. By contrast, the past thirty years have seen a dramatic increase in production due to the introduction of higher-yielding plants that grow in full sun. In addition to the massive deforestation required to cultivate these varieties, petrochemical fertilizers have been introduced to boost yields even higher. Most growers sell to middlemen, who pay them pennies on the dollar, and then sell to companies like Maxwell House (Kraft Foods) and Folgers (Procter & Gamble). Those two companies supply 56 percent of the U.S. market. Fair

Trade products, certified in the United States by the nonprofit organization TransFair USA, cuts out middlemen and brokers, getting growers their fair share of the final market value of their products.

A SYSTEM FROZEN IN TIME On an April day, a slave ship carried several dozen boys and girls from Benin, West Africa, bound for plantations where they were destined to work as unpaid laborers. The year was 2001, and the plantations were cocoa farms in Central Africa. The ship was denied entry to several ports, and the case focused world attention, briefly, on the trafficking of child slave labor in a little-discussed industry. The cocoa industry, which produces products for the $13 billion United States cocoa and chocolate market, is one of the most egregious abusers of child labor. In Ivory Coast, which supplies 43 percent of the world's cocoa, one-third of farmers' children have never attended school. Most farmers employ their own children in dangerous machete harvesting of crops and distribution of toxic pesticides. It doesn't have to be this way.

Fair Trade demands that its farmers adhere to strict child labor standards. No child under the age of eighteen may harvest with machetes or other dangerous tools or apply pesticides. Children under fifteen may work on the farm only if their education is not jeopardized. American consumers do have a choice when buying chocolate. We must exercise it. Stores like those in the Wild Oats Marketplace chain, Starbucks coffee stores, and Whole Foods and Fairway markets always carry Fair Trade items. Mainstream supermarkets like A&P carry some. In coffee alone, Fair Trade has channeled $34 million in additional income to small-scale family farmers over the last five years by certifying their coffee as Fair Trade.

But Fair Trade isn't the only ethical certification agency. The Rainforest Alliance (www.rainforest-alliance.org) is also making a big difference by certifying foods produced with environmentally sound methods in tropical rain forest areas.

Coffee America's favorite hot beverage presents more ethical choices than many people know. Beyond the usual agricultural considerations, like organic versus nonorganic and domestic versus imported (yes, the United States does produce coffee beans, in Hawaii), come other issues of environmental impact, exploitative labor practices, and sustainable use of resources at home. Even sweetening and lightening a cup of joe involve choices that have real impact on the environment and our fellow human beings.

Like having to choose between buying local or buying organic, shopping for coffee often forces us to prioritize our concerns. Are we more worried about habitat destruction and loss of biodiversity in South American rain forests than we are about pesticide runoff in Asia? Does addressing near-slavery working conditions in one place take priority over stemming the tide of deforestation elsewhere? These are all issues connected to the global trade in coffee. The good news is that you can make a difference in more than one area with a single choice.

Sustainable coffees include three main approaches: organic coffee, Fair Trade coffee, and shade-grown coffee. All of these coffees are produced in ways that mitigate problems, both in the environment and in the livelihood of the most vulnerable workers in the industry, that conventional production systems cause. Shoppers can find labels indicating which of these approaches was applied to production on packages of coffee in most outlets. Organic coffee is the most widely available, followed by Fair Trade, and then shade-grown (sometimes called "shade coffee").

Because organic coffee is produced with methods that preserve the soil and prohibit use of chemical pesticides and fertilizers, its production helps preserve a clean environment for workers and indigenous peoples. Fair Trade coffee is purchased

Can Organic Chocolate Be Good Chocolate?

I've searched high and low for good organic Fair Trade chocolate. For years, what I found always came up wanting. Most of the organic products had a waxy and distinctly unsexy mouth feel. I was beginning to think that some nonorganic process was absolutely essential to produce luxuriously silky, sophisticated chocolate like that made in Belgium and France. There wasn't. It just took a lot of searching to find the right one.

Dagoba chocolate, manufactured here in the United States (Central Point, Oregon, to be precise), induces the reactions that only exceptional chocolate can elicit. The company's 73 percent cacao content dark chocolate may be the best chocolate of any kind I've ever tasted. It's at once fruity, smoky, exceptionally chocolatey, and pleasantly sweet.

It melts on the palate at room temperature, and remains deliciously al dente when chilled (my favorite way to eat chocolate—each bite lasts longer, and I love the transition from firm to chewy to molten to pleasant memory that accompanies each chilly morsel).

Dagoba markets their 73 percent cacao bar under the name Conacado, which is the name of the cooperative of Dominican Republic growers that raises the organic, Fair Trade cacao beans used in the bar. As with all Fair Trade participants, these growers are paid a guaranteed, predetermined fair price ($1,750 per metric ton, $1,950 per metric ton organic, and scaled to rise higher if world cocoa prices rise above $1,600 per metric ton). Harvesters are never slaves, and they earn significantly more than the near-slave wages paid to many of the underage workers in Ivory Coast and other African cocoa-producing nations. The premium price the chocolate maker pays these farmer-owners has almost no effect on the retail price of the finished chocolate, because he is dealing directly with the farmers, saving intermediary costs. The bars (two ounces) go for about $3 apiece. That's a few cents higher than France's fine Valrhona brand, but worth every penny. This is a perfect example to hold up to nay-sayers who claim that organics and Fair Trade make running a business too expensive. Buy Dagoba chocolates online at www.dagobachocolate.com or order from the company at (541) 664-9030.

Another organic chocolate of good quality is Newman's Own brand (go to www.newmansownorganics.com). Sweeter and with a more toasty flavor than Dagoba, it's also significantly better than most of the organic chocolates I've tasted. Though it's not certified by Fair Trade or Rainforest Alliance, the company, founded and run by actor Paul Newman and his family, asserts that the Central and South American sources for its cocoa are "slavery free." Newman's Own requires its producers to certify that the cocoa they produce is made without the use of forced labor. In addition, Newman donates all of the royalties he receives from the sale of the chocolate to educational and charitable purposes.

A particularly important aspect to buying organic chocolate is its sugar component. The American sugar industry is one of the worst agricultural actors in the country, polluting and degrading the sensitive wilderness areas of south Florida and the Mississippi Delta. Organic sugar production is much more environmentally sound. Newman's Own sources their sugar from organic farms in Mexico and Paraguay. Perhaps the competition from abroad will force the American sugar industry into more responsible, sustainable methods.

directly from cooperatives of small farmers that are guaranteed a minimum contract price, with some of the profits being invested in education and health care for those grower communities. In return, they are encouraged, trained, and usually expected to grow the coffee using sustainable, ecofriendly practices. Shade-grown coffee is grown in shaded forest settings that are good for biodiversity and birds. Such settings preserve quality of life for native peoples, and help ensure that their livelihoods won't be exploited out of existence.

Some brands are twice blessed: They produce organic coffee that is *also* Fair Trade certified and/or shade grown. Soleil Levant coffee, from Switzerland-based La Semeuse, is organic coffee grown according to Fair Trade standards in Colombia, Peru, and Indonesia. It's available from www.CafeLaSemeuse.com in both whole bean and ground forms. Café Mam is a Mexican coffee producer that sells only shade-grown, organic, Fair Trade–certified coffee from www.cafemam.com. Coffees are all triple-certified (organic, Fair Trade, and shade grown) at www.cafecanopy.com.

ORGANIC COFFEE Coffee, the world's second-largest traded food commodity after grain, is also one of the most chemically treated. Many producing countries have few or no regulations on spraying and the use of the most powerful chemicals, including DDT, Diazinon, paraquat, and active ingredients from Agent Orange. I don't believe that total conversion of all conventional farming to organic farming is feasible or desirable, since judicious use of the right pesticides is necessary to keep crop yields high and prevent further encroachment on wild lands. But the unregulated coffee industry is doing great harm to the environment and farmworkers with its excessive use of these chemicals for the sake of profit only. By choosing organic coffee, you're cutting down on the use of these synthetic chemicals in the global environment at a time when their use is out of control. See Sources for a list of roasters that produce organic coffees.

FAIR TRADE COFFEE Economic development is a double-edged sword. On one hand, greater wealth leads to greater consumption, and to a heavier drain on resources. A poor peasant won't be able to afford disposable diapers for her six children, so she'll wash cloth. But, on the other hand, statistics show that greater economic development leads to smaller families. A smaller number of consumers, all enjoying better health care, creature comforts, and education, is a more humane approach to conservation than sustained poverty is.

Currently, most coffee is grown, picked, and processed by subsistence-level workers in bleak conditions. In the 1980s, when coffee experienced a burst of popularity worldwide, Third World governments encouraged their peasantry to invest their lives in coffee production. Many farmers in the poorest parts of Central America, South America, Africa, and Southeast Asia were lured into the industry by the promise of a better life. But when overexpansion led to a glut of coffee beans in the late 1990s and early 2000s, they ended up deep in debt, burdened with products that cost them more to produce than they could earn by selling them. The rush to production had also eroded their land and deforested their countryside. They were worse off than they were before coffee came into their lives.

Fair Trade organizations stepped into this devolving situation with a sensible solution: If growers would agree to raise better-quality beans in an environmentally sensitive way, then the organizations would help them start cooperatives, guarantee them a higher set price for the product, and market it to wealthy connoisseurs in developed countries. Branded Fair Trade coffee would provide those consumers with a premium product that was produced in a more environmentally responsible way than the lesser product they'd previously chosen. Win-win. One company dealing only in Fair Trade coffee is Mountain View Coffee Roasters (www.mountainviewcoffee.com).

Product and sourcing information about Fair Trade products in the United States is listed at www.transfairusa.org, and names of firms and individuals registered with Fair Trade certifying agencies worldwide are at www.ifat.org. A list of companies whose products are all Fair Trade–certified is at www.globalexchange.org. A wider listing of companies that deal in goods that are produced using Fair Trade principles can be found at www.fairtradefederation.com, though not all are certified.

One issue the Fair Trade movement takes very seriously is child labor. Many of the commodities with which Fair Trade organizations are involved, like coffee, cocoa/chocolate, bananas, and sugar, are often produced through the use of exploitative child labor practices. In the worst cases, this child labor is modern-day slavery. A consumer's decision to purchase a Fair Trade–certified product assures that

that purchase price does not support a producer who employs those egregious practices.

Latin American nations are far and away the largest participants in Fair Trade programs. Guatemala leads the way in Fair Trade coffee production, followed by Costa Rica, Mexico, and Colombia. All of Asia produces 15 percent of Fair Trade coffee, and Africa 10 percent. Vietnam, whose farmers plunged into the coffee business with substantial World Bank and government support, has been among the worst stewards of the land, shortsightedly clearing huge swaths of jungle for high-yield, low-quality coffee that quickly saps the land of nutrients. Fair Trade represents a 58 percent increase in wages, but only a 1 percent increase in product price to retailers, according to an October 2001 PricewaterhouseCoopers report. The consumer pays about $1 per pound more.

SHADE-GROWN COFFEE Shade-grown coffee represents the smallest segment of the sustainable coffee market, and the one most susceptible to corruption. With so many assertions and claims being touted by producers, roasters, and retailers about sustainability, the need for accountable certifying agencies is great. A study commissioned by The Nature Conservancy, in cooperation with The Summit Foundation and several other concerned groups, found that widespread use of the terms "shade-grown" and "bird-friendly" by firms with only a few trees or trees of all the same species on their farms was watering down the meaning of those terms. This is a problem, even with the existence of two recognized international certifications, Rainforest Alliance's "Eco-OK" for shade grown, and Smithsonian Migratory Bird Center's "Bird-Friendly" seal.

Water

A recent ad campaign pokes fun at people who missed great investment opportunities because they didn't see the potential in a timely idea. To illustrate the point, there's a flashback to the 1970s. A possible investor responds to an entrepreneur with the comment, "Who would buy water in a bottle, when perfectly good water is free?" Modern viewers laugh to themselves, knowing that bottled water now represents the fastest-growing segment of the beverage industry. More than half of Americans drink bottled water regularly, and it represents a $35 billion industry worldwide, with nearly $10 billion of that in the United States.

The Natural Resources Defense Council (NRDC) conducted a four-year study of bottled water purity claims, and found that bottled water "was not necessarily safer than tap water." But the perception among consumers is that it is. As a private chef, I've cooked in homes where I was not only expected to cook *with* bottled water, but to cook *in* bottled water. Since the sweet flavor of water becomes an essential part of the flavor profile of any dish made with it, the culinary sense of making soups, stocks, and sauces with the best-tasting water is self-evident. But I defy any gastronome to distinguish vegetables boiled in quality tap water from ones boiled in bottled water. With the exception of certain highly distinctive mineral waters, most bottled water imparts virtually no flavor to foods cooked in it. Even spring water, defined as water that rises from underground to the Earth's surface under natural pressure, seldom bears any noticeable difference from filtered tap water in this regard. Yet the plastic containers for bottled water continue to pile up in landfills (few deposit systems include noncarbonated beverages).

The environmental effects of the bottled water revolution ripple out from the source of the water. Trucking water, which is heavy, requires large amounts of gasoline and diesel fuel. Shipping of water across continents and oceans burns up oil that would never be needed if consumers simply turned on the tap. Along the way, the trucks, cargo ships, freight trains, and delivery vans leave oily wakes, many of which run off into fresh waterways with the very next rain. Ironically, consumers of bottled water are adding to the pollution of our country's fresh water. Petrochemicals, used in the manufacture of plastic bottles, and the disposal of those bottles after one use, compound the pollution. The least a consumer can do is to choose bottled water that comes from a local source, minimizing transportation pollution.

Even the marketing of bottled water adds unnecessary ecological impact. Every billboard, magazine page, and flyer promoting these products adds to the needless pollution generated in printing, distribution, and litter. Until now, tap water needed no promotion. Now, it competes with plastic-clad rivals to quench Americans' thirst.

CULINARY USES FOR WATER There's no denying that water has flavor. Its taste can range from sweet and pleasantly mineral-laced to sulfuric and, in many cases, chlorinated. In some cases, bottled water has valid culinary value. Broths and stocks benefit from water of utmost purity. Water, served as a beverage, should taste great. But sensible consumers will taste their own tap water, passed through a filter, before deciding that it cannot be delicious. Even the Culinary Institute of America, America's preeminent culinary college, uses tap water for its fine preparations.

I've never worked in a professional kitchen that used bottled water for cooking. And, despite easy access to bottled water at no cost, most of the chefs I've worked with drink tap water as a beverage. Perhaps I've been lucky, working in cities like New York and Boston, where the flavor of tap water is good. But even when I worked in San Diego, where high mineral content gave the water a different taste than I was used to, I quickly adapted, and joined my fellow cooks in drinking filtered tap water as a matter of course. Cooks, by the way, drink an enormous amount of water during a ten-hour shift. If the thousands of gallons consumed by us taste-a-holics over a year all came in ten-ounce bottles, we'd have generated mountains of useless plastic waste.

The flavor of certain foods, such as soups, stews, and broths, is so tied to the water used that if filtered tap water doesn't taste excellent, another source may be needed. I wouldn't make a consommé with water that had any undesirable taste or smell. Try to buy from the nearest source available. But make sure you try filtering the tap water yourself first. The Brita tabletop water filter I use practically eliminates the taste of chlorine from treated municipal water. For a comparison of widely available water filters, check out www.waterfiltercomparisons.net.

SOME SUGAR ISN'T SO SWEET People of conscience around the world are taking steps to slow the damage agriculture has been doing to waterways, estuaries, lakes, seas, and oceans. Consumers can stand up and be counted in the fight to protect Earth's water, whether by stirring Fair Trade unrefined cane sugar into their coffee or bulking up their salad with cabbage instead of water-intensive lettuce.

An excellent example of the effects of conventional agriculture on the environment may be found in the Florida Everglades. This area includes fresh and saltwater rivers, lakes, ponds, sawgrass marshes, small tree islands, sloughs, mangrove swamps, open prairies, rocklands, and offshore coral reefs. The Florida Everglades are also the largest remaining subtropical wilderness in the lower forty-eight United States and are home to wading birds, grassland birds, alligators, crocodiles, tropical fish, crustaceans, and mammals, among others. They are also home to fifty-six endangered or threatened species, four national wildlife refuges, two national parks, and one national marine sanctuary. This fragile and complex environment has shrunk to less than half of its original size in the past hundred years because of the encroachment of the sugarcane industry.

This industry enjoys federal quotas on sugar imports and subsidies while the wading bird population has fallen 90 percent in the last twenty years. The destruction of this ecosystem from nearby farms is caused primarily by water diversion to the very thirsty sugarcane crop and from chemical runoff that contaminates the Everglades' water supply. Nitrogen and phosphorus fertilizers used on sugarcane fields pollute the Everglades, causing algal blooms and declines in productivity in the aquatic ecosystems. In addition to being polluted, the water in the rivers, streams, wetlands, and marshes is diverted to the agricultural fields, with the help of federally supported drainage and flood control projects and cheap water prices.

Like reasonably priced prescription drugs, Fair Trade sugar, that is raised responsibly, must be purchased from Canada. It's available from www.lasiembra.com, www.levelground.com, and www.marquisproject.com. American-produced organic sugar, called "evaporated cane juice," has become available here, and is a good second choice. It's available online from www.wholesomesweetness.com.

FARMING OUR DRINKING WATER TO DEATH Irrigation flushes water through the soil, washing away nutrients and prompting the farmer to apply more chemical fertilizer. The manmade water flow also helps pesticides flow into the nearby rivers and streams and enter the groundwater supply. In the United States, the Sierra Club describes agriculture as the largest source of water pollution. According to an April 2001 NRDC Report, agricultural operations are among the top five sources of groundwater pollution in California. And in a state where the groundwater amounts to six times the volume of all the surface water reservoirs combined, groundwater pollution is a problem. The EPA has also detected seventy-four pesticides in the groundwater of thirty-eight states. Contaminants found in groundwater also tend to persist in the environment for hundreds or possibly thousands of years if they are not mediated. Pollution is not the only consequence of heavily irrigated agriculture. Erosion is also a by-product.

Alfalfa is one of the most water-intensive crops grown, along with rice, sugarcane, and turmeric. It is in fact the most water-intensive crop grown in the state of California. Although alfalfa does maintain soil health, prevent soil erosion with its extensive root system, and provide wildlife habitat aboveground, it uses approximately one-quarter of California's irrigation water. It also covers more land than any other single crop in the state. Alfalfa cultivation is not handled very well; 26 percent of this water-intensive crop is grown in California's southern deserts, and most growers use the inefficient and wasteful flooding irrigation technique, although better ways to water the plant are available. This water-costly crop is also of low value and accounts for only 4 percent of the state's farming revenues. In addition, 70 percent of the alfalfa grown goes to feed dairy cows, whose manure is thought to threaten 65 percent of California's drinking water. And the Central Valley dairy farms produce as much waste as a city of 21 million people.

One of the least water-needy crops is sorghum, a drought-resistant cereal and the fifth most important crop in the world, behind wheat, rice, maize, and potatoes. A number of institutions, including the Hermitage Research Station in Warwick, Texas Tech University, Texas A&M University, and the University of Missouri, are studying the drought-resistant properties of an Ethiopian strain of sorghum. They have found a few "stay-green" traits that allow it to survive on very little water. These traits retard the onset and rate of leaf death, and affect transpiration rates and nitrogen levels in the plants, allowing the leaves to survive longer in drought conditions. Other "dry crops" are peanuts and corn.

WATER, WATER EVERYWHERE Food production both relies on and affects water quality in America. It requires about 600,000 gallons of water each year to grow one acre of virtually any crop, according to a study by Penn State's College of Agricultural Sciences. In agriculture, the vast majority of water consumption goes into livestock production, either in the form of feed production (growing corn and soy) or in the care, processing, and cleanup required for the animals. A late 1990s study in *New Scientist* (1/2/97) reported that a kilo of feedlot beef takes about fifty times as much water to produce as a kilo of soy or rice. The numbers they cited are:

- Potatoes: 500 liters

- Wheat: 900 liters

- Sorghum: 1,110 liters

- Maize: 1,400 liters

- Rice: 1,910 liters

- Soybeans: 2,000 liters

- Chicken: 3,500 liters

- Beef (feedlot): 100,000 liters

Livestock forage production is one of the biggest water demands on desert regions. A February 2003 study by Sandia National Laboratories reported that 75 percent of surface water withdrawals and 53 percent of groundwater withdrawals in 1995 were for irrigated agriculture, largely for fields of alfalfa and other livestock forage. The labs have developed a protected agriculture system that conserves water by growing crops in a controlled environment—essentially a modified greenhouse that has the added advantage of protection from adverse weather conditions.

In partnership with 3M and the government of Chihuahua, Mexico, Sandia has created greenhouses that filter the sunlight that reaches crops, allowing only the parts of the spectrum required by the plants. The resulting reduction in greenhouse temperature greatly reduces required cooling and evaporation. The technology could have a dramatic effect on agricultural water usage. That reduction could, in turn, relieve tensions along many of the world's national borders.

Many scientists believe that competition for water will become the most serious resource-related issue facing mankind in the coming decades. Solutions like Sandia's protected agriculture will be an essential part of keeping the peace. We regularly read reports of the water wars in the Southwest, among Arizona and California, New

Mexico, Texas, and Mexico. Consider the fast-growing populations of the Middle East, Asia, and Africa. Their water demands far outstrip supply right now. By comparison, the United States is awash in fresh water. General Electric has recently acquired a major water processing company, and Wall Street continues to push prices of water-treatment-company stocks to record highs.

Think Globally, Act Locally

"Seasonality" has become a catchword for modern chefs seeking to prove the authenticity of their regional foods. But many consumers ask, "Why not use Costa Rican asparagus in midwinter if it looks good?"

We may ultimately choose to enjoy these fruits of the overnight shipping age, but first we'll consider the petroleum consumed to ship our goods around the globe, the copious packaging required to ensure their unblemished arrival, and the other hidden costs of instant gratification. Luscious, plentiful local fish like porgies, bluefish, and blackfish often languish in coastal fish markets while threatened foreign species like Patagonian toothfish (a.k.a. Chilean sea bass) and North Atlantic cod get all the attention.

It's absurd that California oranges are sold in Florida supermarkets, but they are. The Sunshine State that's synonymous with citrus fruit processes 96 percent of its oranges into juice, which is routinely sold in California. It's as if you made a pie at home, packed it in bubble wrap, shipped it cross-country, and then bought someone else's pie, baked thousands of miles away, for your own dessert that same day.

In the peak of the August peach season in the Northeast, produce departments are brimming with air-freight peaches. In urban greenmarkets, like New York's Union Square market, local cherries thrill the few food enthusiasts in the know, while Washington State cherries take the lion's share of the mainstream market. In June, New England strawberries are rarely found in mainstream Boston supermarkets, relegated instead to occasional county festivals and farm stands.

Four percent of our national energy budget is used to grow food, while 10 to 13 percent is required to put it on our tables. This illustrates the true cost of our food. While massive production systems may ensure a lower-cost product for the consumer, air, land, and water are despoiled along the way through trucking, packaging, and distribution. The cheap oil we've come to rely on for our way of life has blinded us to the absurdity of what our food distribution has become.

On July 21, 2004, the *New York Times* reported that the last wholesale produce dealers, who dealt primarily in local and regional goods at the nearly abandoned Bronx Terminal market, were about to be evicted to make way for a retail center and park. They were unable to compete with the colossal Hunt's Point market, the distribution center that sells produce from around the world to nearly all of New York's food outlets. Local producers couldn't deal in the huge volume that Hunt's Point market demands. Ironically, the soon-to-be-homeless vendors were too *big* to sell to city greenmarkets, which conduct only retail trade.

Every New York State apple that you buy in New York and every Illinois squash you buy in Chicago can make a difference. It's one less fruit or vegetable that diesels its way across America to the supermarket. New York City is funding research into centralizing distribution of locally produced food. It's a step in the right direction. But individual action on the part of consumers will be the key to reinvigorating local produce industries. When greenmarkets become so well-attended that they can't keep up with demand, local-produce wholesalers like those from Bronx Terminal will find markets for their goods. When supermarket chains lose business because they don't carry enough local goods, they'll start to carry more of them.

That scenario has already happened with organic foods, and is a selling point for increasingly popular socially responsible supermarket companies, like the sixty-four-store, family-owned Wegman's chain. The company gives their produce managers bonuses for meeting quotas of locally grown food. The stores have responded by setting up separate sections just for local produce, complete with pictures of the farmers who grew it. The rapidly growing Whole Foods market chain also sources a notable portion of its produce from local farms. Putting a farmer's face to the food adds to consumer appreciation of the food. Once they've tasted fruit that ripened on the tree, instead of fruit that was shipped hard and ripened in a gas-filled truck, most consumers see the benefits that go beyond reducing dependence on oil and supporting local farm economies.

Seek out the sources of local produce, and get to know them. It may not be feasible to buy all your produce from farm stands and greenmarkets, but buy all you can. No one doubts the convenience of supermarket shopping, but until local produce is available with that convenience, make a personal choice to do the right thing whenever possible. Assess your options for buying foods grown in a two-hundred-mile radius of your kitchen. Make the first step right at your local supermarket, by choosing wisely there. State-of-origin and country-of-origin labeling is increasingly clear. It will be the law soon, if obstructionists in Congress don't derail pending legislation. Read those labels, and use the information to select Florida oranges in Florida, and California orange juice in California.

Markets often carry both homegrown and imported versions of the same produce. With the increased branding of fruits and vegetables, you often need only look at the package to see how near to home a product is grown. While I lament the disposable culture that has brought us cellophane wrap on cauliflower and polyethylene sacks of potatoes, I always read the tag to see where the farm is, and choose the one nearest my home.

To find local growers' markets where you live, check out databases on these Web sites: www.localharvest.org, www.foodroutes.org, and www.sustainabletable.org. From farmers' markets in Casper, Wyoming, to natural food co-ops in Atlanta, Georgia, these sites have clickable maps with locations, contact information, directions, and descriptions of sources in every state. Links to each individual market tell you not only where to go, but what to expect when you get there, with seasonality charts listing crops that are available in particular months. Just browsing these sites may inspire a market adventure, opening new culinary possibilities. Included in the listings for the Austin, Texas, Farmers' Market are local farmers' fruits and vegetables, herbs, eggs, cheeses, "kindly raised poultry, lamb, beef and buffalo," and local honey. City chefs are at the market, giving cooking demos. There are gardening workshops, children's activities, and live music from Austin's best local bands.

Community-supported Agriculture Your local university/college agricultural office will have names of farmers in your region. The USDA's Cooperative State Research, Education and Extension Service (CSREES) supports programs at over a hundred land-grant colleges and universities. These extensions' century-old mission is to solve public needs on the local level with college or university resources. CSREES partners with state Cooperative Extension Services (CES). Go to either www.csrees.usda.gov/qlinks/partners/state_partners.html or www.gardenersnet.com/atoz/ces.htm to find partner extensions.

These USDA extensions can direct consumers not just to farm stands and farmers' markets, but also to another fantastic resource: community-supported agriculture (CSA) farms. Thousands of small farms sell produce direct to consumers, through CSAs. What they are is a mutual support system between growers and consumers of farm products that provides a conduit for food from field to table. It's the ultimate in "putting a face to the food." Consumers pay the farmer an annual membership fee, which helps him run the farm. In return, the member receives a weekly share of the harvest during the local growing season. There's both a shared bounty and a shared risk, since an abundant, fine crop brings extra benefit to the member, and the membership income defrays costs during lean times for the farmer. The system benefits the ecosystem in many ways: Most farms involved in CSAs grow organic produce, protecting the land and water, and shipping is inherently minimal, protecting the air and natural resources.

Members buy an annual "share," which yields enough weekly produce to feed a family of four, or a couple on a vegetarian diet. Depending on the farm and the region, shares can range from $300 to $600. Sometimes, half-shares are available. In terms of cost, the produce usually ends up averaging about the same as conventional produce purchased at the supermarket. Buying organic anywhere is good. But buying from a source that circumvents the environmental costs of transporting, processing, and distributing the food is especially beneficial to the environment. While organics are still less than 3 percent of the $900 billion annual U.S. food market, at the present rate of growth, sales of organics could outstrip conventional foods within twenty years.

The CSA movement actually began in Japan, where a women's group concerned with use of pesticides and the invisible costs of imported produce started a movement called *teikei* (essentially meaning "food with the farmer's face on it"). They started their CSA in 1965. Twenty years later, a Swiss environmentalist who had started a community-supported agriculture group near Zurich brought the idea to a Massachusetts farm, and started the first CSA in the United States—Indian Line Farm in South Egremont. Today, there are more than two thousand CSAs in North America. They exist in every state. To find one near you, go to www.csacenter.org or www.nal.usda.gov/afsic/csa/.

No Free Ride

Ethical produce is often more expensive than conventional produce. Ethical meats almost always are. America's food is so cheap in part because so many ethical corners have been cut to make it that way. Fossil fuels are cheap, so the maximum amount of them are used to lower food prices. Small farms employ more hand labor than factory farms, which is important since farm machinery represents 12 percent of all diesel fuel consumed in our oil-thirsty country. Mass production makes widespread crop dusting with insecticides and herbicides economically feasible, so pesticides that pollute land and water make conventional crops cheaper. Concentrated feeding and slaughter operations and animal by-product–based feed make livestock production cheap, and meat overabundant and cheap.

Americans spend less on food than people in any other country. Most of us spend about 10 percent of our family income on food. This is a recent development. In 1950, about 21 percent of income was spent on food. This, despite the fact that more meals are eaten in restaurants now than ever before. The period from 1950 to 2002 saw the percentage of family income spent on food at home fall from 16.9 percent to 6.2 percent. In developing countries like India and China, families spend as much as 50 percent of their income on food.

Most of us can afford the extra few dollars a week it would cost to buy the right ingredients, the ethical ingredients. Organic milk and cage-free organic eggs cost roughly double their conventional counterparts. If most Americans could see the hideous conditions that hens are subjected to in order to keep egg prices low, almost anyone would agree that it's a small price to pay. If they could see the squalor of the life of a conventional dairy cow, almost everyone would pay the extra $2 a gallon to be sure that it came from a cow that wasn't confined to a windowless barn clamped to a milking machine 24/7. They might not be able to taste the difference between that milk and milk from a cow that roamed the grass in the light of day (although some can), but they'd feel better about themselves.

The Hidden Costs of Cheap Food Sometimes local *is* the economical option. When popular local crops like summer corn, berries, tree fruit, and root vegetables are at their season's peak, they can be substantially cheaper than imports. Why, then, would West Coast peaches at $2.99 a pound represent 75 percent of the peaches in a New York City supermarket in August, when sweet, tree-ripe New Jersey peaches, selling for $1.49, are so delicious? Part of the reason involves consumer expectation. Seasonal produce grown on small farms lacks the uniform shapes and sizes many consumers have come to expect. It may seem that picture-perfect skin and coloration indicate superior fruit. But any home gardener who's picked an oddly-shaped ripe tomato from the vine and compared it with the "perfect" hothouse specimen from Holland knows that looks can be deceiving. Supermarkets also favor suppliers who can deliver consistent products in predictable quantities. By shunning local growers whose quality is better but crop size is unpredictable, these markets are starving the local farm economies, making the farms ever less able to produce the desired volume.

Thoughtful consumers should expect to pay a premium for buying locally, because it's simply a different system of production, with less mechanization, less yield-boosting pesticides, and other higher costs. Unfortunately, there's an internal mechanism in all of us that tends to prioritize dollar costs above all other costs.

Take it from me. I've been a personal chef to clients who represent the top one percent of U.S. income, and they're more concerned about the price of milk than the middle class is. I've been told by multimillionaires that I shouldn't pay a few extra dollars for more expensive organic ingredients. The food-cost difference to their meal may have been small, but it was the *principle* of spending those dollars that irked them. To be fair, once I explained the environmental rationale for choosing the organic products, most of my clients endorsed them, agreeing that they should have "the best."

When the Union of Concerned Scientists (www.ucsusa.org), a nonprofit group of scientists working for solutions to environmental problems, addressed the costs of industrial agriculture, it revealed the unseen price tags on cheap food. Their report, "The Costs and Benefits of Industrial Agriculture" (March 2001), noted that "a full accounting would include not only the benefits of relatively cheap prices consumers pay for food, the dividends paid to the shareholders of fertilizer and pesticide manufacturers and the dollars earned by exporting American goods abroad, but also the offsetting costs of environmental pollution and degradation." They concede that the costs are difficult to assess. Water pollution and global warming are influenced by many factors. Many of industrial farming's effects are felt far from the farms themselves, such as when nitrogen compounds from Midwestern farms travel down the Mississippi and degrade coastal fisheries in the Gulf of Mexico. They cite costs including:

- Damage to fisheries from oxygen-depleting algae fed by fertilizer runoff

- Cleanup of surface and groundwater polluted with animal waste

- Increased health risks suffered by agricultural workers and farmers exposed to pesticides

- The high energy requirements of industrial agriculture, such as running giant combines and harvesters

- Energy used to produce and transport pesticides and fertilizers, and to refrigerate and transport perishable produce across the country and around the world

- Global warming gases and ozone pollution produced by tillage; effects may already be occurring in the form of increased violent weather and rising oceans

Seas Are Local, Too

Nothing benefits more from timely consumption than fresh fish. In summer, when bluefish are running up the Atlantic coast, their thriving fishery provides abundant, inexpensive, delicious pleasure to savvy East Coast fish lovers. Porgies also thrive in Eastern summer waters. The idea of choosing South American, Chinese, or South African fish when these exceptional local fish are in season is like buying California oranges in Miami. Likewise, when icy midwinter waters ensure the cleanest, clearest, briniest Eastern oysters, mussels, and clams, that's the time to skip the Pacific varieties for a while in New England. And the same goes for the Left Coast. Fall and early winter are still the best times for Western oysters from Puget Sound, Wescott Bay, Hog Islands, and Shoalwaters, even though modern technology has brought nonspawning (all-season) oysters to Oregon and Washington State waters.

Getting to know and use what's local and abundant in your own region also relieves overtaxed fisheries elsewhere. Choosing to dine on local, fresh Atlantic mackerel relieves pressure on stocks of overexploited red snapper in the Gulf, Chilean sea bass in South America, and other trendy fish. It also reduces transportation pollution.

Grains, Beans, and Legumes

A basic premise of this book is that while we are on Earth to enjoy life, we have a responsibility to enjoy it without ruining it. We can live without causing undue harm to other living things and our ecosystem.

We know that animals will inevitably suffer as we raise and slaughter them for food. But some of that suffering is needless, and we can bring about a more humane system by supporting ranchers, farmers, and meatpackers who operate humanely. However, while we can limit animal suffering and environmental degradation caused by meat production systems, the single most effective step we can take is to eat less meat.

For most of us nonvegetarians, meat, poultry, and fish are here to stay. And there's nothing wrong with that. Thousands of noble beasts eat meat, and they are no less noble because of it. It's life in the food chain. It's hypothesized that our species' adoption of dietary meat was a key factor in our evolutionary success. The taste of meat is also one of the great pleasures of our lives. A grilled prime rib-eye steak with herb vinaigrette, meltingly tender lamb shanks with artichokes and giant Sicilian olives, crunchy fried chicken, fresh seafood chowder—these foods are a joy, and can be eaten ethically.

Whether an animal is preyed upon in the African savanna or slaughtered for meat in America, we regret that some creatures must die to give others sustenance. The better part of our nature laments the suffering of any creature, even if that suffering is at our hands. To reconcile our two desires—both to eat meat and to minimize the suffering and environmental impact of doing so—we need to reassess the place meat holds in our diet.

The goal here isn't to eat *no* meat—it's to eat *less* meat. If, instead of putting a one-pound lamb shank in front of every guest, you divide one shank among four people as part of a rustic pasta dish (see page 166), you've reduced the animal suffering and environmental damage linked to that meal by 75 percent. If one steak, instead of being one serving, is sliced into four gorgeous, satisfying portions, that meal causes only a quarter of the suffering and pollution that would otherwise be generated. When the main course of dinner is a pilaf of ancient grains, redolent with herbs, spices, nuts, and dried fruits, and is paired with sweet caramelized roasted beets (see page 152), then the intensely flavored steak will be a dynamic part of the meal, rather than the raison d'être. The key is to approach the meat differently, giving it more impact on the palate—and making it more memorable. At the same time as it's cutting out needless suffering, this change is bringing our diet back into a healthier balance. Our overemphasis on meat in this country is a major cause of the epidemic of heart disease (America's number one cause of death) and obesity. We can be lean, and less mean.

For most Americans, meat is the main course, and all other items served at a meal are "side dishes." In most other cultures, it's the other way around: Meat and fish are accompaniments to the meal—the "side dishes," so to speak. In China, the world's most populous nation, rice is the center of the meal, augmented by vegetable dishes, bean curd dishes, and meat (mostly homegrown pork) or fish dishes. Millet, teff, sorghum, barley, and other grains, cooked as cakes, porridge, dumplings, and flatbreads, make up the staple diet of most East African peoples. Again, they're served with vegetable stews and sometimes meat or fish. Latin American diets are based on whole grains, tubers, nuts, vegetables, and fruits, with poultry and fish served alongside, and sometimes meat. Southern Italians make handmade pasta the center of the plate, not just a vehicle for sauce. By using the best semolina flour, they create a food whose greatness deserves center stage. A chorus of flavors serves to frame it rather than disguise it. The same is true of the risotto and polenta of central and northern Italy.

Anyone who has experienced the cuisines of China, Africa, Latin America, or Italy knows the exquisite, dynamic, intricate, and varied flavors and textures of their foods. Those foods are at least as delicious and varied as our own. Their meat, fish, and poultry dishes are often more complex and interesting than mainstream American dishes. They stand out, providing a big impact on the palate, even if they're only a small fraction of the total meal. In fact, they have that impact *because* they comprise only a small fraction of the meal.

Meat plays a smaller role in most cuisines because, in most places, it's more expensive than grains, vegetables, and fruits. In the United States, that's no longer the case. Our mass-production system, so beneficial when applied to cars, iPods, and washing machines, cheapens production of meat. But the cost in animal cruelty is high, and the quality of the resulting meat is often dismal. Not only do we contribute to the suffering of livestock and the degradation of the environment when we buy this meat, but we support a system that has introduced new and needless levels of suffering to the herds.

The solution to this needless suffering is to seek out and use a better quality of meat and make it a different, smaller part of the total meal. We won't stop the killing of animals and the pollution inherent in livestock production altogether, but we can ensure that our footprint on the Earth is as small as it can be, and that the animals live with the dignity they deserve. The change can be a wonderful culinary discovery for lovers of fine foods. Focusing on the new center of the plate—diverse whole-grain sautés and pilafs, concentrated vegetable flavors, and texturally rich foods like marinated tofu, spiced nuts, and beans—can open new worlds of cookery.

The New Center
Whole grains carry much greater gravitas on the palate and much more resilience in their bite than processed rice and other American staple starches. Discovering and learning how to cook grains like amaranth, spelt (a.k.a. farro), whole barley, quinoa, oats, and numerous varieties of wheat was an epiphany for me. My classical training at the Culinary Institute of America and fifteen years in restaurant kitchens, plus many more as a private chef, brought me only an introduction to the diverse flavors, textures, and aromatic possibilities of these grains. My voyage of discovery continues. The recipes I developed from those discoveries are the basis of many of the recipes on these pages. I've grouped many of the most complementary recipes, so that the whole meal can be seen at a glance. Of course, you'll interchange the elements of the plates at will as I do. Mushroom-Barley "Risotto" (page 82) pairs as wonderfully with venison as it does with bison, beef, free-range turkey, pan-seared tofu, or grilled portobello mushrooms.

Some of the menus are substantial vegetarian fare, with beans and grains paired to provide all the protein without the meat. More and more nonvegetarians are enjoying occasional meatless meals without redefining their diets. Another way of reconfiguring the plate is to serve a meat or fish appetizer, followed by a meatless main course. Soups and stews are another way of bringing the flavors and textures of meat into the picture without using very much of it. Many great stew and soup recipes originated in lean times, when meat was a luxury and had to be stretched thin. Now, ecofriendly cooks are turning to the same techniques for different reasons.

MAKE THE MEAT MEMORABLE AND THE MAIN INGREDIENT UNFORGETTABLE

Bold flavors make a lasting impression on our palates and minds. Complex tastes spur us to examine and think about what we're eating. To make a single steak satisfy a number of people, each bite has to say something to the taster. We remember special occasions more than ordinary ones, so these dishes have to feel like a special occasion.

Quality ingredients are indispensable. It makes good sense to buy organic chicken, even at more than twice the price of conventional, if its deeper flavor makes each bite more satisfying. Such a bird can satisfy many more people than a cheap chicken would. By making dinner with superior ingredients, it becomes precious.

The famed white truffles of Alba are treasured as much for their rarity as for their heady aroma. Chefs use specially designed devices to dispense tiny shavings onto plates of delicate food because the impact of the truffle is so great. Once we appreciate the true value of other foods that come at great cost, we can view them in the same reverential light, and utilize them with the respect they deserve.

This concept is especially true if we serve such respected ingredients in exceptionally satisfying dishes that are ethically beyond reproach. For grains, vegetables, and legumes to move to the center of the meal, they must feel like a main course. We're so used to noodles or potatoes being an afterthought that many of us take them for granted. But a rosemary-laced ragoût of choice potatoes, steeped in shallots, leeks, and shiitake mushrooms, is unforgettable. Homemade pasta is another perfect centerpiece.

GRAINS AT THE CENTER OF THE PLATE Grains are an even easier way to re-design the plate. Let's face it: There's not much you can do with Uncle Ben's that will make it memorable. But use Bhutanese red rice (see www.worldofrice.com or www.lotusfoods.com) and the grassy flavor of the rice adds an intriguing element to any dish. The rice's pliable hull adds resilient texture, giving the dish a more substantial feel. It becomes a meal.

Say "oats" and people think of horses. But oat groats, like rice, can be cooked into pilafs with a nutty flavor and enjoyably chewy texture. The plants are hardy and able to thrive in poor soil conditions where other crops can't. They also happen to be highly nutritious and filled with cholesterol-fighting soluble fiber. Their longer cooking time is a blessing in disguise, since it allows for whole spices like cardamom or cinnamon to fully release flavors into the dish as it simmers. Serving cooked oats with savory red bean stew makes a gorgeous presentation with sprigs of cilantro or chervil. That main course pairing might be accented by a sweet beet salad and some small slices of roast pork with an intense, garlicky vinaigrette. Positioning the oats as a main course makes the pork into the side dish. Once again, this is the healthy way to eat: No one needs a sixteen-ounce steak for dinner.

The Most Ethical Proteins: Grains, Beans, and Legumes
Rigidity was big at the Culinary Institute of America when I studied there in the late 1980s. "Forget everything your previous chefs taught you about method and ingredients," I was told. The only way to make food was the CIA way. The system had its merits, including establishment of a lingua franca among professional chefs in America, like the one the apprenticeship system had created in Europe. But one rigid rule sticks in my craw to this day: the dinner plate triad.

The rule went *exactly* like this: "Every dinner plate must have a protein, a starch, and a veg." Those were the terms we used, and the implication was that these categories were mutually exclusive. A steak, a potato, and broccoli. A salmon fillet, pasta, and spinach. Tofu, rice, and bok choy. Among ourselves, we actually argued over which categories certain foods belonged in. Dictums came from on high to settle things once and for all. Yes, carrots were starchy, but they were a vegetable. Yes, parsnips were really, really similar to carrots, but they were a starch. Corn? Don't get me started.

The most contentious category was protein. From the way our chefs talked about meat being "a protein" and fish being "a protein," you would have thought that protein was a single substance, like modeling clay, that God shaped into a thousand different things. We never even discussed the protein *content* of the "starches" or the "vegs." Since then, the CIA's view of the plate has evolved, and so has mine.

Once relegated to the starch category, grains and beans actually have sufficient protein elements to support healthy human life all by themselves. Legumes (seed-bearing pods like string beans) may fit the vegetable segment of the triad, but they're also good sources of complex carbohydrate energy (starch) and are building blocks for protein. The enlightened view is that the meal should contain a balanced menu of nutrients. A dish of beans and rice with sautéed garlic chives is a dinner, CIA triad or no CIA triad.

Grains, beans, and legumes alone, once labeled starches, can serve as all three elements of the meal quite nicely. All this is to say that, while vegetarianism isn't the only lifestyle, it is a nutritionally valid one, and naysayers who raise concerns about protein deficiency are wrong. In fact, the average American consumes more than twice the amount of protein that is the absurdly oversized U.S. Recommended Daily Allowance (RDA). Even a vegan diet, without any supplements, can easily fulfill daily protein needs. The idea that every dinner plate must have meat, fish, or "a protein" per se is just wrong. Make one or two days a week your "vegetarian days." You won't be missing anything, and you'll be improving your health.

Beans and grains are high in protein, composed of the amino acids we need to build our bodies. While it's true that meat contains the complete package—all eight essential amino acids—we also get those amino acids separately from vegetarian sources, especially grains and beans eaten in combination.

Biting the bean doesn't mean biting the bullet. These are exceptional foods to which Americans are underexposed. I tend to start with dried beans, since I like the taste better than canned. I occasionally use canned beans in dips because I like their texture, but I prefer the taste of dried. I love discovering and experimenting with new beans. I found bright yellow canary beans at the store recently. They made great soup with saffron.

The biggest myth about beans is that you have to soak them. I've soaked and not soaked, and there's no difference, except in cooking time. Beans that break up when you cook them without soaking would have broken up even if you had soaked them. Believe me, I've tried. Many a broken bean has passed my lips after it had had a thorough overnight swim. And cooking evenly? If your beans still have a hard core after the outside starts to disintegrate, it's because they were too old, not because they were too dry. I remember reading about some archaeological site discovered from a camp of early humans, where they actually found still-usable beans that had been their food. At the time, I thought the report implied that the beans could still be eaten. Who were they kidding?

Even though U.S. government sources say that "dry beans will keep indefinitely if stored in a dry place," I contend that dried beans get even drier the longer they sit around. Try to cook a package of beans that has sat on your shelf for three or four years, and you'll see what I mean. They never soften, no matter how long you cook them, and they taste like cardboard. This is the voice of experience talking. I now use a magic marker to scribble the date on every bag of beans before I put it into the cabinet. Anything closing on two years, I use it or lose it. But if dry bean shelf life is measured in years, not millennia, then cooked bean shelf life is measured in days, not weeks. Cooked beans really only last four or five days, unless you put enough salt in them to give an elephant hypertension.

One more note on soaking beans. I don't mean to imply there's anything *wrong* with soaking them. I just don't think it's necessary in most cases, and often turns off people who look at a recipe on the day they want to make something, only to see the dreaded word "overnight" in the recipe. But there are certain preparations starting with raw beans that do require soaking. Falafel, the Middle Eastern spiced chickpea fritter that makes exquisite pita sandwiches with sesame sauce (tahini) and salad, is made of seasoned ground, raw chickpeas. You'd stand a better chance of turning ball bearings into flour than turning unsoaked dried chickpeas into falafel batter. Also, if you have the foresight to soak beans, you can cut their cooking time in half. Just remember never to cook the beans in the same water they were soaked in. It makes the beans much gassier. One final tip: If you need soaked beans in a hurry, boil dried beans for five minutes in a pot of water that covers them by two inches or more, and then cover them for one hour. They'll behave just like beans soaked overnight.

Whole-Grain Health Bread

YIELD: 2 LOAVES When making yeast-risen breads, dough ingredients need to be adjusted by feel. You might wish for a scientific formula, but the perfect dough comes with the give-and-take of added liquid or flour as you mix and knead. The moister the dough, the crisper the crust and the lighter the bread will be. But it should be dry enough that it's easy to knead without getting stuck all over your hands. I generally err on the side of moister dough, and then sprinkle the work surface copiously with flour as I knead. Anna and David Kasabian taught this recipe to me. All grains and flours for this bread are available from www.arrowheadmills.com.

1 cup raisins

2 cups warm milk

Two ¼-ounce packets active dry yeast

¾ cup whole wheat flour

⅓ cup quinoa

⅓ cup amaranth

3 cups bread flour

¾ cup spelt flour

¾ cup brown sugar

1 tablespoon kosher salt

1 cup chopped walnuts

Vegetable oil for greasing bowl and pan

Plump (soak) the raisins in 1¼ cups of the milk for 30 minutes. Drain, reserving the milk. Combine the yeast, whole wheat flour, and remaining ¾ cup milk. Let stand for 30 minutes until very foamy. Meanwhile, bring 2 cups water to a boil in a small saucepan. Add the quinoa and amaranth and simmer, uncovered, until the grains are tender, about 10 minutes. Remove from heat and let stand covered until the water is completely absorbed, 10 minutes; cool.

Combine the bread flour, spelt flour, brown sugar, and salt in a mixing bowl. Add the yeast mixture and ½ cup of the raisin-plumping milk; knead for 30 seconds. Add the quinoa, amaranth, raisins, and walnuts; knead until the dough comes together and forms a slightly tacky ball of dough, adding additional plumping milk as needed. Knead for 6 minutes by hand, sprinkling with bread flour if the dough becomes too sticky.

Transfer the dough to a greased mixing bowl; turn to coat with oil. Cover with plastic wrap; allow to rise in a warm place for 1 hour, until nearly doubled. Turn out onto an unfloured work surface. Punch down the dough and divide it in half. Grease two 8½ X 4½-inch loaf pans; shape the dough into two loaves and place in the pans. Cover with greased plastic wrap; allow to rise for 2 hours, until more than doubled. When the dough has almost finished rising, heat the oven to 350°F.

Bake in a 350°F oven for 50 to 60 minutes, until golden brown and internal temperature reaches 190°F. Test by knocking on the loaf—it should sound hollow. Cool on racks.

Canary Bean and Garlic Soup with Saffron

SERVES 8 When I found bright yellow canary beans in my local market, I couldn't wait to see what they tasted like. With copious amounts of garlic and a pinch of saffron, they made a powerfully *umami*-flavored soup. (*Umami* describes a taste, roughly translated as "meaty" or "savory," that is found in certain foods, especially garlic, shellfish, and mushrooms.) Organic garlic is available from www.thegarlicstore.com or www.garlicgourmet.com. Dried canary beans can be found at www.goya.com.

2 tablespoons olive oil, plus more for serving

2 cups chopped onions

2 heads garlic, cloves peeled and thinly sliced (about 1 cup)

½ teaspoon crushed saffron threads

8 cups stock, cooking liquid from beans, or water

1 cup tomato sauce

1 cinnamon stick

2 teaspoons ground cumin

2 cups dried canary beans, simmered until very tender, drained, or
two 28-ounce cans garbanzo beans, drained

Salt and freshly ground black pepper

½ cup chopped fresh cilantro

Heat the olive oil in a large, heavy-bottomed pan for 1 minute. Add the onions and garlic and cook over medium heat until the onions are soft and juicy, but not browned. Soak the saffron threads in ¼ cup warm water for 5 minutes; add to the onions along with the stock, tomato sauce, cinnamon, cumin, and beans.

Bring to a boil; lower the heat. Transfer a third of the soup into a blender and puree until very smooth. Pour the puree back into the soup pot. Simmer gently, uncovered, for 30 minutes. Season to taste with salt and pepper.

Serve garnished with chopped cilantro and a drizzle of olive oil.

Mini Lentil-Scallion Pancakes with Cumin Cream

SERVES 8 AS AN APPETIZER Almost any grain or bean can be made into pancakes by binding it into a batter with flour, eggs, and milk. More egg makes the pancakes hold together better, but undermines the crunch that less eggy bean pancakes attain. However you make them, these hors d'oeuvres will appeal to fine-food aficionados and comfort-food lovers alike.

1 cup brown lentils, cooked until soft but not broken

3 scallions, chopped fine

1 tablespoon curry powder, toasted in a dry pan until fragrant

Pinch of cayenne

1 teaspoon salt

¼ cup chopped fresh cilantro or flat-leaf parsley

1 large egg, beaten

1 tablespoon milk or water

1 tablespoon all-purpose flour, plus more as needed

3 tablespoons olive oil

1 cup sour cream

2 teaspoons cumin seeds, toasted briefly in a dry pan and then ground, or 2 teaspoons ground cumin, toasted in a dry pan until fragrant

Gently combine the lentils, scallions, curry, cayenne, salt, and cilantro in a mixing bowl. Mix in the beaten egg and milk with your hands, then dust with enough flour to form a cohesive batter.

Heat the olive oil in a large nonstick skillet until hot, but not smoking. A bit of the batter should sizzle when placed in the oil. Drop teaspoonfuls of batter into the pan; flatten them and shape them into round cakes with the back of the spoon. Some lentils may fall away, but the cakes will stick together once they're cooked. Leave at least 1 inch of space between cakes. Fry 2 to 3 minutes per side, until lightly browned and crisp. Drain on paper towels.

Whisk together the sour cream and cumin. Arrange the lentil cakes on a serving platter and top each with a dollop of cumin cream.

Bean Dips

SERVES 8 AS AN APPETIZER A cheerful little Southeast Asian/Mexican fusion restaurant in New York City, the Bright Food Shop, serves each guest a freshly cooked tortilla chip with a spoonful of dip as an *amuse-bouche* before every meal. These dips are addictive vegetarian snacks created by co-owner Dona Abramson. One or several of them, combined with a grain pilaf or whole-grain breads and vegetables, make a complete vegetarian meal.

Organic beans are available from www.beanbag.net; chipotle chiles in adobe sauce can be found at www.mexgrocer.com.

Chickpea Dip

1½ cups cooked chickpeas or one 14-ounce can, drained

Pinch crushed red pepper

2 tablespoons sour cream

1 scallion, chopped fine

1 tablespoon chopped roasted red bell pepper (bottled pepper is fine)

½ teaspoon ground cumin

½ teaspoon red wine vinegar

1 garlic clove, chopped

1 tablespoon chopped fresh cilantro

Salt and freshly ground black pepper

In a food processor, combine the chickpeas, red pepper, sour cream, scallion, roasted pepper, cumin, vinegar, and garlic. Pulse until smooth.

Fold in the chopped cilantro with a wooden spoon or rubber spatula. Season liberally with salt and black pepper. Serve with warm breads or tortillas.

Pinto Bean Dip

1½ cups cooked pinto beans or one 14-ounce can, drained

2 tablespoons sour cream

¼ cup buttermilk

¼ teaspoon ground cumin

½ teaspoon red wine vinegar

1 tablespoon chopped fresh cilantro

2 tablespoons finely diced red onion

1 pickled jalapeño, finely chopped

Salt and freshly ground black pepper

Mash the beans in a mixing bowl. Then, using a wooden spoon, mash the sour cream, buttermilk, cumin, and vinegar into the beans.

Gently fold in the cilantro, onion, and jalapeño. Season to taste with salt and pepper. Serve with warm breads and tortillas.

White Bean Dip

1½ cups cooked small white (navy) beans or one 14-ounce can, drained

1 teaspoon orange juice concentrate

Juice of half a lime

1 tablespoon sour cream

Grated zest of 1 orange

1 chipotle chile in adobo sauce, pureed or finely chopped

2 tablespoons chopped fresh cilantro

¼ cup finely diced white onion

Salt and freshly ground black pepper

In a food processor, combine the beans, orange juice concentrate (you can make your own by simmering the juice of one orange until it has a syrupy consistency), lime juice, sour cream, orange zest, and chipotle. Puree until very smooth.

Transfer the mixture to a bowl and fold in the chopped cilantro and onion. Season well with salt and pepper. Serve with warm breads and tortillas.

Sesame Rice

SERVES 8 This rice carries enough flavor and nutrition to make it a main course. Try it with some stir-fried Asian vegetables, such as Napa cabbage, young bok choy, and mustard greens. You can find organic Japanese short-grain rice, or *koshihikari,* from www.yatatex.com.

2 cups Japanese short-grain rice

1-inch piece kelp (optional)

1 teaspoon oil

2 large eggs, beaten

1 tablespoon sesame seeds (preferably Japanese)

2 tablespoons Asian toasted sesame oil

¼ cup chopped scallions

Pinch of salt

In a bowl or pot, rinse the rice very well under cold running water, agitating it with your hands until all the starch has washed off and the water runs clear; drain. Place the rice and kelp (if using) in a pot with a tight-fitting lid. Add 2½ cups water. Cover the pot and bring to a boil; lower to a simmer. Cook until all the water is absorbed, about 10 minutes. Remove from heat. Let stand, covered, for at least 10 minutes.

Lightly oil a small skillet and cook the beaten eggs until firm; transfer to a board and roughly chop. Heat a small skillet over medium-high heat; toast the sesame seeds in the dry skillet until fragrant and just starting to brown. Transfer the rice to a mixing bowl. Gently toss the rice with the eggs, sesame seeds, sesame oil, scallions, and salt.

Coconut Rice

SERVES 6 A discovery of richness for anyone who thought rice was just steamed starch, this tropical preparation is the basis for a Thai rice salad made in combination with Southeast Asian Slaw (page 109). It is also good with sautéed mushrooms and stir-fry dishes. You can find organic brands of coconut milk, jasmine rice, and coconut at www.villageorganics.com.

One 14-ounce can coconut milk

1½ cups jasmine rice

1 cup unsweetened shredded coconut

1 teaspoon salt

Combine 1 cup water, the coconut milk, rice, shredded coconut, and salt in a heavy-bottomed saucepan with a tight-fitting lid. Place over a low flame. Bring to a simmer; cook, covered, very gently for 20 minutes.

Remove from heat; let stand 10 minutes. Fluff with a fork before serving.

Coco-Vegetable Rice with Tamarind Chicken Skewers

SERVES 8 This main course pairs a small amount of intensely flavored chicken with a substantial portion of rice-vegetable salad. Serve it with hot sauce on the side. Organic sesame oil is available from www.edenfoods.com.

2 tablespoons vegetable oil

1 small onion, chopped

2 teaspoons chopped garlic

2 tablespoons tamarind concentrate

1 tablespoon Thai or Vietnamese fish sauce

1 teaspoon honey

½ teaspoon Asian toasted sesame oil

1 teaspoon Asian hot chili paste (such as Sriracha brand)

1 pound boneless chicken (preferably dark) or rabbit meat, sliced into 16 thin strips

1 recipe Coconut Rice (page 61), warm or at room temperature

1 recipe Southeast Asian Slaw (page 109)

Fresh cilantro sprigs and lime wedges

Heat 1 tablespoon of the oil in a small skillet over medium heat. Add the onion and garlic; cook until very soft and beginning to brown, about 10 minutes. Transfer to a blender or food processor; add the tamarind, fish sauce, honey, sesame oil, and chili paste. Puree until smooth. Mix with the sliced chicken and marinate for at least 2 hours (or overnight).

Heat the oven to 350°F. Reserving the marinade, thread the chicken onto 8-inch bamboo skewers. (The skewers can be soaked in water for 30 minutes to prevent them from burning at the ends, but this is not necessary.) Heat the remaining oil in a large skillet until a piece of vegetable sizzles when added. Brown the chicken on both sides, working in small batches. Transfer to a baking dish, baste with the excess marinade, and finish in the oven, no more than 5 minutes.

Combine the Coconut Rice and Southeast Asian Slaw. Serve the chicken skewers on a bed of Coco-Vegetable Rice. Garnish with cilantro and lime.

Pumpkin Basmati Rice Pilaf

SERVES 8 Master the pumpkin and you'll eat locally all winter. Squashes, gourds, and pumpkins keep for months in cold weather and get sweeter as they age, as their starches convert to sugars. They are usually interchangeable, so try this recipe with delicata, dumpling, kabocha, turban, calabaza, or any other winter squash that looks good in the market. Serve this pilaf with beans for a wholesome, protein-complete vegetarian meal.

Organic basmati rice is available from www.diamondorganics.com.

3 tablespoons unsalted butter

1 large Spanish onion, chopped (about 3 cups)

2 pounds pumpkin or winter squash, cut into ½-inch dice (about 4 cups)

1 teaspoon salt

1 bay leaf

2 cups basmati rice

3 cups vegetable stock or water

Melt the butter in a large saucepan with a tight-fitting lid over moderate heat. Add the onion, pumpkin, and salt; cook gently until the onion is soft, about 10 minutes. Add the bay leaf and rice. Stir to coat; cook 5 minutes, scraping the bottom of the pot regularly with a wooden spoon.

Add the stock; stir, and bring to a boil. Lower the heat and simmer, covered tightly, very slowly for 20 minutes. Remove from heat; let stand 5 minutes. Fluff with a fork before serving.

Creamy Polenta with Butter and Cheese

SERVES 4 Delicious as a base for stews and ragoûts, such as chunky tomato sauce, sautéed wild mushroom ragoût, or vegetable stew, polenta is also excellent when it is chilled, then cut into pieces and grilled or fried.

4 cups water or stock

1 teaspoon salt

1 cup coarse yellow cornmeal (polenta)

½ cup grated Parmesan cheese

1 tablespoon unsalted butter

Bring the water to a boil in a large saucepan; add salt. Whisking constantly with a stiff wire whisk, gradually pour in the cornmeal in a steady stream, working out any lumps. Continue whisking constantly until mixture thickens noticeably.

Lower the heat to a very low simmer. You should see only the occasional bubble plopping up through the polenta. Beware: The polenta is molten lava at this point, and spattering can be hazardous. Stir regularly with a wooden spoon until full thickening is achieved, about 25 minutes. Stir in the cheese and butter; remove from heat. Serve immediately, or cool for grilling or frying.

Vegetarian Chili

SERVES 12 Chili, like many stews, tastes better the second day. Make this ahead, and serve it either souplike, in bowls, or saucelike, over rice. I like to puree a few tomatoes and cook them in with the rice to be served with the chili. A few teaspoons of olive oil in the rice cooking water also adds another dimension.

Chipotles, or canned smoked chiles, are in the Spanish foods sections of most supermarkets and can also be found at www.ethnicgrocer.com. If not available, add extra crushed red pepper.

¼ cup olive oil

2 cups chopped onions

1 cup chopped carrots

1 cup each chopped green, red, and yellow bell peppers

2 teaspoons salt

1 tablespoon chopped garlic

2 chopped, seeded jalapeños

1 tablespoon ground ancho chile or ½ teaspoon crushed red pepper

1 chipotle chile in adobo sauce, chopped

1 tablespoon cumin seeds, toasted briefly in a dry pan and then ground, or 4 teaspoons ground cumin, toasted in a dry pan until fragrant

One 28-ounce can plum tomatoes, roughly chopped, juice included

One 16-ounce can each red kidney, cannellini, and black beans, rinsed and drained, or 1½ cups cooked beans of each variety

1 cup tomato juice

Sour cream (optional)

Finely chopped red onion

Chopped fresh cilantro

Heat the oil in a heavy-bottomed Dutch oven or soup pot. Add the onions, carrots, bell peppers, and salt; cook 15 minutes over medium heat, stirring occasionally, until the onions are soft.

Add the garlic, jalapeños, ancho chile, chipotle, and cumin; cook 5 minutes more. Stir in the tomatoes, beans, and tomato juice. Simmer about 45 minutes. Serve garnished with sour cream (if using), red onion, and cilantro.

Dominican Stewed Red Beans

SERVES 8 A pairing of beans with a grain, such as rice or barley, provides all of the essential amino acids for complete protein. This classic Caribbean pairing is a main course, great served with various salads and side dishes such as fried yuca (cassava root) and ground plantain cakes (called *mofongo*), which may or may not include meat.

Sazón or Accent is optional, but will make the dish more authentic. Also, don't neglect to soak the beans; long soaking is traditional for this dish.

3 tablespoons olive oil

1 medium onion, chopped

3 garlic cloves, sliced

1 teaspoon dried oregano

2 bay leaves

One 8-ounce can tomato sauce (such as Goya Spanish style)

2 teaspoons adobo (seasoned salt) or salt and pepper to taste

½ teaspoon Goya Sazón or Accent seasoning (optional)

½ small bunch fresh cilantro, including stems, roughly chopped (optional)

2 cups (1 pound) dried red beans, soaked overnight in 1 quart cold water, drained

Heat the olive oil in a pot large enough to hold all the ingredients. Sauté the onion and garlic over medium heat for 5 minutes. Add the oregano, bay leaves, tomato sauce, adobo, and Sazón (if using). Bring to a simmer and add the cilantro (if using) and beans, adding enough water to cover (about 3 cups).

Bring to a boil, then reduce to a low simmer and cook 1½ hours, covered, until the beans are tender enough to mash between two fingers.

Amaranth Cake with Cinnamon Banana Sauce

SERVES 8 Momo Attaoui, a colleague with a deep love of whole-grain cookery, convinced me that whole grains can be the basis for every course. He proved it with this dessert, whose sweetness comes from fresh and dried fruits and just a touch of honey. Amaranth is a fine grain that looks like porridge when it's cooked, but has a delightful crunch. Drain it well, and it can be molded to create this handsome composed dessert. Organic amaranth is available from www.arrowheadmills.com.

1 cup amaranth

½ cup pumpkin seeds

2 tablespoons honey

3 tablespoons pumpkin seed oil or other dark nut oil

1 ripe banana

¼ teaspoon ground cinnamon

½ cup soymilk or milk

25 pitted dates, crushed with your hands

3 kiwi fruit, finely diced

Bring 2 cups water to a boil; add the amaranth and simmer 20 to 25 minutes, until it has a tender, porridgelike consistency. Strain. Cool. Stir in the pumpkin seeds, honey, and 1 tablespoon pumpkin seed oil.

In a blender, puree the banana, cinnamon, and soymilk together.

On a dessert plate, use a 3-inch ring mold (or a tuna can with both ends removed) to form 3 tablespoons of the amaranth mixture into a disk. Spoon on 1 tablespoon of the crushed dates, press flat, then top with 2 tablespoons of the diced kiwi. Carefully lift the ring mold or can to reveal the cake. Repeat to form seven more cakes, each on its own plate. Garnish with the banana sauce and remaining pumpkin seed oil.

Chopsticks

Twenty billion pairs of disposable chopsticks are used once and thrown away every year in Japan alone. As Asian foods become more popular in the West, so do *waribashi,* the individually wrapped single-use chopsticks common at ramen noodle shops, sushi bars, and other Asian restaurants. They're cheap, attractive, and require no washing after use. It's surprising, though, that such a wasteful item would become so ubiquitous in Japan, where environmental concern has led to obsessive recycling, super-efficient cars, well-financed alternative fuels projects, and ultra-low-flow toilets. But in fact, Japan is the world's largest importer of temperate and tropical hardwoods. After construction, disposable chopsticks are the number one use for imported wood.

A CULTURE OF WASTE IN A LAND OF ENVIRONMENTALISTS

Culture plays an important role in the popularity of *waribashi* in Japan. A Shinto precept that chopsticks are a link between mankind and the deity fuels a perception that the chopstick is a deeply personal item. Most Japanese would consider it rude to be served with anything other than unused chopsticks, even in a fine restaurant. When hosting guests, even very fine reusable sticks are slightly insulting. Using reusable chopsticks is viewed as akin to borrowing used gym socks. This view has emerged since the 1870s, when *waribashi* were invented as a thrifty way to utilize scrap wood from the lumber industry. Ironically, what began as a sensible recycling step has grown into a destructive national obsession.

Concern is rising in China, where throwaway chopsticks are used in all but the poorest and fanciest restaurants. Low-end eateries still use reusable bamboo sticks (which are given only a cursory washing between uses, in many cases), and fine restaurants present expensive lacquered chopsticks. The rest of the restaurants in urban China, as in Japan, use *waribashi*. The country fells 25 million trees annually to produce 45 billion pairs, two-thirds of which are used in China. Most of the rest go to Japan, which also sources sticks from mostly deforested Southeast Asia and North America. China is facing a deforestation crisis, with twelve of the nation's forty state-owned logging companies having nothing left to fell. In amount of forest land per capita, China ranks 121st in the world. Still, its disposable chopsticks cost one-fifth the price of Japanese-made sticks in Japan.

The Canadian Chopstick Manufacturing Company, a subsidiary of corporate giant Mitsubishi, makes among the most highly prized *waribashi* from virgin aspen wood. Eighty-five percent of the timber is wasted because it doesn't meet the company's standards. Mitsubishi is the largest wood exporter from the United States, shipping out mountains of processed wood from Alaska and the Pacific Northwest. U.S. taxpayers subsidize logging in national forests by constructing logging roads that help timber companies access unexploited areas. Political candidates supported by huge logging companies' donations seem to be winning election after election. These bad corporate citizens are considered among the most polluting industries in the American West.

In our throwaway society, disposable chopsticks are catching on. Supermarkets, take-out shops, delicatessen salad bars, and chic eateries now habitually slip them in with customer orders, often in addition to forks. If the customer doesn't use them, they're thrown away anyhow. Do not become inured to the waste of these throwaways as the Japanese have done, and the Chinese are starting to do. Take a stand now, while we still have a culture that accepts reusable utensils.

SOLVE THE PROBLEM YOURSELF

Concerned Japanese and Chinese are taking to carrying their own chopsticks with them to dine. Chopstick cases are widely available, and the sticks wash quickly and easily after meals. The important thing to remember is to refuse the *waribashi* when they're offered. Even untouched *waribashi* will likely be cleared into the garbage when the table is bused. In Japan, where conformity is highly valued, bringing personal chopsticks will draw stares. But many habits we now consider mundane were ridiculed only a generation ago. Consider the now-routine use of seatbelts: In the sixties and seventies, only "sissies" would don them. Nowadays, they're expected.

If carrying chopsticks in a purse or pocket seems ungainly, throw authenticity to the wind and request a fork. While restaurants that put out disposable chopsticks seldom have reusable ones on hand, most will bring a reusable fork to a guest who requests one. Even in Japan, there's virtually no stigma about reusing Western eating utensils, only chopsticks.

Cumin-laced Root Vegetable Couscous with Apricots

SERVES 8 TO 10 AS A MAIN COURSE In winter, when farms in most parts of the country are quiet, local root vegetables and dried fruits are still for sale in greenmarkets. These make some of the most comforting, hearty winter dishes, like this Moroccan-inspired pilaf. Serve with dark greens, balsamic vinaigrette, and slices of rare seared duck breast if desired.

1 onion, roughly chopped

2 carrots, diced

½ pound celery root or potato, diced

2 parsnips, diced

1 white turnip, diced (about 1 cup)

1 pound diced rutabaga (yellow or "wax" turnip), about 2 cups

½ teaspoon turmeric

1 cup dried apricots, diced

¼ cup olive oil

2 cups couscous

½ teaspoon ground cinnamon

1 teaspoon ground cumin, warmed in a dry pan until fragrant

¼ cup roughly chopped fresh flat-leaf parsley

Juice and zest of 1 lemon

Salt and freshly ground black pepper

In a medium saucepan, combine the onion, carrots, celery root, parsnips, turnip, rutabaga, and turmeric with lightly salted water to cover by 1 inch. Bring to a boil;

simmer until tender, about 10 minutes. Pour the cooking liquid into a measuring cup and add water to equal 3 cups. Bring this liquid to a boil in another saucepan.

Stir the apricots, olive oil, and couscous into the boiling liquid. Remove from heat and cover tightly. Let stand 5 minutes, or until all the liquid is absorbed. Combine the couscous with the cooked vegetables, cinnamon, cumin, parsley, lemon juice, and zest. Season with salt and pepper.

Mexican Frijoles Refritos (Refried Beans)

SERVES 4 These luxuriously unctuous beans form a complete protein when served with brown rice. Simmering time for the beans varies, depending on how old the beans are and which brand you use. Taste-test one to be sure it is cooked: It should be easy to mash against the roof of your mouth with your tongue. Some chefs mash the beans with an old-fashioned potato masher for a smoother texture. These are great as a dip for tortilla chips; as a filling for bean tacos, burritos, or Mexican Pinto Bean Tortas with Pickled Jalapeños (page 76); or as a simple dinner, with brown rice and a tomato salad. Canned beans could also be used.

¼ **pound dried pinto beans (slightly less than 1 cup), washed**

1 **tablespoon salt**

1 **large white onion, roughly chopped (about 2 cups)**

1 **tablespoon vegetable oil**

6 **tablespoons olive oil**

Radishes, lettuce, shredded *queso blanco* **(a fresh Mexican cheese sold in most Hispanic food sections) or feta cheese to garnish**

Bring the beans and 5 cups water to a boil in a 2½-quart pot with the salt, 1 cup of the onion, and the vegetable oil. Lower the flame and simmer 2 to 3 hours, until very tender, skimming occasionally and adding water if necessary to keep the beans brothy. Cool the beans in their cooking liquid.

Heat the olive oil in a 10-inch cast-iron skillet over medium heat; cook the remaining cup of onion until translucent. Add the beans with their cooking liquid 1 cup at a time, mashing with a wooden spoon over high heat.

Constantly mash and stir until the beans dry out and sizzle around the edges. They should start coming away from the surface of the pan. Rock the pan back and forth to make sure they loosen. Turn them out, omelet style, onto a warm serving platter.

Garnish with radishes, lettuce, and shredded cheese. Accompany with brown rice.

Mexican Pinto Bean Tortas with Pickled Jalapeños

SERVES 4 Mexican hot sandwiches, called *tortas,* combine bold-flavored ingredients like pickled jalapeño peppers and feta cheese with earthy bean purees and bright cilantro. They're a meatless hot meal from a place where meat has traditionally been a secondary source of protein.

4 crusty rolls, such as Kaiser rolls

2 tablespoons olive oil

1½ cups cooked pinto beans or Mexican Frijoles Refritos (page 74), kept warm

4 pickled jalapeños, sliced

¼ pound feta cheese, crumbled

1 cup Salsa Fresca (recipe follows)

8 fresh cilantro sprigs

Heat the oven to 400°F. Slice open the rolls; scoop out a small amount of the insides. Drizzle the bottoms with olive oil and distribute the beans among them. Sprinkle some jalapeños and cheese over each bottom. Close the sandwiches.

Place the sandwiches on a baking pan and heat in the oven until hot, about 5 minutes. Serve garnished with salsa and cilantro.

Salsa Fresca (Pico de Gallo)

YIELD: ABOUT 1 CUP This simple salsa pairs magnificently with burritos, tacos, empanadas, tortilla chips, and all kinds of other Mexican savories. For smoky, deeper spiciness, add the chipotle puree, available from www.ethnicgrocer.com.

2 large tomatoes

1 small onion, finely diced

1 or 2 jalapeño peppers, finely chopped

½ teaspoon fresh lime juice

Salt and freshly ground black pepper

½ teaspoon pureed chipotle in adobo (optional)

Quarter the tomatoes. Remove the seeds and their pulp; reserve. Cut the tomato flesh into fine dice. Puree the seeds and pulp in a food processor until smooth. Toss together with the diced tomato, onion, jalapeño, lime juice, salt, pepper, and chipotle (if using). The salsa keeps in the refrigerator for two days, but is best used the day it's made.

Toasted Hard Red Wheat Pilaf with Caramelized Shallots, Figs, and Brazil Nuts

SERVES 8 AS A MAIN COURSE Wheat berries are widely available in health food stores and online; see Sources. Hard wheat has a pleasantly chewy texture when cooked, and makes excellent pilaf. Hard winter wheat is similar to hard spring wheat—it's just planted at a different time of year. Soft wheat is starchier and has a more ricelike texture when cooked; it can be substituted in this recipe. This is a complete vegetarian meal, excellent with a lemony salad. Wheat berries are available from www.sunorganicfarm.com, www.greenmountainmills.com, www.barryfarm.com, and www.greatgrainsmilling.com. Organic Brazil nuts are available from www.truefoodsonline.com.

2 tablespoons grapeseed oil, peanut oil, or Clarified Butter (page 223)

1 tablespoon yellow mustard seeds

4 whole cloves

1 stick cinnamon

8 green cardamom pods

2 bay leaves

1 pound dried figs, halved and soaked 6 to 8 hours or overnight in enough water to cover by 1 inch

2 cups red wheat berries, soaked overnight, drained

1 teaspoon kosher salt, plus more to taste

Freshly ground black pepper

½ pound shallots, peeled and halved lengthwise

1 tablespoon olive oil

2 cups whole, shelled Brazil nuts

Heat the grapeseed oil, mustard seeds, cloves, cinnamon, cardamom, and bay leaves in a large, heavy-bottomed pot over medium-high heat until the mustard seeds begin to pop, about 4 minutes. Add the figs with their soaking liquid, the wheat berries (wash them well first under running water), salt, and 6 cups water. Bring to a boil; cover and lower to a simmer. Cook until the wheat berries are tender, about 1¼ hours. Season with salt and pepper. Drain off any excess liquid.

While the wheat is cooking, heat the oven to 375°F. Toss the shallots with olive oil; spread in a small baking pan. Roast until lightly browned, turning once, about 20 minutes. Add the Brazil nuts and roast 5 minutes more, until the nuts are shiny.

Add half of the shallot-nut mixture to the cooked wheat and toss; adjust seasoning. Serve garnished with the remaining shallots and nuts.

Wheat Pilaf with Cumin Lamb

SERVES 8 The bulk of this hearty dinner is a robust wheat pilaf (not technically a pilaf, since it's cooked in two separate pots, and pilaf is a one-pot dish) flavored with nuts, vegetables, and dried fruits. Lamb serves as a flavor and texture element, adding its unique dimension to the dish without dominating it.

See Sources for suppliers of organic wheat berries and humanely raised lamb. Organic Brazil nuts and dried figs are available from www.truefoodsonline.com.

2 cups red spring or winter wheat berries or other whole grain

8 cups stock or water

2 teaspoons salt, plus more to taste

1 cup whole, shelled Brazil nuts

1½ pounds shallots, peeled (about 24)

4 tablespoons olive oil

2 teaspoons cumin seeds, toasted in a dry pan until fragrant

1 small boneless loin of lamb (about 2 pounds)

Freshly ground black pepper

2 large onions, chopped (about 4 cups)

2 pounds white mushrooms, sliced

4 tablespoons chopped fresh rosemary, or 2 tablespoons dried

6 garlic cloves, finely chopped

16 fresh or dried figs, quartered

Chopped fresh flat-leaf parsley

Heat the oven to 400°F. Wash the wheat berries well under running water. In a medium saucepot with a tight-fitting cover, bring the stock to a boil; stir in the wheat berries and salt. Simmer for 1½ hours, or until the grains are tender; drain. Meanwhile, spread the nuts on a small baking pan and toast them in the oven for 10 minutes until they sizzle; set aside.

While the wheat berries are cooking, toss the shallots with 1 tablespoon of the olive oil and place in a baking pan. Roast 40 minutes until tender. Once they're cool enough to handle, peel any leathery outer layers.

Combine 1 tablespoon of the olive oil with the cumin seeds, and rub the mixture onto the lamb loin. Season the loin well with salt and pepper. Sear the lamb on all sides in a heavy skillet over high heat, transfer to the oven, and cook to medium rare, about 15 minutes (adjust time downward if your roast is smaller, or cut into smaller pieces). Let the loin rest for 10 minutes before slicing as thinly as possible.

In a large skillet, heat the remaining 2 tablespoons olive oil until very hot, almost smoky. Add the onions and mushrooms. Cook without stirring for 5 minutes, allowing the vegetables to brown. Stir in the rosemary and garlic; cook for 5 minutes more, stirring occasionally, until the onions are very soft. Combine the wheat, figs, and vegetables; season to taste with salt and pepper.

For an attractive presentation, mold the pilaf into 8-ounce cups, and unmold onto serving plates. Arrange the roasted shallots and lamb slices around the pilaf, then sprinkle with nuts and chopped parsley.

Mushroom-Barley "Risotto"

SERVES 4 AS A MAIN COURSE Italian culinary purists are up in arms about supposed American abuse of their cuisine, with dishes like this one being held up as evidence of sacrilege. So lambaste me, but not until you've tasted this dish, which resembles risotto in texture, but definitely is *not* risotto. Similar dishes are appearing with increasing frequency on the tables of restaurants with open-minded chefs. Serve with crisp vegetables, such as sliced fennel, dressed with olive oil, lemon, and shaved Parmigiano-Reggiano cheese.

1 tablespoon olive oil

2 cups chopped onions

2 garlic cloves, finely chopped

4 cups mixed mushrooms, such as chanterelle, cremini, morel, and oyster,
cut into bite-size pieces

1 cup pearl barley

3 cups vegetable stock or water

1 teaspoon kosher salt

½ teaspoon turmeric

½ cup grated Parmigiano-Reggiano cheese

½ teaspoon freshly ground black pepper

1 tablespoon unsalted butter, chopped

Lemon wedges

Heat the oil in a heavy-bottomed saucepan over medium heat until a piece of onion sizzles when added. Add the onions; cook until lightly browned, about 5 minutes. Stir in the garlic and cook until it turns white, 30 seconds. Add the mushrooms; cook until soft, about 5 minutes more. Stir in the barley to coat.

Add the stock, salt, and turmeric; bring to a boil. Lower to a simmer. Cover and cook, stirring occasionally, until the barley is tender and liquid is absorbed. Remove from heat.

Stir in the Parmigiano-Reggiano, pepper, and butter. Serve with lemon wedges.

Spelt Pilaf with Mushrooms, Almonds, Dried Fruit, Roasted Onions, and Eggplant

SERVES 4 AS A MAIN COURSE Whole-grain pilafs make great main courses when they're crafted as flavorful dishes rather than afterthoughts. This sweet, vegetable-rich, complexly spiced dish stands on its own, with or without a meat accompaniment. Spelt is sold either unprocessed or with the outer hull polished off (pearled).

3 tablespoons olive oil

3 whole cloves

1 cinnamon stick

5 whole allspice berries

3 celery ribs, diced (about 2 cups)

4 carrots, cut into bite-size pieces

1 tablespoon kosher salt

4 cups mixed mushrooms, such as shiitake, cremini, and oyster, cut into bite-size pieces

2 cups whole-grain spelt or wheat berries, soaked overnight

½ cup white wine

4 cups vegetable stock or water

8 pitted prunes

12 dried apricots

4 onions, sliced ½ inch thick

½ pound Japanese eggplant, cut into large chunks

½ cup whole, shelled almonds, lightly toasted in a dry pan until shiny

Heat 2 tablespoons of the olive oil with the cloves, cinnamon, and allspice in a heavy-bottomed pot over medium heat until fragrant, about 1 minute. Add the celery, carrots, salt, and mushrooms. Cook until the vegetables release their juices and become soft, about 10 minutes.

Stir in the spelt until coated with juices. Add the wine; cover and simmer 5 minutes to steam out the alcohol. Add the stock, prunes, and apricots; cover. Lower the flame; simmer until the spelt is tender and liquid is absorbed, about 1½ hours (less for pearled spelt).

While the spelt is cooking, heat the oven to 400°F. Toss the onions and eggplant with the remaining tablespoon of olive oil. Spread on a baking sheet; roast until tender and caramelized, about 20 minutes. Serve the pilaf topped with almonds, roasted onions, and roasted eggplant.

Tuscan White Beans with Onions and Thyme

SERVES 4 AS A MAIN COURSE If you are unable to locate great Northern beans, navy beans, though smaller, are fine. As far as the soaking controversy, I stand firmly on the don't-soak-but-cook-for-hours side of the fence. If you must soak, then cut the cooking time for the beans accordingly (soaked navy beans will cook in slightly under one hour). These beans make a protein-rich component of a vegetarian dinner plate, paired with dishes such as sautéed escarole, roasted tomatoes, and a barley pilaf. You could also serve them as a handsome vegetarian appetizer, garnished with sprigs of fresh thyme, or pair them with two pieces of simply grilled shrimp. (Information on organic shrimp is available from www.oceanboyfarms.com. The shrimp are sold at all Publix supermarkets and many other fine stores.)

1 cup dried great Northern (Tuscan) white beans or navy beans

10 bushy sprigs fresh thyme

2 large Spanish onions, one left whole and one chopped

¼ cup fruity extra virgin olive oil, preferably unfiltered, plus more for serving

3 garlic cloves, finely chopped

Salt and freshly ground black pepper

Pick through the beans to remove any stones. Wash thoroughly under cold water, and place in a large pot with 2 quarts water, 4 sprigs of the thyme, and the whole onion. Bring to a boil, cover, then simmer until very tender, about 2½ hours. Cool the beans in their cooking liquid. Drain. A cooked bean should mash easily between two fingers.

Heat the oil in a large skillet until it shimmers but does not smoke. Add the chopped onion, garlic, and 2 sprigs of thyme. Cook over medium heat until the onion is soft and translucent, about 10 minutes. Add the cooked beans, salt, and pepper. Transfer to plates, remove any stray thyme stems, and garnish with the 4 remaining thyme sprigs. Drizzle the beans with additional olive oil at the table.

Vegetables

If you call the Sierra Club and ask for suggestions in choosing foods ethically, they'll tell you to eat vegetarian. So maybe you'll shop for tofu, lettuce, and strawberries. You'll reward yourself with some chocolates.

But there might be a catch or two: The lettuce was grown unsustainably in arid lands that were irrigated by depleting Western river habitats. The strawberries, one of the most pesticide-intensive crops, may have come from farms doused in noxious chemicals that are seeping into groundwater and running off into estuaries. The soybeans for the tofu were grown on farmland created by clearing wetlands. And the chocolate's production might be contributing to slavery in Africa and rain forest degradation in the Amazon.

These are hypothetical examples, but real ethical choices exist, even for vegetarians. For example, eating a nectarine is more ecologically sound than eating a peach, since peach production uses nearly twice as much pesticide as nectarine production (though differences in amount of residue left on them are negligible). A cabbage salad or slaw represents a better use of natural resources than a lettuce salad, since cabbage uses water very efficiently, while lettuce is the most water-intensive crop grown, especially in the dry Western states where it's cultivated in the U.S. Cabbage also contains many more nutrients and antioxidants, making it a healthier salad ingredient to boot.

Cultivation of crops for use in other products is another issue. For example, growing of grapes for wine uses lots of pesticides and chemical fertilizer. Organic wine is available from the Organic Wine Company (www.ecowine.com).

The Four Tiers of Ethical Produce
Organic isn't always a panacea. Sometimes other considerations trump the growing method when deciding which product is better for the environment, your community, and the world as a whole. For example, if you have a choice between two bunches of beets, one organic and the other not, all other things being equal, the organic beets would be the logical choice, since their production can be assumed to be more benign to the soil and water. But if the organic beets were grown thousands of miles away, while the conventional beets are from a local farm stand, you have to consider the pollution gen-

erated in bringing them to you. A lot of organic produce is now shipped to the U.S. from places as far away as New Zealand. That's a long way, and a lot of fuel, for a fresh vegetable. In this case, the conventionally grown local beets are the more ecologically sound choice.

Some organics advocates argue that the corporatization of organic production is pushing small, local organic farmers out of business. If they can't compete with agribusinesses like Dole and ADM on prices, they say, they'll be unable to survive. But local farms have an advantage in quality, and chefs and savvy home cooks know that. Alice Waters, the groundbreaking organic/local-sourcing chef of Berkeley's Chez Panisse, and Michael Romano, the organic/local-sourcing chef of New York's Union Square Café, aren't about to start bargain-hunting in the A&P. Small local farmers have been a niche market for my whole life, and they've seen a resurgence in recent years because of the specialty crops they grow. Maybe corporate potato giant Simplot will convert some of its fields to organic production to meet growing demand, and to reap the higher market price that organics command, but I don't see them investing too heavily in the organic French fingerling potatoes or the heirloom purple Peruvian spuds that small specialty farmers grow for restaurants and gourmets. The small local farmer niche will not swamp mainstream supermarkets with products, now that consumers recognize the USDA certified-organic label on foods. But neither will they become extinct, as some have been predicting since the 1960s.

Let's celebrate the increasing share of America's farmland that's being cultivated organically, without chemical pesticides or fertilizers. And let's support the efforts of agribusinesses that are doing the right thing by producing organically, even if they're doing it for the money. We all benefit from greater availability of organic products, and from more organic land. While some activists advocate a return to an agrarian America, complete with home canning, root cellars, and greens-less winters, that's not a realistic scenario. Yes, ethical consumers should source as much as possible from local producers. And yes, organic local is better than organic agribusiness. But there's no sense in cutting off our nose to spite our face. Mainstream organic production holds greater promise of cutting into *conventional* foods' market share than it has for putting the fifty-acre organic farm out of business.

What we do have to fight, however, are efforts by powerful players in the food industry to weaken USDA Organics Standards. Efforts are under way in Congress to loosen organics definitions to allow small amounts of synthetic or nonorganic ingredients into certified organic foods. Write your congressmen and senators. Tell them that's not acceptable.

Small local farms have been competing with industrial agriculture since the "green revolution" in the 1960s, when new seed varieties, better irrigation, chemical fertilizers, and pesticides radically increased crop yields and cut the cost of large-scale farm production. But for crops with the best flavor, and special regional appeal, small farms continue to draw loyal customers. Don't write the epitaph of the locally grown, organic candy-cane striped beet yet. Where there's demand for the product, there'll be someone to produce it. To condemn large-scale producers of the new generation of organic foods because they compete on broccoli is counterproductive. What has kept local growers in business for the past thirty years has been their ability to provide a different, better product. I endorse choosing local, small-farm-grown products over mass-produced. But I also endorse mass production of organic foods.

Ethical choices at the market involve numerous decisions. Organic agribusiness broccoli trumps conventionally raised agribusiness broccoli. If you're shopping at the supermarket, where your local growers' produce never appears, then factory-farmed organic presents a better option. It's progress. Embrace it. Organically raised lamb from Pennsylvania is certainly a more ecologically sound choice than similarly raised organic lamb from New Zealand. But conventional lamb from a humane domestic producer might also be a better choice than the imported product from overseas. A 747 jet flight from the other side of the globe consumes about 50,000 gallons (950 oil drums) of fuel (11.6 times as much as rail transport).

Organic products are the fastest-growing sector of the food market. Consumption of mainstream companies' organic products will lead to increased product range. At the current rate of growth, organic sales could outstrip conventional sales within twenty years. No one expects the organic sector to sustain its current breakneck pace, but it's likely that, within our lifetimes, conventional growers will be crying that they can't compete with organics. Organic meat has an even bigger impact on the environment than organic fruits and vegetables.

There's an easy way to prioritize food purchases. To ensure that the largest share of your food dollar goes to the most ethical producers, use a four-tier decision tree to guide purchases. It takes into consideration pollution, ecologically sound production, and support of deserving economies. It can be applied to fresh produce, meat and dairy, fish and seafood, and packaged goods with equal confidence. The priorities run in the following order.

1. **Local organic:** If you live in a region where organic food is grown or produced nearby, that's the gold standard. Map an area within 50 miles of your home, and source all that you can from organic producers in that zone. If you're in an urban area, where farms and farm stands aren't nearby, set a range of within 200 miles of your home. Organic goods grown within that distance will not employ the massive cross-country trucking system that pollutes the air and increases our dependence on petroleum. And foods that are shipped in by airfreight are the worst offenders. One 747 arriving and departing produces as much smog as a car driven 5,600 miles, and as much nitrogen oxides as a car driven nearly 26,500 miles.

2. **Local:** Even if the farmers in your area use conventional methods (read: pesticides and chemical fertilizers), buying direct from small local farms benefits the environment. Half of the air pollution in the United States is generated by motor vehicles. The less gasoline burned to bring your goods to you, the better. Also, small farms tend to use more environmentally sound farming practices, because they have a bigger stake in the sustainability of their farm. From a culinary standpoint, fresh foods taste superior to older ones. Not only are the natural sugars and essential oils of most fruits and vegetables at their peak at picking, but produce can also be picked at or close to perfect ripeness when it doesn't have to travel far. Foods intended for shipping are intentionally picked unripe, so that they can withstand the slings and arrows of shipping. Fresh-picked fruits and vegetables have a tender, more delicate texture, more appealing natural aroma, and deeper taste than artificially ripened ones.

3. **Organic:** All other factors being equal, choose organic foods over conventional. The energy used to manufacture chemical fertilizer and pesticides is enormous, and the unintended effects of those chemicals can be terrible. While some longtime sup-

porters of the organics movement decry the corporatization of large-scale organic farming, there's no denying the benefit of turning more acres over to organic production. Maybe the agribusiness companies are only in it for the money, but sometimes people do the right thing for the wrong reason. I, for one, look forward to the day when organic production is considered mainstream, and pesticide/chemical fertilizer farming is the exception (though I believe there will always be a place for limited use of these technologies). If such a system competes with small local growers, they should welcome the competition. Ethical shoppers will still opt for foods grown close to home, and everyone benefits from an overall cleaner environment.

4. **Produced by ethical methods:** Try to make every item you buy make a difference in the world. If it can't be organic or local, then try to find Fair Trade, Rainforest Alliance, or other products that address a problem. Buying Fair Trade–certified foods helps alleviate poverty and end inhumane, unsustainable farming practices in the developing world. It's like using a credit card that donates one percent of purchases to a good cause (check out www.workingassets.com). Get to know which companies are socially responsible, and support them with your food basket. Information and names of who's doing it right can be found on Web sites like www.greenpages.org.

WARNINGS ON GENETICS AND FARMING Since the introduction of the "Flavr Savr" tomato in 1994, the first genetically modified (GM) food to be approved for commercial sale, numerous red flags have been raised about the possible effects of genetically modified organisms (GMOs) on human health and the environment. Concerns include, but are not limited to, unintended cross-pollination of conventional crops with genetically modified ones, negative impacts on beneficial species that come in contact with insect-resistant crops, corporate ownership of patented seed strains, and unknown potential consequences to human health.

An early study of the effects of insect-resistant corn raised concern that its pollen, aerially transported to wild milkweed leaves, could decimate populations of migrating monarch butterflies, which rely entirely on milkweed for their nutrition. This raised the bigger question of what other unintended ripple effects might go undetected in the environment until it was too late to take remedial action. Just as fertilizer runoff in heartland states flows downriver to the Gulf of Mexico, causing fish kills unknown to the upstream farmers, transgenic pollen could be transported to remote places where it could do undiscovered harm.

Pollen from GM corn has already infected conventional cornfields. In a high-profile case in Saskatoon, Canada, biotech giant Monsanto actually sued a farmer for raising crops with its patented genetic modification, even though the farmer's crops were accidentally cross-pollinated by airborne elements from an adjacent GM field. That brought the issue of seed ownership to the fore also.

In countries like India, 80 percent of seed is still saved by farmers. These farmers and their allies have developed strains of crops to resist salt, drought, flood, rocky soil, and a host of other natural occurrences. The introduction of registered patents in those places has put farmers in the position of having to defend their right to plant crops that they've grown for generations. In the U.S., patent protection of seeds dates back to the Plant Patent Act of 1930. But both that and the Plant Variety Protection Act of 1970 specifically excluded seeds from "utility" patenting. Those laws, while patenting new development in hybrid species by breeders, allow for seed saving and exchange by farmers. Nonetheless, the Supreme Court in 2001 upheld the right of breeders to patent GM seed that can't be saved for the next year's crop. Critics of that Supreme Court decision argue that GM plants are different, and should be treated differently, because breeders can now modify seeds to grow for only one season (with a "terminator gene").

Of the thousands of new foods introduced every year, those made with GMOs have raised concern among citizens and scientists around the world over the possibility of long-term health risks. No one knows what effects these transgenic plants could have on our species. Just as pesticide contamination has led to mutation in river fish species, perhaps GMOs could have some effect on future generations of people.

These questions are raised amid a long list of claims by supporters of genetic developments. They say that this field of science has produced crops that resist insects without excessive insecticide; remain fresh longer without preservatives, preventing waste; have higher nutrition; and protect wild lands by giving higher yields per acre, reducing the need for farmland encroachment. There are good arguments on both sides. Obviously the millions of tons of pesticides used annually are a known evil, and reducing that abuse should be a goal. And loss of habitat is the main threat facing endangered species today, so the advantages of using already-cleared farmland more efficiently are great. But each person has to decide for himself where the risks of new technology outweigh the benefits.

Rethinking Tillage and Pest Management

Scenes of the plowman turning the soil conjure feelings of harmony with the land. Farming is so intertwined with the romantic lore of our agrarian history that many are shocked to learn that breaking up the ground to turn under weeds is a major cause of soil erosion and release of greenhouse gases. Up to 30 percent of the soil from a plowed field, along with any residual pesticides it contains, can end up in rivers, harming river life as it washes away from the farm where it's needed. Sediments muddy the waters, and excessive nutrients alter the balance of life in the river. Back on the farm, the upturned soil releases carbon gases, a leading cause of global warming.

But that soil can be saved, and the carbon can remain locked in the ground where it belongs, through a different kind of plowing called *conservation tillage.* The EPA defines it as any tillage and planting system that covers 30 percent or more of the soil with crop residue after planting to reduce soil erosion by water and wind. The system encourages water to seep into the soil and return to the rivers as groundwater. Soil remains soil, not runoff or dust in the wind. Conservation tillage benefits the farmer by preserving precious topsoil, and benefits the atmosphere by capping loose carbon in the ground. The system also uses half as many tractors as conventional tillage, which means lower fuel consumption. The Nature Conservancy, which trains and supports farmers in conservation tillage, reports that the practice can cut annual soil erosion by four to seven tons per acre.

Preparing the fields before planting usually involves some form of tillage. *Traditional, intensive,* or *conventional* tillage disturbs the entire soil surface in the full width of every row. It leaves less than 15 percent residue cover after planting, and involves numerous tillage trips. Multiple tillage operations take place over many months, and occur before, during, and after planting. Farmers have always loved this method because turning up the earth this way simultaneously creates seedbed, controls weeds, and removes unwanted crop plants from the previous season. It also incorporates plant residues into the soil, along with fertilizers and soil-applied pesticides, and creates the soil configurations that generations of farmers have customarily used for planting, drainage, and harvesting operations. New approaches to tillage, in light of what we now know about soil erosion, pesticide abuse, and pollution in the farming industry, translate into a learning curve for farmers. To their credit, huge numbers of farmers are getting on board.

Conservation tillage can be accomplished through several methods: *no till, strip-till,* or *ridge till.* Each has its advantages and disadvantages. No-till farming, the most extreme form of conservation tillage, leaves the soil undisturbed from harvest to planting. At planting time, specially equipped planters deposit seeds into a narrow strip, forming narrow rows.

The process reduces labor by eliminating the need for multiple plowing trips, which saves an average of 3.5 gallons of fuel per acre by keeping machinery idle. Greater carbon retention in the soil increases organic matter, essential to future crops. The shade provided by crop residue on the ground surface reduces water evaporation, so farmers can net up to two additional inches of water in the late summer. Because conservation tillage reduces soil erosion, it improves water quality—by holding soil along with its component nutrients, it reduces herbicide runoff into surface water by as much as half. Microbes that live in carbon-rich soils quickly degrade pesticides. Also, crop residues left on the ground, especially the larger amounts left in no-till farming, protect against wind erosion, thus lowering the amount of dust in the air and improving air quality. But the biggest benefit is the system's effect on soil erosion.

Soil erosion is of greater concern than herbicides. Biologist David Pimentel, professor of agriculture and agricultural services at Cornell University, is a strong proponent of pesticide reduction. But, while he's asserted for years that the United States could cut its pesticide use (currently at 1.2 billion pounds annually) in half without significantly affecting food production costs, he concedes that we have bigger problems to tackle than overuse of pesticides. "It takes approximately five hundred years to replace just one inch of topsoil in agriculture. So when you've lost that topsoil, it's something that you don't turn around quickly," he says. "With herbicides, you can stop using the material, and within four or five years the soil will be decontaminated.

Looking at it in the long term, soil erosion is a far greater problem than pesticides." He also points out that eroding soils get into our water, forming sediments that kill fish and "contaminate our ecosystem broadly." Judith D. Soule reports in *Farming in Nature's Image* (Island Press, 1992) that in the last forty years, about one-third of the world's arable land has been lost to erosion. And, she warns, the trend continues at a rate of more than ten million hectares a year, a rate of loss that is seventeen times faster than the average rate of formation.

To get an idea of what soil erosion means, it's believed that the entire population of Easter Island was forced into starvation and cannibalism after deforestation-driven soil erosion wiped out arable land on the island.

Since a primary reason for plowing is weed suppression, conservation tillage relies more on herbicides to control weeds than conventional tillage does. This is a troubling element of the system that has yet to be completely resolved. Dan Towery, a natural-resources specialist at the Conservation Technology Information Center, a nonprofit group that promotes conservation tillage, says that not all herbicides are created equal. He differentiates between what he calls "old chemistry" and the newer generation of herbicides developed with sustainability in mind.

"The only folks who don't use [chemical] herbicides are organic producers," says Towery. "In conventional tillage, where all crop residue is incorporated into the soil, they're still using herbicides." The difference with no-till, the least soil-disruptive of all conservation tillage methods, he says, is that farmers commonly do what's referred to as a "burn down," where a weedy field is cleared by one application of herbicide prior to planting. The most widely used, by far, is glyphosate (which sells under the brand name Roundup, among others). As soon as it comes into contact with clay particles in the soil, it becomes bound to it. "There are no water-quality issues associated with the use of Roundup," Towery asserts. "It's environmentally benign." Since conservation tillage increases organic matter in the soil, it promotes the growth of microbes that live in carbon-rich soils. Such microbes quickly degrade herbicides such as Roundup.

Genetically modified crops that are not affected by Roundup were introduced in the 1990s. The herbicide can be applied to a planted field, and it will kill the weeds without doing any harm to the crop. "Ninety percent of the soybeans planted in the U.S. are 'Roundup-Ready,'" says Towery. "Normally, you can spray Roundup, and anything that's green, Roundup kills. But alter one gene, and then spray Roundup on the soybeans, and it doesn't faze them at all. Some farmers don't use any other herbicide."

Roundup isn't a panacea. He concedes it's not completely effective on some weeds. In some cases, it's used in combination with another agent. A handful of resistant weeds are also a problem. The EPA uses what Towery characterizes as a simplistic way of measuring herbicides: It measures pounds of active ingredient. Are fewer pounds of herbicide being applied today than five years ago? There's an assumption by the public, he says, that fewer pounds translate to a reduced environmental threat. "But," he says, "all herbicides differ in their toxicity level, their residual [how long they last in the environment], and in their pounds of active ingredient. Some newer herbicides are applied at one ounce per acre—a very low rate. Most of what I refer to as 'old chemistry' herbicides," he says, "are the ones that have long residual [they remain in the soil without degrading], and medium or high solubility. Those are the ones where we have environmental issues associated with runoff. The most common one out there is atrazine. It's got a residual of nine weeks, it's fairly soluble, and it's used on 90 percent of corn acres because it's effective and it's cheap. Atrazine attacks weeds such as foxtail, lamb's quarter, and velvetleaf—the weeds that most often affect yield reduction. Weeds compete for light, space, and water with the crops that you plant. If weeds are growing faster than the crops, then you can have significant yield reduction." USDA reports indicate that, pound for pound, more Roundup is needed to control weeds than other chemicals. That higher poundage raises flags from many environmentalists. But we need to look at the whole picture. While some would argue that all agriculture should revert to organic production, I contend that that's neither practical nor good for the environment in every case. Unless we plan to level every forest and wild area for low-yield farm production, we need a combination of agricultural methods.

GMO Fear Factor If wheat were introduced into the market today, it would probably be banned because of all of the food allergens it contains. Sometimes fear of the unknown is more of a hindrance than a help to society. While testing of new foods makes sense, such caution should be balanced with a reasonable cost-benefit

analysis. Before gene-splicing ever existed, scads of new foods were introduced every year without testing. Crossbreeding small seedless oranges with big seeded oranges to produce big seedless oranges is certainly a form of genetic engineering. It's just done without gene-splicing. Problems might be discovered in genetically modified foods, but no health risks have been found so far. Meanwhile, the well-documented damage caused by chemical pesticide abuse is going on right now.

Over the last decade, farmers and food scientists have fast-forwarded natural selection in the laboratory by a process known as gene splicing. Desirable traits of one plant or animal can be brought out in another by transferring the gene responsible for those traits from one organism to the other. In one example, a beneficial bacterium called *Bacillus thuringiensis* (Bt) produces a protein toxic to corn-borer pests but not to people or other animals. Organic farmers have applied the Bt bacteria to their crops for years, because it's harmless to humans, animals, and most other eaters. But, when the gene that produces the active Bt protein is introduced into the genetic makeup of, say, corn, the result is corn that resists the corn borer worm.

The technology isn't perfect. Yields of some GMO crops are lower than those of conventional crops, leading critics to ask whether previous higher pesticide use on non-Bt corn wasn't a better system. It wasn't. Farmers have consistently found ways to improve crop yields, and they will again, this time with fewer pesticides.

The importance of reducing dependence on chemical pesticides cannot be overstated. Unlike Bt, widely used chemical pesticides like organophosphate, carbamate, and pyrethroid insecticides cast a wide net, killing many different kinds of insects and beneficial invertebrates such as spiders. Different Bt subspecies are so species specific that, even if characterized as "dipteran-active" (active only against flies), they are active only against certain members of the species. For example, they will be effective against mosquitoes but have no effect on houseflies, fruit flies, or stable flies.

In order for the proteins to be effective, they must be "activated" in the alkaline environment of the insect's gut. In an acid environment, such as a mammal's digestive tract, there is no toxicity. In a rare human experiment, subjects consumed a thousand times the dose of Bt that a person would consume by eating fresh vegetables immediately after field application, to no effect. In forty years of use, Bt has caused no confirmed human infections or deaths. Just one chemical pesticide alone, methyl parathion, is blamed for hundreds of illnesses and five to ten deaths annually (mostly in farmworkers). Adoption of Bt by farmers is, in fact, beneficial to the environment, as it reduces use of broad-spectrum chemical insecticides. It is estimated that, in 1999, use of Bt cotton in the United States reduced chemical pesticide application by 2.7 million pounds (15 million less applications, or 20 percent fewer sprayings than before Bt cotton introduction).

With all the environmental advantages Bt has over chemical pesticides, one would think environmentalists would embrace it. It hasn't quite worked out that way. Although some environmental groups' leaders have expressed tentative support for the principle of using biotechnology to mitigate the worst forms of pesticide use, most have derided genetically engineered crops as environmentally unsound. Among the chief concerns about Bt crops is that they might lead to Bt-resistant insects. Any pests that could consume Bt crops with no ill effect would survive, breed, and lead to resistant generations. This problem has plagued farmers since the widespread use of chemical insecticides began after World War II. Increases in resistant populations led to the adoption of ever-more-lethal chemicals over time—a cycle that came to be called the "pesticide treadmill."

While the possibility of Bt-resistant bugs is real, the problem of massive ecological destruction by chemical pesticides is immediate. If the pest resistance wasn't produced by the plant, it would be sprayed onto the crop by other means, none of which are particularly ecofriendly. Small-scale organic farmers may use low-tech means of applying Bt bacteria to their crops, but most farms will dust aerially, using much more product and fuel in the process.

Caution, not fear, should guide decisions on GM technologies. While deliberate research and justified concerns have driven the policies of environmental groups in the past, there seems to be a circling of the wagons about GM foods. Despite copious study, testing, and evidence of safety and environmental benefits of some of these crops, Sierra Club, Greenpeace, and other defenders of the environment continue to assert that the risk is too high to allow further introduction of them into agriculture. It seems like the one issue where the environmental mainstream is working against the environment. By obstructing the replacement of some conventional crops with insect-resistant ones, the "greens" are encouraging the continued use of substances that are proven to be much more devastating to the environment.

BIODIVERSITY AND GM CROPS Biodiversity and crop diversity are two separate issues. Just as the hundreds of breeds of dog exhibited at shows and competitions were all cultivated from a single wild strain by our ancestors to address their own needs, so have we developed tens of thousands of food crops from wild plants. A single wild plant species, *Brassica oleracea,* has given birth to countless cabbages, Brussels sprouts, broccoli, cauliflower, and kohlrabi. The sweet corn varieties we eat today bear little resemblance to the hard varieties passed on to us by Native Americans. Tomatoes, which can now be grown the size of small melons, were little more than berries when European explorers encountered them a few hundred years ago.

Although dozens of varieties of corn have been grown in America's history, the vast majority of corn plants grown today belong to only four species. Some would point to this as evidence of loss of biodiversity. Rather, it is a loss of crop diversity, based on the needs and tastes of the market and the ecosystem. The real loss of biodiversity is occurring daily in rain forests, wetlands, and other wild places that are being cleared for agriculture and development. Those interested in preserving strains of food crops developed by past generations should certainly proceed with that mission, as concerned culinary historians at places like the Seed Savers Exchange (www.seedsavers.org) do. But introduction of new crops that meet today's more fragile environment, such as higher-yield or pest-resistant transgenic crops, should not be squelched because of a perceived threat they pose to currently cultivated varieties.

After the Fall American vegetable farms are no Gardens of Eden. Let's clear up that illusion right away. They're largely coated with powerful pesticides, and draw nourishment from a mixture of earth and chemical fertilizer that pushes growth to maximum velocity. These compounds keep crop yields high and production fast. So let's dispel any fantasies about keeping mad scientists out of our food chain. They've been putting their products there for generations.

The idea of crops that resist pests without pesticides, and grow rapidly without chemical fertilizers, is generally a good one. If you were a fish in an American river or stream, you'd jump for joy at the thought of it, since much of the stray pesticide dusted over crops runs off into waterways. We use far more pesticides now than ever before. And our produce is cheaper than ever before, too. Farmers wouldn't spray the stuff if it weren't cost-effective. But they are inexpensive in only one sense of the word.

In fact, pesticides are very expensive. They're a huge financial burden for most farmers. One reason so much of the Third World is in famine is because, year after year, crops fall victim to insect plagues before harvest. If the farmers of Africa could afford pesticides, they'd use them. It would help stabilize their food supply, even while it poisoned their water supplies (sound familiar?).

Chemical fertilizers, also very costly, enable smaller plots of land to generate much greater crop yields. In countries where such products are unaffordable, larger swaths of land are cleared to produce the same amount of food that could be grown on smaller, fertilized plots. In the Amazon basin, locals burn down rain forest to clear land for crops. They move on to new virgin lands regularly, as the nutrients in the soil are spent. If they could afford chemical fertilizers, they would use them. In a way, employing those powerful compounds might be a more ecologically sound choice, on balance, than continuing the slash-and-burn method of today.

But the optimum solutions to insect, rodent, weed, and other plagues, low crop yields, and easily exhausted soil are better-adapted crops. When a crop that provides nutrition and quality food for people is neither nourishing nor appealing to pests, pesticides will become obsolete. When a crop planted every two inches can produce just as much food per plant as a similar one planted every six inches, then undeveloped land will be safe from the ax.

When feasible, organic agriculture is certainly the best option. By cultivating crops that naturally repel pests along with crops that would be threatened by those pests (think marigolds and tomatoes), organic farmers minimize crop loss to insects. By rotating crops so that soil regenerates and fields stay fertile naturally, sensible farmers have reduced the need for new land. But these are only partial solutions. Other forms of ingenuity may help in other ways, if allowed to flourish. The time is now for government and independent agencies to subject genetically modified crops to practical testing. If proven safe for the environment, they hold great potential to reduce man's already-negative effect on global ecology. An October 2004 study by the National Center for Food and Agriculture Policy concluded that biotechnology-derived crops had directly reduced use of pesticides in 2003 by 46.4 million pounds.

While there are real problems, the goal of pesticide-free fields warrants further exploration of GM technology. Ultimately, solutions to the competition between mankind's need for cropland and the natural environment's tendency to reclaim it will have to be process based (inventive farming), rather than product based (inventive crops). But until farming techniques can achieve that balance, GM technology will remain a tool for helping reduce our invasive impact on nature. Many modern farmers are introducing combinations of technologies and environmentally sensitive techniques (such as resistant plants, beneficial insects, natural enemies, physical barriers, repellent sounds, and biological and conventional pesticides) in a system known as Integrated Pest Management (IPM) to battle pests and agricultural sprawl.

A FINAL GM NOTE Profit isn't the only motive behind genetic modification of foods. "Golden rice," which contains a gene that develops vitamin A, has been tremendously successful in wiping out deficiencies of that essential nutrient in children throughout Asia. In Kenya, the stem borer worm kills hundreds of children with a poison it leaves behind in corn. Modified corn that resists the stem borer is staged to eliminate that problem, and reclaim the 15 percent of crops once destroyed by this worm, thanks to grants from the Rockefeller Foundation and cooperation from socially responsible companies.

NOURISHING OUR CROPS WITH MIDDLE EASTERN OIL More unintended harm takes place in the production of chemical fertilizers. To replenish one acre of exhausted soil, it takes 5.5 gallons of oil-produced nitrogen fertilizer (think how many acres we have under cultivation). Alternative fossil fuels are no better. The production of 5.5 pounds of nitrogen fertilizer takes 2,200 pounds of coal, making this the most energy-intensive process on most farms. Many pesticides are also fossil-fuel-derived products.

PESTICIDES KILL MORE THAN JUST PESTS Insecticides are also liberally applied to soil. These pesticides kill beneficial insects as well as those that eat or otherwise destroy crops. Bees, needed to pollinate the plants so that they can produce their fruit, are often wiped out by insecticides applied for other pests. Many insecticides are poisonous to other forms of life as well. For example, permethrin, used on 77 percent of head lettuce and 37 percent of fresh tomatoes, is highly toxic to fish and terrestrial wildlife. Methomyl, also widely used, kills birds, fish, aquatic invertebrates, and mammals. Many of these pesticides are applied to young plants before they bear fruit, and thus are mostly absent from washed produce at market.

Another danger of insecticides involves their intended goal of eliminating certain insects. During nesting season, insects are a major food source for newly hatched birds. When insecticides have killed off most of the insects, there's a lack of food for the growing birds, hampering their growth and indirectly reducing the bird population. Biologist David Pimentel estimates that 67 million birds are killed annually in the United States alone.

WHICH CROPS USE THE MOST PESTICIDES? America spends $8 billion a year on herbicides, insecticides, and fungicides, a third of the world market in dollar terms (a quarter in active ingredient terms). Pesticides fall into five categories: herbicide, insecticide, fungicide, nematocide (kills nematodes, wormlike organisms that eat roots), and rodenticide. None of these substances make particularly good eating, and if you're concerned about ingesting them, memorize the twelve foods found to contain the most residue (dubbed "the dirty dozen" by the Environmental Working Group, www.foodnews.org, a nonprofit that compiled the list, based on USDA and FDA data): apples, bell peppers, celery, cherries, imported grapes, nectarines, peaches, pears, potatoes, red raspberries, spinach, and strawberries. Those found to have the least pesticide residue are asparagus, avocados, bananas, broccoli, cauliflower, corn (sweet), kiwis, mangoes, onions, papaya, pineapples, and peas (sweet).

Pest-control substances spread beyond farm boundaries through aerial disbursal, runoff, seepage, and the movements of animals. When it comes to animals' pesticide intake, the amount of pesticide used in the production of the food is more important than the amount found on it. The trace amounts of pesticides left on produce at the market are seldom associated with human side effects, but the more concentrated residues on growing crops are harmful to farmworkers who handle the plants, and to smaller, more-vulnerable animals and microorganisms that eat the crops immediately after the pesticides are applied.

BUY ORGANIC Organic farming in the United States makes good sense, because we are not a country starved for farmland. The amount of land under cultivation has actually declined in recent years, as advances in crop yields (partly due to bioengineered crops) have reduced the need for land. The post–World War II "green revolution" combined modern farm machinery, modern pest control (including chemical means), and modern soil management (including various tillage and fertilizing methods) to make American land the most productive in the world. While Amazon rain forests burn (the United Nations estimates that 37.5 million acres are lost annually—rain forests could be completely gone within ten years), American farmland converts back to grassland and wetland (one notable exception is sugarcane cultivation, whose encroachment on Florida wetlands is downright criminal), thanks to one of the few good provisions of the 2002 Farm Bill. The bill provides for easements that encourage farmers to convert unused farmland back to wildlife habitat. Before the bill, nearly 1.1 million acres had become eligible for easements. The bill doubles this successful program, which has been embraced in every state except Alaska, bringing eligible acreage up to 2.2 million acres. But by and large, the door is open to organic farming. Land that has been freed up elsewhere allows organic farmers to expand land under cultivation without a net loss of wild land nationally. While an overall decrease in cultivated land would be best, organic farming's encroachment into uncultivated lands is okay with me if it replaces an equal amount of pesticide-controlled lands.

Although yields will be notably lower than in conventional farming, there is room for organic production to increase in the United States. Part of the green revolution involved a consolidation of farms, and the phasing out of a storied institution: the family farm. Much of the increased productivity of American land was the result of large-scale, high-tech equipment unaffordable to small farmers. The USDA's standards for certified organic products have, ironically, pushed independent small farmers further out of the mainstream. Small farmers now represent a small niche in a large industry. In some ways, that's a distinct loss for the ethical consumer, whose local options (almost always the ecological and culinary best choice) are more and more limited. But in other ways, it may hasten the dawning of a new era for responsible food production. The key will be for mainstream "factory farms," which control the vast majority of American agricultural production, to move in an ethical (read: organic) direction.

Already, Heinz has introduced an organic ketchup line and Gold Medal sells organic flour. Dole's organic lettuces, spinach, and bananas are currently on market shelves, and Muir Glen, the country's largest processor of organic tomatoes, is now owned by General Mills. Dean Foods, parent of Borden and Land O' Lakes, bought Horizon Organic Dairy in 2004 for $216 million, and assumed the milk producer's $40 million debt. (Note: I recommend Organic Valley brand over Horizon, because Organic Valley is committed to humane treatment of dairy cows and support for small farmers on a level that Horizon is not.)

Know the Codes

Well-Kept Secret: Those PLU (product look-up) code numbers that appear on produce stickers tell a tale, if you know their secret. They tell the savvy consumer whether the fruit or vegetable is organic, conventional, or genetically modified.

Designed by the Produce Marketing Association, the codes mainly benefit grocery store checkout workers, who no longer have to remember prices of every item sold. But they indicate the mode of production too, so knowledgeable consumers can classify food by the codes.

PLU codes that begin with the numbers 3 or 4 and are four digits long are conventionally grown. Organically grown produce bears the same four digits plus the number 9 at the beginning, for a total of five digits. Genetically modified fruits and vegetables bear five-digit PLU codes beginning with the numeral 8. For example, conventional bananas would be code 4011, organic bananas would be code 94011, and genetically modified bananas would be 84011.

Summer Radish Soup with Berries and Balsamic Syrup

SERVES 4 White radishes, including daikons, make a great base for soup. The spicy leaves that come with them give the soup great color and zing. The tart-sweet berry flavors complement the spicy flavor of this soup. I strongly urge you to buy organic berries, since conventional strawberries and raspberries are highly pesticide-intensive crops.

¼ cup balsamic vinegar

1 tablespoon olive oil

2 garlic cloves, thinly sliced

2 cups chopped onions

Salt and freshly ground black pepper

1 pound radishes (preferably white) with greens, radishes thinly sliced

1 teaspoon fresh thyme leaves

1 quart chicken, mushroom, or vegetable stock

½ cup assorted berries, such as raspberries or strawberries

In a small pan, simmer the balsamic vinegar until it reaches a syrupy consistency. It should reduce to about a teaspoon. Cover it and set it aside.

Heat the olive oil in a medium saucepan; add the garlic and onions. Sprinkle with salt and pepper to taste and sweat (cook slowly, without browning) for 5 minutes, until the onions are soft and juicy. Add the radishes, radish greens, thyme, and stock. Bring to a boil, then lower to a simmer; cook 10 minutes, until the radishes are soft.

In a blender at high speed, puree the soup in batches until very smooth. Return to the pot and reheat. Serve the soup in shallow bowls, and arrange a small group of berries in the center of each portion. Drizzle a few drops of balsamic syrup over the berries just before serving.

Fresh Fig Soup with Sheep's Milk Yogurt

SERVES 8 The season for fresh figs is short—early to mid summer. This refreshing dish makes the best use of that moment. Look for figs that are slightly overripe, making them sweeter and juicier. Figs can, in fact, be frozen for later use. Once defrosted, their texture will be too soft to eat them whole, but since they are pureed for this soup anyway, it's of no consequence if they're too soft to handle without breaking.

¼ cup raisins

¼ cup dark rum

2 pounds fresh or frozen figs (about 4 cups)

1 quart apple juice or water

Salt and freshly ground black pepper

1 cup sheep's milk yogurt or other plain yogurt

Combine the raisins and rum. Soak 1 hour or more until plump (this can be done well in advance). Drain and set aside. Wash the figs well, if fresh, and remove any stems. Cut them roughly into quarters.

Puree the figs in a food processor; add apple juice to achieve a pleasing consistency similar to a thick milkshake. Season with a pinch of salt and black pepper. Chill.

Serve garnished with yogurt and the soaked raisins.

Flavor Salads with Flair

Salads have often been relegated to side status. But main course salads have become so popular that even fast-food restaurants now include them on the menu. Most restaurants that serve Caesar salads now offer slices of grilled chicken or shrimp as an accompaniment for a small additional charge. The salad is the main course, and the chicken or shrimp is a garnish.

A Roasted Quail Salad with Spiced Cashews (page 186) commands center stage. A single quail is often served as an appetizer. It joins with a salad, however, to become a main course. Garnishing a large salad of dark leafy greens like arugula, spinach, or beet greens with a savory quail makes sense, since this delectable, diminutive game bird is a pleasant project to eat, and its deep flavor is nicely balanced by refreshing dressed greens.

When *pavés* (rectangular cuts of a fillet) of salmon or bass are sautéed and placed immediately on salad greens, the residual heat from the fish softens some of the leaves, making them juicy and tender. Juices from the fish begin to dress the salad. Splash some fine vinegar into the fish's cooking pan to deglaze the concentrated fish flavors from the bottom. Swirl it into a quick natural dressing to spoon over the rest of the salad, heightening the drama. The proportion of fish to other ingredients is small, but the fish's effect on the dish is grand. Nutritionists recommend eating meat and fish in portions of no more than three ounces (the size of a deck of cards), so this portion size is not only ethical, but healthful too. With a meal like this, four people can enjoy delicious fish, and leave three times as many untouched fish swimming in the sea. Everyone benefits.

Southeast Asian Slaw

SERVES 4 AS AN APPETIZER Besides being a great first course or snack, this slaw works as an ingredient in many other dishes. In place of lettuce leaves, try a pinch for crispness in a sandwich. Toss it with Coconut Rice (page 61) as a main course, accompanied by barbecued fish or Tamarind Chicken Skewers (page 62).

¼ head (about ½ pound) Napa or other cabbage

½ carrot, grated

1 small red onion, cut into julienne

1 small Thai "bird" chile or jalapeño pepper, finely chopped

¼ cup chopped fresh cilantro

Juice of 1 lime

1 tablespoon rice wine vinegar

1 teaspoon sugar

1 teaspoon vegetable oil

A few drops of Asian toasted sesame oil

½ teaspoon salt

Shred the cabbage as fine as you possibly can, using a knife, mandoline, or slicing machine. Combine with the carrot, onion, chile pepper, and cilantro.

Dress with the lime, rice vinegar, sugar, vegetable oil, sesame oil, and salt; toss thoroughly. Let rest, refrigerated, for at least 30 minutes before serving.

Caramelized Apples and Yams

SERVES 8 AS A SIDE DISH This warming, hearty winter vegetable sauté pairs beautifully with Savory Corn and Vegetable Pudding (page 174) for a rustic dinner, with or without Rosemary Pork (page 176).

1 pound yams or sweet potatoes, sliced into ½-inch-thick rounds

1 pound apples, such as Rome Beauty, Golden Delicious, or Northern Spy

½ cup (1 stick) unsalted butter

1 large Spanish onion, sliced into ½-inch-thick rounds

½ teaspoon ground cinnamon

Salt and freshly ground black pepper

Bring a pot of water to a boil over high heat. Parboil the yams until they are no longer crisp, but will not break apart, about 5 minutes. Peel and core the apples, and cut them into ½-inch-wide wedges.

Melt the butter in a large skillet. Add the onion and cook over medium-low heat until very soft and juicy, about 10 minutes. Add the apples and yams; dust with cinnamon.

Increase the heat to high and sauté until the ingredients are attractively browned. Season to taste with salt and pepper.

Caraway-Coriander Wilted Savoy Cabbage

SERVES 6 Cooking with whole spices is a foreign concept to many cooks, but it opens up whole new flavor and texture possibilities. Crunchy coriander seeds first flavor the cooking oil in this dish, then marry with more assertive caraway seeds to give the dish complex flavor. Serve it with chewy-textured Bhutanese red rice (available from www.lotusfoods.com) and something tart, like marinated tomatoes or Moroccan-style preserved lemon julienne (available from www.mustaphas.com).

1 medium head Savoy cabbage

¼ cup grapeseed or canola oil

2 tablespoons whole coriander seeds

1 teaspoon caraway seeds

¼ teaspoon freshly ground white pepper

1 teaspoon kosher salt

Bring a large pot of salted water to a boil. Cut the core from the cabbage and discard the outermost dark green leaves. Separate the leaves and cut them into ¼-inch-wide julienne. Blanch the cabbage until crisp-tender, about 1 minute; cool immediately under cold running water. You may need to do this in two batches. Drain.

In a large skillet over medium heat, heat the oil and coriander seeds until fragrant, about 3 minutes (again, this might require two batches, depending on the size of your pan). Add the caraway seeds; heat 30 seconds. Add the cabbage; cook until hot. Season with the pepper and salt.

Focaccia with Cardoons

SERVES 16 Cardoons are distantly related to artichokes. The juicy thistle has been used since ancient Roman times, boiled and dressed with olive oil, lemon, and salt. Like artichokes, the cardoon (sometimes spelled *cardone*) has a slight bitterness in its sophisticated flavor. The vegetable looks like oversized celery, and is in season from late fall to late winter. (Ocean Mist uses responsible Integrated Pest Management to grow cardoons, and their cousins, artichokes, in California—visit www.oceanmist.com/cardone.htm). If you use artichoke bottoms for this focaccia, you can cook the artichokes whole, then peel off the leaves and scoop out the "choke" in the center before slicing.

Focaccia dough is very soft and wet. Keeping your hands oiled is the best way to handle it. This vegetable bread makes handsome sandwiches with tomatoes, blanched broccoli rabe, and shaved Asiago cheese. It's also a fine appetizer, served with Simple Tomato Sauce (page 114) for dipping.

Coarse sea salt

Juice of 2 lemons

2 cups diced cardoons or 2 medium artichoke bottoms, sliced 1 inch thick

5 ounces potato, roughly diced (about 1 cup, or 1 small potato)

One ¼-ounce packet active dry yeast

2 teaspoons sugar

2 tablespoons olive oil, plus more for oiling bowl and pans

1 teaspoon table salt

4 cups bread flour

1 cup Simple Tomato Sauce (recipe follows)

Freshly ground black pepper

Bring 3 quarts water to a boil; add 2 tablespoons salt and the lemon juice. Boil the cardoons until very tender, about 10 minutes. Drain.

Simmer the potato with 1 cup water in a covered pot until very soft, about 15 minutes. In a bowl, combine the yeast, sugar, and ¼ cup warm water; let stand until it becomes foamy.

Transfer the potato, along with the cooking liquid and the olive oil, to a standing mixer with a whisk attachment. Whip on high speed until smooth, 5 minutes. (This can also be done by hand, in the cooking pot, using a stiff hand whisk, or in a food processor.) Exchange the whisk attachment for a dough hook; add the yeast mixture, salt, flour, and a scant ¾ cup water. Knead on medium-low speed (speed #2 on KitchenAid) until the flour is completely incorporated and the dough is wet, sticky, and elastic, about 10 minutes. (This can be done by hand, with a wooden spoon, for about 15 minutes.) Oil a large bowl and, using well-oiled hands, transfer the dough to the bowl. The dough will be quite soft.

Cover the bowl and place in a warm area. Let the dough rise until doubled in volume, about 1 hour. Liberally oil two 9½-inch round cake pans with olive oil. Divide the dough between the two pans, and allow to rise until doubled in size again, about 45 minutes.

Heat the oven to 400°F. Using well-oiled fingers, poke a pattern into the dough to create a dimpled surface. Spread the tomato sauce over the dough, leaving a ½-inch border. Distribute the diced cardoons over the focaccia, allowing some pieces to fall into the dimpled markings. Season assertively with sea salt and pepper.

Bake until golden, about 30 minutes, rotating the pans halfway through.

Simple Tomato Sauce

YIELD: ABOUT 3½ CUPS

2 tablespoons olive oil

1 tablespoon chopped garlic

2 pounds tomatoes (preferably Roma plum tomatoes, but any are fine), chopped (about 4 cups)

½ teaspoon salt

Heat the olive oil and garlic in a medium saucepan over medium heat until the garlic sizzles.

Add the tomatoes and salt. Cook over medium heat for about 15 minutes, until the tomatoes are all soft and saucy. Voilà!

Eggplant Caviar

SERVES 8 AS AN APPETIZER This savory eggplant spread gets its name from the tiny round seeds of eggplant that give it a caviarlike look. Every cocktail hour should have at least one vegetarian hors d'oeuvre, and this one makes the perfect, low-maintenance choice. Either spoon it onto toasted rounds of French bread and garnish with chives, or put out a dish for people to serve themselves. It also makes fantastic vegetarian sandwiches on crusty whole-grain bread, such as Whole-Grain Health Bread (page 51).

1 large eggplant (about 2 pounds)

2 tablespoons olive oil

1 large onion, finely chopped

3 garlic cloves, finely chopped

1 tablespoon tomato paste

Salt and freshly ground black pepper

Heat the oven to 400°F. Place the eggplant in a baking dish, and roast on the middle rack of the oven until very well done, about 1 hour; cool. Cut the eggplant in half and scoop out the soft pulp with a serving spoon. Place on a cutting board and chop thoroughly, until it has the consistency of oatmeal.

Heat the olive oil in a large skillet over medium heat 1 minute. Add the onion; cook until very soft, but not brown, about 10 minutes. Add the garlic and cook 1 minute more. Stir in the tomato paste; cook another minute.

Add the chopped eggplant and cook until the mixture is thickened. An indentation should remain when a spoon is depressed into the mixture. Season to taste with salt and pepper. Serve with crackers or sliced French bread.

Vegetarian Peking Duck

SERVES 4 AS AN APPETIZER, 2 AS A MAIN COURSE Duck, when cooked in the Peking style, has a crispy skin, a juicy bite, and a woodsy, smoky taste. In this mock duck, a crunchy outer bean curd skin, filled with earthy mushroom and bamboo shreds, provides the crisp, juicy, woodsy effect. Wrapped in a tortilla with hoisin (Chinese dried plum sauce), scallions, and cucumber, you won't believe it isn't the real deal.

Bean curd sheets, called *fu jook* in China and *yuba* in Japan, are available from Asian grocers and from www.orientalpantry.com. But if you can't find them, use spring roll wrappers to replicate crispy skin instead. Dried black mushrooms are the beloved fungus of China and Japan. Fresh, they're sold as shiitake mushrooms here. Once you hook into a source for dried black mushrooms, you may never want fresh again. When sliced, they add a pleasantly chewy texture to anything you cook. Like good risotto, they're soft when you bite down, but resistant at the middle. Bamboo shoots have a crunch, making your "duck" more dynamic yet. I shred them with a knife, but you can use a grater or food processor if you wish.

Rolling these quackers is like making spring rolls—fold the sides in first to ensure that filling doesn't fall out during cooking, then roll them into a not-too-tight cylinder. Set the steamer basket on a counter, where the rolls can air-dry as they cool a bit. To soften the tortillas (an essential step, unless you're into eating leather), I like to place them directly over a low heat on the stovetop, and flip them back and forth until they puff and blister on both sides and have some brown or charred spots. Alternatively, you could steam them or toast them in the oven. Bean curd sheets are great wrappers for crisp rolls. Fresh ones are pliable, but they dry quickly. If they crack when bent, steam them for five to seven minutes.

6 dried black Chinese mushrooms

4 teaspoons light soy sauce

1½ teaspoons sugar

1 teaspoon salt

1 tablespoon peanut oil

1 cup finely shredded bamboo shoots

1½ teaspoons cornstarch

½ teaspoon Asian toasted sesame oil

2 fresh bean curd sheets, approximately 12 inches square (if they are dry and crackly, steam to soften for 5 minutes)

2 cups peanut oil for frying

4 flour tortillas, quartered

2 scallions, cut into thin strips

1 cucumber, peeled, seeded, and sliced into thin matchsticks

Hoisin sauce

Soak the mushrooms for 15 to 20 minutes in boiling water to cover. Drain, reserving the liquid; then shred very finely (about ½ cup).

Combine 2 teaspoons of the soy sauce, ½ teaspoon of the sugar, ½ teaspoon of the salt, and 1 tablespoon of the mushroom soaking liquid in a small bowl. Heat the peanut oil in a skillet, add the shredded mushrooms, and stir-fry a few minutes. Add the bamboo shoots and the soy sauce mixture. Cook 1 minute more. Remove from heat.

In a small bowl, mix together the cornstarch, remaining 1 teaspoon sugar, 2 teaspoons soy sauce, and ½ teaspoon salt, the sesame oil, and a tablespoon of mushroom soaking liquid. Brush this mixture onto the bean curd sheets and spread the cooked vegetables over the sheets, leaving a 1-inch border around the sides and bottom, and a 3-inch border along the top. Fold the sides in to seal in the filling and roll, jelly-roll-style.

(continued)

Heat the peanut oil to 375°F in a high-sided medium skillet. Cook the rolls until browned and crisp (careful: they spatter; use a screen if you have one), about 5 minutes, turning once. Set on paper towels to drain excess oil. Slice into eight pieces each (a serrated knife is best).

Soften the tortillas by either steaming them or heating them directly atop a stove burner. Serve each slice wrapped in a tortilla quarter with scallion strips, cucumber sticks, and hoisin sauce.

Wild Mushrooms

Perhaps no wild food has been more misrepresented than wild mushrooms. Much of what consumers think is drawn purely from nature are actually cultivated products that never even existed in the wild. Other times, they see farm-grown fungi (derived from once-wild species) that never saw a forest floor. Over the last fifteen years, successful cultivation of varieties that had resisted captivity has revolutionized the mushroom-farming world. Search all you want for wild portobello mushrooms. You'll come up empty, because they were developed by breeders. So were their miniature offspring, creminis. Both are variants of the familiar white button mushrooms. Enoki mushrooms, those slender, elegant, wispy white hatpins, trace their origins back to a lab also. The wild species from which they're derived are orange to yellow in color.

While wild shiitakes exist, they're virtually never foraged or sold in America. The cultivated ones are too good and too cheap to justify the hunt. Ditto with oyster mushrooms. Hen-of-the-woods (maitake), bluefoot, and yellow chanterelles are also cultivated now (although there is still a thriving market for truly wild chanterelles of both colors, foraged in fall and winter).

Like truffles, morels—the handsome honeycomb-textured brown cones with a profound, woodsy flavor and aroma—still defy large-scale cultivation. When you see them, they're probably truly wild. The same is true of cèpes (called *porcini* in Italy). Their complex flavor and irregular shapes are dead giveaways that they haven't yet been tamed.

Mushroom farming is an environmentally sustainable form of agriculture that requires almost no pesticide because the product grows so fast. Foraging, however, sometimes takes a toll on the forests where it's done, as huge teams of foragers trample young shoots as they turn the woods upside down in search of black gold like wild morels. Mostly, though, foraging is done on a small scale. I consider both foraged wild mushrooms and cultivated exotic and domestic mushrooms to be sustainable foods, and good choices for the environmentally concerned.

Mushroom-Tofu Halupki (Stuffed Cabbage)

SERVES 6 Mushrooms, carrots, celery, and tofu may not boast a 20 percent fat content, but otherwise, they're just as juicy as most other potential cabbage fillings. These rolls rest in a sweet tomato sauce with plump raisins, offhandedly delivering twice the recommended daily allowance of vitamin C and enough antioxidants and fiber to do battle against cancers of the esophagus, stomach, and colon. If that doesn't make you hungry, I don't know what will.

Wrapping these cabbage bundles is easy. Just place some filling on each leaf, fold in the sides, and roll the *halupki* into a neat cylinder. Serve the finished dish with a glass of "bull's blood," a Hungarian red wine that will stand up to the sweet-tart flavors of this dish.

2 cups tomato sauce

2 teaspoons brown sugar

¼ cup raisins

1 head green cabbage, ragged outer leaves discarded

2 celery ribs, roughly chopped

2 carrots, roughly chopped

1 medium onion, roughly chopped

3 medium portobello mushrooms (about 12 ounces), roughly chopped

3 tablespoons extra virgin olive oil

2 teaspoons dried oregano

1½ teaspoons salt

1 cup cooked rice

½ pound firm tofu, cut into ¼-inch dice

2 large eggs, beaten

Freshly ground black pepper

Make the sauce by combining the tomato sauce, brown sugar, and raisins in a medium saucepan; simmer for 3 minutes, until hot. Set aside. Bring enough water to a boil to submerge the cabbage head. Cut around the core of the cabbage to detach the leaves, and submerge it for 2 minutes. Gradually remove twelve or so leaves as they soften, placing them directly into a bowl of icy cold water to stop the cooking. Take off four more leaves, and chop them roughly.

Pulse the celery, carrots, onion, and chopped cabbage in a food processor until very finely chopped (or chop by hand). Separately, process or chop the mushrooms to the same fineness. In a large pot, heat the olive oil until it shimmers but doesn't smoke. Add the chopped vegetables and mushrooms. Cook undisturbed for 5 minutes; add the oregano and salt, toss, and cook 10 minutes more. Set aside to cool slightly. Add the rice, tofu, eggs, and pepper. Taste and adjust the seasoning.

Heat the oven to 400°F. With the stem end of the leaf facing you, place about ½ cup of filling on the lower third of each blanched cabbage leaf. Fold 1-inch flaps in from the sides to lock in the filling, then roll the leaf away from you to form a cylinder. Line a 9 x 13-inch baking dish with the sweet tomato sauce. Arrange the rolls atop the sauce, cover with foil, and bake for 1 hour.

Moroccan Squash Tagine with Couscous

SERVES 8 The first dish I ever tasted in Paris was not French cuisine. It was this brothy Moroccan comfort food, served in one of the many North African holes in the wall in the artsy Left Bank neighborhood near the Sorbonne. It was as restorative after a long flight as anything I've ever eaten.

3 tablespoons olive oil

2 onions, chopped (about 4 cups)

4 garlic cloves, sliced

1½ pounds organic pumpkin, butternut, delicata, dumpling, or other squash, skin on, cut into large chunks

2 large carrots, cut into 2-inch sticks (about 4 cups)

8 small red potatoes, halved

1 teaspoon ground cumin

1 teaspoon ground ginger

1 teaspoon ground cinnamon

1 tablespoon kosher salt, plus more to taste

6 tomatoes, roughly chopped

½ pound fresh fava beans or frozen lima beans

One 14-ounce can chickpeas, drained

1 quart vegetable stock

Pinch of saffron steeped in ¼ cup warm water

¼ cup roughly chopped fresh flat-leaf parsley

Juice of 1 lemon

Freshly ground black pepper

Harissa (Middle Eastern hot chili paste) to taste

1 pound couscous, cooked according to package directions

Heat the oil in a Dutch oven; add the onions, garlic, pumpkin, carrots, potatoes, cumin, ginger, cinnamon, and salt. Cook gently for 10 minutes, until the mixture is softened and the vegetables have released some of their juices. Add the tomatoes; cook 3 minutes. Stir in the fava beans, chickpeas, stock, and saffron.

Bring the mixture to a boil. Lower heat to a simmer; cover and simmer 30 minutes. Finish by stirring in the parsley and lemon juice; season to taste with salt and pepper. Mix a small amount of broth with the harissa, and serve it on the side. Accompany with heaping plates of couscous.

Mediterranean Vegetables

SERVES 6 AS A MAIN COURSE The balance of sweet, tart, and onion flavors makes this play on ratatouille a satisfying vegetarian entree. Preserved lemon adds a salty, tangy element to many Southern European and North African dishes. It is available from www.mustaphas.com, www.pointshop.com, and www.cybercucina.com.

2 large zucchini

1 large fennel bulb, cut into ½-inch dice

1 preserved lemon, cut in half

4 ripe tomatoes, seeded and chopped

2 small shallots, finely chopped

2 tablespoons small capers, drained

3 tablespoons olive oil

1 tablespoon finely chopped fresh flat-leaf parsley

Cut the green sides from the zucchini, slicing them off in ¼-inch planks. Discard the seedy inner core. Cut the zucchini into ½-inch dice. Bring a large pot of salted water to a boil; blanch the zucchini until crisp-tender, about 3 minutes. Cool immediately in ice water, then drain. Blanch and cool the fennel in the same manner. Scoop the inner pulp and white from the preserved lemon; blanch and cool the yellow part. Cut into fine julienne.

Combine the blanched zucchini and fennel with the preserved lemon, tomatoes, and shallots in a small saucepan over medium-low heat. Add the capers and olive oil. Heat until the vegetables are just warmed through. Do not cook them further. Stir in the parsley.

Manchego-Potato Tacos with Pickled Jalapeños

SERVES 4 AS A MAIN COURSE, 8 AS AN APPETIZER Mexican cooks at restaurants where I worked always taught me a few of their native dishes. One cook used to grill chicken strips and stuff them into corn tortillas with potatoes, cheese, and pickled hot chiles. Then he'd cook the tacos on a griddle until they were crisp. I prefer them this way, without the chicken. You can find pickled jalapeños in supermarket Mexican sections, ethnic specialty stores, or online from www.kitchenmarket.com.

8 soft corn tortillas

1 cup mashed potatoes

¼ pound Manchego or sharp Cheddar cheese, cut into 16 small sticks

16 slices pickled jalapeños

4 tablespoons (½ stick) unsalted butter

Soften the tortillas by briefly toasting them directly over a burner on the stove (electric is fine) for a minute or two, flipping frequently. Spoon 1 tablespoon of mashed potato into the center of each tortilla. Flatten out the potato, leaving a 1-inch border. Lay 2 pieces of Manchego and 2 slices pickled jalapeño onto each tortilla, and fold into a half-moon shape.

In a large skillet over medium heat, melt half the butter. Gently set four of the tacos in the pan and cook until nicely browned, 3 to 4 minutes on each side. Drain on paper towels. Repeat with the remaining butter and tacos. Cut the tacos in half before serving with salsa (such as Salsa Fresca, page 77).

Ragoût of Fingerling Potatoes, Niçoise Olives, and Sweet Onions

SERVES 4 AS AN APPETIZER, 2 AS A MAIN COURSE Though common culinary terms for potato texture like "starchy" and "waxy" are oddly unappetizing, they convey the experience on your palate very well. Fingerlings *do* have a texture that resists the bite only a little, but never becomes crumbly like a baking potato or mushy like a Maine potato. Some waxy potatoes are French fingerlings, Yellow Finnish, Red Bliss, and round white. They're wonderful in stews (such as this ragoût) because they hold their shape and take on the flavors with which they're cooked. This recipe can be cooked a day ahead and reheated just before serving.

1 pound French fingerling or other waxy potatoes, cut into ½-inch slices

4 teaspoons olive oil

1 fresh rosemary sprig (about 4 inches)

2 bay leaves

3 Vidalia or other sweet onions, sliced into ½-inch-thick rings

4 garlic cloves, sliced

½ cup Niçoise or other black olives, pitted and halved

½ teaspoon all-purpose flour

¼ cup dry white wine

1 tablespoon unsalted butter

½ cup roughly chopped fresh flat-leaf parsley

Salt and freshly ground black pepper

Bring a pot of lightly salted water to a boil. Parboil the potatoes until tender but firm. Drain, toss with a teaspoon of olive oil, and set aside.

Heat the remaining tablespoon of olive oil in a 12-inch skillet or Dutch oven over medium heat. Add the rosemary and bay leaves; warm until the rosemary sizzles. Add the onions, garlic, and olives. Cook slowly and gently, sweating the onions until they are translucent and very soft, about 30 minutes. Sprinkle in the flour and stir once to incorporate; cook 1 minute more.

Splash in the wine; simmer to steam out the alcohol, 1 minute. Add the potatoes; simmer until heated through. Stir in the butter and parsley. The dish should have a saucy consistency—add a few drops of water, if necessary. Season liberally with salt and pepper.

Roasted Portobello Mushrooms with Fresh Fava Beans

SERVES 4 AS A MAIN COURSE Farmers plant fava beans in late October, so they're one of the first crops to come up in the spring. The beans are ready for harvest in April (they're available from www.harvestsensations.com). Removed from their velvety, oversized pods, they're bright green gems sheathed in dull, translucent skins. The skins are edible, but I always peel them off, because they detract from the delicate texture of the vegetable. Favas' flavor is very earthy, making them a great match for meaty portobellos. Serve with creamy polenta or angel hair pasta.

1 cup shelled fresh fava beans (about 1 pound, unshelled)

4 large portobello mushrooms (the size of a CD)

2 tablespoons peanut oil or other vegetable oil

2 garlic cloves, finely chopped

1 tablespoon soy sauce

1 teaspoon honey

Lemon wedges

Bring a large pot of water to a rapid boil; blanch the fava beans for 5 minutes. Transfer immediately to a basin of ice-cold water to stop the cooking. The bright green beans will slip easily out of their dull skins with a pinch between two fingers, so skin them if desired. (This step is optional, since the skins are edible, but it makes the dish much more beautiful.) Keep the hot water on the stove to reheat the beans later.

Heat the oven to 425°F. Remove the mushroom stems by wiggling them gently back and forth; discard stems. Wipe the caps clean. Stir together the oil and garlic; brush this mixture liberally onto the mushroom caps, top and bottom. Arrange the caps, top side down, in a roasting pan or baking dish; roast 10 minutes, until they begin to sizzle. Combine the soy sauce and honey. Brush the mushrooms with this mixture; cook 5 minutes more.

Transfer the mushrooms to serving plates, top side up (this side should be nicely browned). Drizzle with any remaining garlic oil and soy glaze. Quickly dip the fava beans into the reserved hot water to warm them; spoon them over the mushrooms. Serve with lemon wedges (not just for looks; this dish benefits from a squeeze of lemon).

Wild Vegetables

Wild vegetables, like wild animals, have a much different taste from cultivated ones. Savvy gourmets seek out foraged delicacies like tender, earthy fiddlehead ferns and pungent ramps (wild leeks), intense wild strawberries and delicate wild asparagus. These gifts from nature offer modern diners a taste of the dynamic essential range of edible plants in our land. While loss of habitat has severely limited the availability of such treasures, they remain a renewable resource for the lucky (savvy) few who enjoy them. True wild rice, hand-harvested in Minnesota from canoes by Native Americans, has a deep, nutty flavor that's noticeably different from the cultivated machine-picked variety.

Miso Eggs Benedict

SERVES 2 AS A MAIN COURSE Miso has a salty flavor that replaces the Canadian bacon used in traditional eggs Benedict. Have all of the ingredients ready to go, and start toasting the English muffins when you put the eggs in to poach, so you can place freshly poached eggs on freshly toasted muffins. Organic eggs are preferable, of course; look for the "Certified Humane Raised & Handled" seal of approval.

Eggs can be poached up to a day in advance and stored in the refrigerator, submerged in cold water. To reheat, gently place in fresh poaching water for a minute before using.

¼ cup white vinegar

2 tablespoons salt

4 extra-large eggs

2 English muffins, split

1 tablespoon miso paste

3 tablespoons unsalted butter, softened to room temperature

½ cup store-bought or homemade Hollandaise Sauce (recipe follows)

Chopped fresh chives (optional)

Hot pepper sauce

Combine the vinegar and salt in a deep skillet with 3 to 4 inches of water (about 2 quarts). Crack each egg into its own teacup or egg cup. When the water boils, lower the flame as low as you can. Gently pour the eggs from the cups into the water. Set the muffins to toast.

Poach the eggs for no more than 3 minutes, then remove them with a slotted spoon, allowing excess water to drain back into the skillet. Transfer the eggs to a towel-lined plate to drain completely. Mash together the miso and butter; spread this mixture onto the toasted muffins. Place one poached egg atop each muffin half. Spoon generous helpings of hollandaise sauce onto each, and serve immediately with a sprinkling of chives (if using) and hot pepper sauce on the side.

Hollandaise Sauce SERVES 8

3 large egg yolks

4 teaspoons fresh lemon juice

½ pound (2 sticks) unsalted butter, melted and kept warm

Salt and freshly ground white pepper

¼ teaspoon cayenne or hot pepper sauce

In the top of a double boiler or in a stainless-steel bowl fitted over—not in—a pot of barely simmering water, whisk the yolks, lemon juice, and 1 tablespoon water. Cook until the mixture begins to thicken, has tripled in volume, and takes on a pale yellow color. Whisking should be rapid and constant. Remove the bowl from the heat when the yolks are the consistency of soft-peak whipped cream.

Secure the bowl on a damp towel. While whisking the yolk mixture vigorously, gradually ladle in the melted butter. If the mixture becomes too thick (denser than mayonnaise consistency) before all of the butter has been added, thin it with a few drops of water or lemon juice.

Season with the salt, pepper, and cayenne. Cover and keep warm until serving (setting the sauce over warm water will work); take care not to place the sauce over direct heat, or it will separate—near a stove or over a pan of warm water is fine.

Vegetable Stew on Polenta

SERVES 4 AS A MAIN COURSE I learned this dish when I cooked at Orso Restaurant in Manhattan. It's a hearty combination of vegetables perfect for cold days. Polenta is soft and creamy when hot, but becomes firm when cooled, and can then be molded or cut into attractive shapes, then fried or grilled. Grilled or fried polenta attains a deliciously crunchy crust.

3 tablespoons extra virgin olive oil, plus extra for serving

Pinch of crushed red pepper

2 fresh thyme sprigs, or ½ teaspoon dried

2 large red onions, cut into 1-inch dice

3 celery ribs, cut into large chunks

4 carrots, cut into large chunks

2 large parsnips, cut into large chunks

½ pound white mushrooms, halved

1 teaspoon kosher salt, plus more to taste

3 garlic cloves, chopped

1 teaspoon sugar

2 cups chopped tomatoes, or one 28-ounce can diced tomatoes (with juice)

1 tablespoon tomato paste

1 cup fresh corn kernels (2 ears) or frozen corn

2 cups chopped asparagus or green beans, blanched

2 tablespoons roughly chopped fresh oregano or flat-leaf parsley

Freshly ground black pepper

1 recipe Creamy Polenta (page 65), kept warm

In a large, heavy-bottomed pot, heat the olive oil, red pepper, and thyme until the thyme sizzles (careful, it pops). Add the onions, celery, carrots, parsnips, mushrooms, and salt; cook 10 minutes, until the vegetables begin to release their juices and the onions are translucent. Add the garlic; cook 1 minute more.

Stir in the sugar, tomatoes, and tomato paste. If using fresh tomatoes, add ½ cup water. Cook 15 minutes. Stir in the corn and asparagus. Bring back to a simmer; season with oregano, salt, and black pepper. Spoon the stew over the polenta. Serve drizzled with extra virgin olive oil.

Meat, Game, and Poultry

Got yak? It's part of a herd of new livestock raised in humane ways, with much less impact on the environment than animals raised under the mainstream feedlot/factory slaughter system. It's an additional choice beyond the humane, ecofriendly options already available in meat production, such as organic pork, bison, lamb, and venison. American farmers and ranchers are now testing the viability of large-scale farming of alternative meats like yak and ostrich—both culinarily valuable ingredients that every food lover should taste. The ethical chef knows that meat is best served as a flavorful but small element of the meal, rather than the main event. Intensely flavored recipes that bring out the most in meats' flavors, such as Chinese Yak Buns with Scallions and Rice Vinegar Dipping Sauce (page 181), illustrate that concept.

Hormones
More than 80 percent of conventionally raised beef cattle are treated with growth hormones. Many of these drugs are the same steroids used illegally by athletes to bulk up. The chemicals have the same effect on the livestock, generating more meat on the cattle for the feed consumed. The USDA's Natural Resources Conservation Service reports that hormones administered to livestock pollute the environment along with manure. Steroid and other hormone residues escape the cattle in the waste stream. Estrogens and androgens excreted into the environment have damaging effects on the reproductive cycles of fish, causing males to become impotent and females to exhibit more masculine characteristics. Other development changes have also been seen.

Better Than "Natural"
The USDA's National Organics Standards (NOS) have ruffled some feathers. But who would have thought it would be organic farmers who would be upset? Part of the problem is that the standards exclude certain farms that had been producing organically for years, because they don't adhere to the letter of the new law.

If you've ever confirmed availability of an item on the phone, and then traveled to the store to discover that the place never carried it, it will come as no surprise to you that many store clerks think their outlet sells organic meat when it doesn't.

People who don't know the definition of either use the terms "organic" and "natural" interchangeably. But the difference is huge. The term reflects not only the contents of the package, but the living conditions of the animal from which it came.

Organic meat refers to meat produced under the general standards of the USDA, and includes practices such as the prohibition of antibiotics and hormones in production, the use of 100 percent organic (and meatless) feed, and no continual confinement. These products appear with a "USDA Certified Organic" label. Read labels carefully, even if they're certified. All organic meat is not equal. For example, one might assume that any organic animal was fed an all-vegetarian diet. But, while the National Organic Standards (NOS) state that organic producers "must not feed mammalian or poultry slaughter by-products to mammals or poultry," there is no restriction against organic livestock feed containing fish products. So an organically labeled meat or dairy product with the added distinction of "all vegetarian diet" is providing additional useful information. The standards also specify gradations of "organic" for processed foods:

- "100 percent organic" must contain 100 percent certified organic ingredients.

- "Organic" must contain no less than 95 percent certified organic ingredients.

- "Made with organic ingredients" must contain at least 70 percent certified organic ingredients.

Organic meat is certified to have been raised without hormones and antibiotics. Antibiotics and hormones excreted by livestock into the waste stream cause changes in wildlife that are just beginning to be discovered. While the majority of concerns reported in the media about antibiotic use on livestock focus on whether that use is creating resistant strains of diseases that affect humans, those substances also serve as an industry fig leaf for cruel and inhumane treatment of livestock. Some antibiotics are applied to treat sick cattle, but most are either "therapeutic" (administered as a preventive measure) or "subtherapeutic" (applied to promote growth). Inhumane conditions lead to greater infection rates, and drive the need for more antibiotics. The Union of Concerned Scientists estimates that overall use of antimicrobials for nontherapeutic purposes appears to have risen by 50 percent between 1985 and 2001. Organic meat is the gold standard. See Sources for a list of producers who sell organic beef.

Natural meat can be many things. There's nothing in the NOS defining or regulating use of the term "natural." The department's Food Safety and Inspection Service (FSIS) regulates the term "natural" on meat and poultry labels and defines it this way:

> *A product containing no artificial ingredient or added color, and is only mini-mally processed (a process which does not fundamentally alter the raw product) may be labeled natural. The label must explain the use of the term "natural" (such as no added colorings or artificial ingredients; minimally processed).*

This doesn't mean that the animal was raised without hormones or antibiotics. Some ranchers producing natural beef use the chemicals, some don't. Since those substances are part of the problem with our factory farming of meat, natural meats produced without them are a better choice for the environment, the animals, and our own health. See Sources for a list of natural beef producers who don't use growth hormones and subtherapeutic antibiotics.

Sustainably-produced meat refers to meat produced using any alternative management practices, such as limiting or prohibiting antibiotic and hormone use, limiting confinement, and so on. These products would generally appear with a "natural" or "negative claim" label, such as "cage free" or "produced without hormones." The FSIS defines the following terms:

- **"Free range" or "free roaming"**: Poultry that has been allowed access to the outside. (The USDA is currently working on finer definitions for these terms, and also for "grass fed." Until they clarify them, the terms can be used pretty loosely. Grass-fed beef may have grazed on nonorganic grass. And only if the label reads "100% grass-fed," "grass-fed only," or "pasture finished" can you be sure that the animal has not spent time in a feedlot.)

- **"Natural"**: A product that contains no artificial ingredient or added color and is only minimally processed (processing that does not fundamentally alter the raw product) may be labeled natural. The label must explain the use of the term "natural" (such as no added colorings or artificial ingredients; minimally processed).

- "No hormones": The term "no hormones administered" may be approved for use on the label of beef products if the producer provides sufficient documentation to the USDA showing no hormones were used in raising the animals. By law, hormones are not allowed in raising hogs or poultry. Therefore, the claim "no hormones added" cannot be used on the labels of pork or poultry unless it is followed by the statement, "Federal regulations prohibit the use of hormones."

- "No antibiotics": The term "no antibiotics added" may be used on labels for meat and poultry products if the producer provides sufficient documentation to the USDA demonstrating that the animals were raised without antibiotics.

Truthful claims of any kind are permitted on labeling. However, alternative labeling claims may not be used to misrepresent a product. Who decides if animals were raised on a "kinder, gentler farm"? In most cases, it's the producer himself. Negative claims, such as "cage free" and "raised in the light of day," are legal if they're not provably false.

Humane Certifications

Free Farmed: The American Humane Association's Farm Animal Services program administers this label, which indicates humane treatment of poultry and cattle. Criteria include access to water, healthy food, rapid medical treatment, and space.

Certified Humane Raised & Handled (CHRH): Humane Farm Animal Care, a non-profit based in Herndon, Virginia, certifies and labels meat, poultry, eggs, and dairy products. Its standards prohibit added growth hormones and antibiotics. The group uses American Meat Institute slaughtering standards, which are higher than those of the Federal Humane Slaughter Act.

Farmers and producers voluntarily submit to inspections and spot checks that ensure that they're treating their animals with respect. In return, they earn the right to display the group's logo on their packaging. The CHRH standards require that livestock

> have access to clean and sufficient food and water, that their environment is not dangerous to their health, that they have sufficient protection from weather elements, that they have sufficient space to move naturally, and other features to ensure the health, safety and comfort of the animal. In addition, the standards require that managers and caretakers be thoroughly trained in animal husbandry and welfare, and have good working knowledge of their system and the animals in their care.

For more on CHRH and a database of retailers carrying Certified Humane products, go to www.certifiedhumane.com. The USDA has a verification role in the CHRH certification program. For more about the government's role in the program, go to www.ams.usda.gov/lsg/lsarc.htm.

American Humane Association

FREE FARMED™ CERTIFIED

CERTIFIED* HUMANE

RAISED & HANDLED

* Meets the Humane Farm Animal Care Program standards, which include nutritious diet without antibiotics, or hormones, animals raised with shelter, resting areas, sufficient space and the ability to engage in natural behaviors.

Home on the Range

Our fertile land supported 60 million bison and 100 million antelope before the arrival of Europeans. For ages, the soil benefited from the constant infusion of natural nitrogen from manure. Today, with the bison all but gone, we consume millions of gallons of petroleum to produce the chemical fertilizer most essential to farming: nitrogen. Meanwhile, the land struggles under the weight of 100 million cattle, whose nitrogen-rich manure is a major pollution problem in our country. According to a 1990 Minnesota Agricultural Statistic Service study, the Minnesota beef industry alone generates approximately 10 million tons of manure annually. That translates to 55,000 tons of nitrogen, 41,000 tons of phosphorus fertilizer equivalent, and 47,000 tons of potassium fertilizer equivalent. That manure could help replace the need for fossil fuel–produced nitrogen on thousands of acres of cropland. It would likely fertilize enough acreage to produce organically fertilized feed for the beef industry there. The USDA's Natural Resources Conservation Service estimates national recoverable nitrogen at 2.5 billion pounds.

It's neither practical nor desirable to aim for manure-based fertilization of all U.S. cropland. The last thing our environment needs is more grazing cattle. But to manufacture excessive amounts of petrochemicals and disregard the fertilizing properties of existing manure is a waste of waste. A well-conceived manure management plan would cut noxious emissions into our waterways, and reduce equally noxious industrial emissions into our air. Organic farms fertilize with manure, and they produce crops that are the envy of the farming world. This kind of integration would make good environmental, business, and culinary sense. Pollution from hog farms is among the worst sources of manure pollution. Ethical producers like Du Breton Farms of Canada (www.dubreton.com) are already composting their manure and using it as fertilizer.

This doesn't mean that increasing meat consumption would be a net benefit to the environment. We've all heard the staggering numbers, first cited in Frances Moore Lappé's *Diet for a Small Planet*—that it takes sixteen pounds of grain and soy, and 2,500 gallons of water, to produce a one-pound steak. About 90 percent of the grain currently grown in America is used to feed livestock. The biggest single contribution individuals can make to the environment, family planning aside, is to reduce the amount of meat they consume.

Ethical Choices Require Constant Decision Making
About now, you may wonder how I can simultaneously argue that local and organic are the right way to eat, that ecologically sound and humane fine foods can be ordered through the Internet, that chemical fertilizers and pesticides play an important role in protecting the environment, that biodiversity must be protected, and that genetically modified crops should be conditionally embraced. As Walt Whitman wrote, "Do I contradict myself? / Very well then I contradict myself, / (I am large, and I contain multitudes)." I believe that ethical choices in dining require regular decision making on a case-by-case basis. If there were a single principle that could sum up ethical food, this book would be unnecessary. We have to consider numerous factors, including taste, when buying food.

With meat, the first consideration has to be a personal one: How big a role is meat going to play in my diet? If you're like most Americans, you eat meat every day, if not at every meal. Nutritionally, there's no need for that much consumption. If you were to set aside one day a week as your "vegetarian day," you could reduce your meat consumption by over 14 percent. Rethink your menu strategy as I describe in this book, and you could cut your meat consumption by 75 percent, and enjoy the meat you *do* consume 100 percent more.

Real Food from Virtual Stores
The biggest single factor in providing access to ethical products is the advent of online shopping. Bison raised humanely in New Jersey can be ordered on Monday and be on the dinner table on Tuesday. People who had little or no access to organic meats can now shop from the best producers, regardless of where they live. Spices, sauces, and condiments are a click away. Though fresh vegetables are rare over the Web, fruit, preserves, and frozen products arrive unscathed.

First, of course, consumers should get to know their best food shops, natural food stores, and farmers' markets. These close-to-home sources should be the first choice. When buying from an online retailer, buy in the largest quantity you think you'll consume, to minimize shipping and thus packaging. Plan and employ practical uses for packing materials, and learn which companies pack in the most responsible way (some pack in popcorn, recycled newspaper, or rice-based, biodegradable "peanuts" instead of Styrofoam). While you want products to arrive fresh, you don't want to support gratuitous packing. Another benefit to buying direct from producers is that intermediate packaging is minimized. In some cases, buying direct from meat producers means buying larger cuts and breaking them down into smaller roasts and steaks yourself. It's akin to buying whole vegetables by the pound, rather than the prepeeled, preshucked, preprocessed packs that supermarkets now also carry.

Help the Environment by Doing Your Own Butchering

Buying what chefs call "primal cuts"—larger sections of an animal, like a hindquarter—is still a hurdle for many home cooks (especially those with little freezer space). This is an issue that ranchers and sellers of grass-fed, pasture-raised meats are still grappling with. Some describe the humane, ecologically sound meat market as being where the organic market was twenty years ago: still trying to find a convenient way to reach the consumer. What cooks need to know is that they can apply a little common sense and a few knife cuts to separate roasts, steaks, and stew meat with ease. They'll even end up with stock bones to boot.

Meat separates easily along natural seams. One of my chefs at CIA used to say,

"As long as you're cutting through connective tissue and fat, you're on the right track, cheffy baby." What he meant was, it's easy to see when you're cutting into the wrong part, because you'll see the grain of the meat. In between the roasts and the other parts, connective collagen tissues define sections that constitute a guide of sorts. Cut along those seams, and you'll have logical smaller cuts. Layers of fat also separate sections, and you can cut along those fat lines for smaller cuts. It's not nearly as daunting as it seems when you first lay eyes on a large primal cut. It's the most economical way to buy grass-fed beef and other meats. See Sources for the best suppliers of grass-fed, pasture-raised meats near you.

Beef

Butchers commonly refer to ground odds and ends of beef as "cheap chop." At $6 a pound plus shipping, Niman Ranch beef is a whole different animal from the $1.59-a-pound family-pack hamburger at the supermarket. These steers may not sleep at the Ritz-Carlton, but they're not locked in a stall with scads of hormone and antibiotic-laced feed to make them fat fast, as most livestock in factory beef production systems are. They graze in pastures, and also eat barley, corn, soy meal, cane molasses, and hay. They aren't poked and prodded with growth-promoting hormones and antibiotics. This ranch, while not organic, provides the kind of humane treatment and healthy diet that factory farms don't, which gives the livestock a better quality of life, and decreases demand for environmentally unsound chemicals.

One of the eeriest "farming" practices revealed during the European crisis over bovine spongiform encephalopathy (a.k.a. mad cow disease) was the feeding of these herbivores to one another. Most consumers were shocked to discover that the remains of some of the cattle were routinely ground and fed back to other cattle, turning the cud-chewing livestock unwittingly into cannibalistic carnivores. Few would argue the ethics of such a practice, but it continues even to this day, and even in the United States. It's a real-life remake of the man-eats-man thriller *Soylent Green*.

To ensure you're not contributing to this reprehensible affair, always know the source of any beef you buy. The new USDA organic certification comes in handy here, since feeding of organic livestock is more closely supervised than that of nonorganic, ensuring greater enforcement of FDA rules prohibiting the practice. Another encouraging development is the branding of beef and other meats (see sidebar, Brand-Name Beef Breeds Accountability), enabling consumers to make informed purchasing decisions. For a "Smart Shopper's Beef & Pork" wallet card with some suggested brands, contact the Green Guide by clicking www.thegreenguide.com or calling them at (212) 598-4910.

GRASS-FED BEEF The flavor of American beef has become so dumbed down that people from lands where concentrated animal feeding operations (CAFOs) don't exist describe it as bland. From a culinary point of view, mass production of U.S. beef has been a losing proposition. As flavor has diminished, fat content has increased. This brings up a tricky issue. Grain-fed beef is distinctly more tender than grass-fed. Its fibers, marbled with fat that doesn't develop in more active animals living on a leaner diet, yield more gently to the knife and the bite than pasture-raised meat does. Even the least "worked" muscles of the pasture-raised animal, such as the tenderloin and rib loin, are less fatty, and so less tender. To achieve equal juiciness when cooked, lean meats need to be treated differently than conventional CAFO meats.

Grass-fed and pasture-raised livestock grow in an environment that straddles a middle ground somewhere between the wild fauna of the untouched prairie and the factory system of modern agriculture. While not truly "wild," their flavor and texture resemble that of wild game more closely than mainstream meat does. For the most part, that's what we experience when we buy so-called game meats now. Bison, deer, quail, and pigeons (squab) are raised on farms, but are mostly free to roam outdoors. Very few of these animals raised for meat undergo the treatments and manhandling associated with mainstream meat production, so they are almost always a more humane choice. Wild boar, which is as close to a wild product as the USDA will allow for public sale, is actually an introduced species from Europe. They roam the Southwestern states, foraging for wild greens, acorns, and roots. They're regularly trapped by ranchers and inspected by the USDA, and then processed and sold to aficionados. Their meat is as far from pork as Chicago is from Brisbane. With a sweet, nutty taste and dark color, it has loads more character than the "other white meat" (American pork producers adopted the slogan to convince consumers that their product was as mild as factory-farmed chicken).

THE PRICE OF SUPERMARKET STEAK Environmental abuses of the mass-production beef industry abound. Oversized herds graze Western pastures down to the dust, leaving no vegetation to keep topsoil from eroding away. As in dust bowl days, the herds just move on to another piece of land to repeat the cycle. Densely packed, they generate concentrations of waste that exceed natural waterways' capacity to absorb it, leaving rivers and streams poisoned open sewers. Flatulence from livestock is a major contributor to total greenhouse gas emissions. New Zealand, a signatory to the Kyoto protocol designed to limit greenhouse gas emissions, imposed a tax on livestock (since repealed) in an effort to lower the country's contribution to global warming. Methane and nitrous oxide from cattle and sheep account for more than half of that country's greenhouse gas emissions.

The conditions under which cattle live are often abominable. During the "feedlot" stage of the production process, the gentle giants are confined in cruel fattening pens to focus them on chemical-laden diets designed to maximize weight and profit.

Feed and Seed Indeed!

I was a volunteer firefighter in my hometown of Farmingdale, New York, when the biggest fire to hit town in my lifetime occurred. At the firehouse, we used to sit around the kitchen table and ruminate on what location would be the worst that fire could strike, and Wagner's Feed & Seed, near the railroad station, always came out on top.

Farmingdale's agricultural roots were still evident from the presence of a state agricultural college in town, the village's charming name, and, of course, in the sizable "feed and seed" warehouse located near the rails. The name of the company conjured up images of hardscrabble farmers in overalls stopping in to buy seed corn, hay, and grain for their chickens. But in the 1980s, the name belied what was a highly dangerous business. The elders in the firehouse knew what was in that building, and spoke solemnly about the potential for disaster. Even thousands of miles from the breadbasket states, the feed and seed outlet was packed with toxic chemicals, pesticides, solvents, and petroleum-generated nitrogen fertilizers like the ones used to blow up the Murrah Federal Building in Oklahoma City in 1995.

When lightning struck the block-long corrugated tin Wagner's Feed & Seed Company building in June of 1985, the place went up like a tinderbox. Minutes after the strike, when our engines pulled up to the scene, the structure was "fully involved" (fire department lingo for "engulfed in flames"). We were prohibited from even approaching the blazing building, as the fumes were known to be filled with lethal gases. Instead, the hazardous materials team was called in from neighboring Hicksville to see if any of the poisonous fuel could be extracted from the inferno. They arrived in their metallic space suits and bravely forced their way into the blaze, emerging seconds later to report that we "must be kidding" if we thought anything could be pulled out of there.

Six fire departments surrounded the building with dozens of trucks linked to hydrants all over Farmingdale, and poured every ounce of water available on the structure (under pouring rain, no less), in what's known as a "surround and drown" operation. The fire took all night and most of the next day to extinguish. For the most part, that fire burned itself out, practically mocking the scores of firefighters attacking it. All that was left was the contaminated ground, which New York State declared a hazardous waste site after the fire.

Chain-link fencing surrounded the deserted site for fourteen years, marked with nothing more than a tin sign warning of hazardous wastes inside. In what many consider an obscene move, developers bought the land after the Wagners finally cleaned it up and the state Department of Environmental Conservation declared it safe, and built senior citizens residences there. Maybe they figured no one there would live long enough to sue if they became ill from any residual toxic waste.

My point here is that "feed and seed" has become a euphemism for dealers in potent toxic chemicals and poisons. "Grain-fed" livestock are actually fed "feed," an industrial cocktail of grain and animal by-products, including their remains and wastes. So-called milk-fed veal is fed "milk" composed largely of cows' blood. I've seen veal sold with labels boasting that it was raised on "top-quality protein." You'd think it was peanut butter. Until we break our cycle of self-deception, we'll continue to view "feed and seed," "grain-fed," "milk-fed," and "protein" as wholesome terms that suggest no harm.

John Mackey, founder and CEO of Whole Foods, says he thinks Americans are in denial about factory farms in the United States. He's a vegetarian who recognizes that not everyone is going to give up meat. Bearing that in mind, he's developing new, stricter humane standards for the meat sold in his stores. Americans don't want to know what's happening in factory farms, he says, because they're not willing to give up eating meat. In an interview on the www.grist.org Web site, he says: "Once we can really have animal-compassionate alternatives where people can buy this product and know that the animal was well-treated during its lifetime, then they'll be willing to look at what the factory farm is all about. I think when that happens across the United States, there's going to be outrage about factory farms."

A necessary first step to breaking free of denial is to find out what label claims and well-known catchphrases really mean. When poultry comes labeled "never administered hormones," be aware that the use of hormones is illegal in poultry, and that none of the producers, not even the cruelest and most egregious polluters, can administer hormones to their chickens. The label might as well say "never basted with rat poison." As long as a label claim is not demonstrably false, the seller can use it. Regulated terms like "organic" and "free range" and the marks of trustworthy independent organizations like Certified Humane and Marine Stewardship Council (MSC) are distinctions worth seeking out.

Brand-Name Beef Breeds Accountability

Years ago, chickens were marketed like a commodity: Shoppers saw only the butcher's price tag on the package, and had no idea who produced the product, or where it came from. Today, most consumers choose between these still-unbranded birds or an array of brands like Tyson, Purdue, Cookin' Good, Murray's, Nature's Farm (organic), Pilgrim's Pride, Bell and Evans (antibiotic free), Ebberly Poultry (organic, free range), and Wise (kosher organic), to name a few. For poultry companies, the move to branding was a double-edged sword.

Although creation of a consumer-recognized brand brought about brand loyalty, it also made it easier to identify whose products were produced in unsavory ways. Tyson has been frequently criticized in the press for pollution and inhumane treatment issues since emerging from anonymity. Consumers can easily vote with their wallets at the supermarket against clearly labeled products. Result? Tyson has not only bowed to public pressure and addressed some long-ignored abuses, but it has launched its own line of organic poultry (Nature's Farm), which prominently displays the Tyson label. But while chickens became branded, beef remained largely a commodity. Until now . . .

Lately, packages with names like Meyer Natural Angus, Oregon Country Beef, Painted Hills Natural Beef, Thomas E. Wilson, and Niman Ranch, among others, have begun showing up, vacuum-packed, in upscale supermarket meat departments. Prepackaged beef, known in the industry as "case ready" since it requires no handling by meat cutters at the point of sale, has been growing by as much as 15 percent annually. This trend bodes well for consumers who want to choose only meats from responsible producers, and hold the companies accountable for their practices. It also opens the door for organic and humane producers, who need not be pioneers in branded beef anymore.

Cardamom-scented Grass-fed Rib Steak with Herb Vinaigrette

SERVES 4 AS A SIDE DISH Roaming the range foraging for grasses makes pasture-raised beef leaner and more intense in flavor. Grass-fed beef, with its lower fat content, cooks differently from conventional beef, so cook it slower, at lower temperatures. Its concentrated flavors make it an exceptional meat to serve in small, sliced portions as a spicy accompaniment to a grain and vegetable main course such as Pumpkin Basmati Rice Pilaf (page 64), Toasted Hard Red Wheat Pilaf with Caramelized Shallots, Figs, and Brazil Nuts (page 78), or Spiced Whole Oats (page 303).

4 cardamom pods, crushed

4 garlic cloves, lightly crushed

2 bay leaves

2 star anise, crushed, or ½ teaspoon anise seeds

2 tablespoons red wine vinegar

¼ cup white wine

1 tablespoon honey or molasses

¼ cup soy sauce

One 1-pound rib-eye steak from grass-fed or pasture-raised beef

3 tablespoons olive oil

1 tablespoon Champagne vinegar or white wine vinegar

¼ cup chopped tender fresh herbs, such as chives, flat-leaf parsley, chervil, and/or tarragon

Salt and freshly ground black pepper

Combine the cardamom, garlic, bay leaves, star anise, vinegar, wine, honey, and soy sauce. Stir until the honey is dissolved. Place the beef in an airtight bag or container with the marinade. Marinate for 8 hours, turning once.

Scrape the marinade from the beef; pat dry. Heat 1 tablespoon of the olive oil in a skillet over medium-low heat 30 seconds, until hot but not shimmering. Place the beef in the center of the pan. Cook slowly for 10 minutes without disturbing. Turn; cook 5 minutes more. Transfer the meat to a board to let it rest for 5 minutes.

Whisk together the remaining 2 tablespoons olive oil, the Champagne vinegar, and herbs. Season with salt and pepper. Slice the beef thinly, and serve dressed with the vinaigrette.

Almond and Golden Raisin Wild Rice with Roasted Beets, Sliced Rare Rib Eye of Beef, and Zinfandel Sauce

SERVES 4 Spicy and bursting with berry flavors, zinfandel is an excellent choice for cooking with beef. An excellent organic zinfandel is available from California's Frey Vineyards (www.freywine.com). Organic options are also available: for organic wine vinegar, www.villageorganics.com; for wild rice, www.truefoodsmarket.com; for almonds, www.woodprairie.com; and for raisins, www.organic-planet.com. You can get organic beef from www.pratherranch.com, and nonorganic but humanely and responsibly treated beef from www.nimanranch.com.

½ cup whole almonds

1 pound beets, greens removed

4 tablespoons (½ stick) unsalted butter

2 tablespoons wine vinegar

2 tablespoons ground coriander

1 teaspoon salt, plus more to taste

½ teaspoon freshly ground black pepper, plus more to taste

2 tablespoons olive oil

One 12-ounce rib-eye steak

1 cup wild rice

1 cup golden or other raisins

½ cup zinfandel or other red wine

Heat the oven to 400°F. Spread the almonds in a small baking pan and toast in the oven until they sizzle, about 10 minutes. Set the beets in another baking pan and roast them until tender, about 45 minutes. Let cool, peel, and cut into 1-inch chunks. Toss with a tablespoon of the butter and set aside.

While the beets are roasting, whisk together the vinegar, coriander, 1 teaspoon salt, ½ teaspoon pepper, olive oil, and 2 tablespoons water; marinate the meat in the mixture for 45 minutes.

Put the rice in a pot of lightly salted water and bring to a boil. Lower the heat and simmer until most of the grains have split open, about 45 minutes; drain. Combine the rice, raisins, almonds, and 2 tablespoons butter. Season well with salt and pepper. Keep warm.

Heat a heavy skillet (preferably nonreactive metal) until very hot over a high flame. Remove the steak from the marinade, reserving the mixture. Sauté the steak to desired doneness, about 3 minutes per side for medium rare. Immediately deglaze the pan by splashing with red wine and leftover marinade. Remove from heat and swirl in the remaining tablespoon of butter. Season with salt and pepper.

Slice the steak across the grain into twelve thin slices. Spoon a portion of wild rice in the center of each of four plates. Arrange three slices of beef in a fan at the six o'clock position of the plate, spoon with sauce, and garnish the rest of the plate with roasted beets. Serve immediately.

Ethical Brown Stock

Classical and winter recipes often call for brown *veal* stock. In some cases, the gelatin in that stock plays a role in giving body to a sauce, or viscosity to a reduction. Veal bones, naturally high in gelatin, are often used to make brown stock. They're roasted until caramelized, along with aromatic vegetables and tomato paste, and simmered until their color, gelatin, and flavor are extracted. A handful of humane farms produce veal without confinement or cruel treatment. If you must use veal, only source bones from these places (www.overthemoonfarm. com and www.meadowraisedmeats.com both sell humanely raised veal). But in most cases, the only roles of brown stock in a dish are color and flavor. For those, any bones will do.

Beef, lamb, or pork stock and even duck, chicken, or turkey stock can be made in the same way as brown veal stock, and will impart rich color and complex flavor to your foods. Buying humanely raised and organic meats is rightly expensive. Never throw away bones. They should be roasted and simmered for stock. The process is mindless simplicity, and fills the house with pleasing cooking aromas. I haven't yet found a good organic beef bouillon cube. But a good homemade beef (or other) stock can be reduced to a concentrated *glace* for the same applications. Stocks and glaces keep frozen for months. Roasting and simmering the bones for stock when preparing any meat meal should become part of your routine.

At the Culinary Institute of America, where I studied cooking, chefs teach that meat dishes should mostly be made with stock from the same animal: duck dishes with duck stock, chicken dishes with chicken stock, venison dishes with venison stock. While they also teach that brown veal and white chicken stocks are flavor-neutral (they can be used in dishes that contain no veal or chicken), having a variety of stocks on hand makes sense. You never know when a lamb recipe will call for brown veal stock, and you'll be glad to have lamb stock on hand to use in its place. With the exception of the small amount of humanely raised meat, sold mostly by mail order, veal is produced in reprehensible ways. I won't go into the details, because by now they're widely known. But suffice it to say that even the culinary arbiters at the CIA would support your use of alternative brown stocks in place of veal stock in meat dishes.

Brown Stock

YIELD: 2 QUARTS Scale this recipe up or down to match whatever bones you have. Even the bones from one chicken make a good quart of strong stock. The perfectly stocked (no pun) freezer contains stock of every meat that is typically cooked in that kitchen.

2 tablespoons oil

2 pounds bones (such as beef, lamb, pork, chicken, or game), cut into 1- or 2-inch pieces

1 large onion, cut into 1-inch pieces (2 cups)

2 celery ribs, cut into 1-inch pieces (1 cup)

2 carrots, cut into 1-inch pieces (1 cup)

3 tablespoons tomato paste

1 sachet d'epices (cheesecloth packet tied with a string) containing 2 parsley stems, 2 thyme sprigs (or ¼ teaspoon dried), ¼ teaspoon cracked black pepper, 1 bay leaf, and 1 garlic clove

Salt (optional)

Heat the oven to 425°F. Heat the oil in a roasting pan in the oven until hot enough to shimmer, but not smoke. Add the bones to the pan and roast, turning occasionally, until they turn a deep brown color. The roasting time varies with the type of bones. Beef bones may take 45 minutes, while chicken bones might take only 25. Transfer the bones to a tall stockpot (set the roasting pan aside for the vegetables), add 3 quarts water (it should cover the bones by 1 inch), and bring to a simmer over low heat. Simmer 4 hours, skimming fat and impurities that come to the surface occasionally.

Add the onion, celery, and carrots to the residual oil in the roasting pan; return to the oven and cook until they are golden brown, about 20 minutes. Stir in the tomato paste, and cook 2 minutes more. Remove the vegetables with a slotted spoon and set them aside. Pour off any fat that remains in the roasting pan (this is called degreasing the pan), then deglaze the pan by pouring in some cool water, and scraping up any browned bits with a wooden spoon.

After the stock has simmered 4 hours, transfer the roasted vegetables (called mirepoix) and the deglazed juices to the pot with the bones, along with the sachet. Simmer the stock 2 more hours. Strain the stock, and season with a tiny bit of salt, if desired.

Lamb

Although mainstream lamb production suffers from some of the same inhumane practices as the beef industry, sheep generally have a better life than cattle. For one thing, few are subjected to the cruelties of factory dairy production. For another, sheep's wool production dictates that the animals be more sanitary and injury-free. For consumers, resources like www.eatwild.com, www.meadowraisedmeats.com, and www.farmtotable.org make sourcing organic and pasture-raised lamb from responsible growers like Amissville, Virginia's Touchstone Farms (www.touchstone farm.org) easy.

Another advantage for the consumer is manageable order size. Many direct farmer-to-consumer operations deal only in larger cuts, like whole, quartered, and halved animals. While not everyone has a large separate freezer capable of storing a hundred-pound forequarter of beef, a quartered lamb easily fits in a standard refrigerator freezer.

The reasons for buying humanely raised, grass-fed lamb couldn't be clearer. Overcrowding and indoor raising of sheep in factory farm operations cause painful injury to the sheep's hooves. To force them to grow fatter and faster, they're fed liquid diets and animal matter, to which their ruminant bodies are unsuited. Merino sheep, prized for their wool, are sometimes subjected to surgery, without anesthesia, to remove folds in their skin. This reprehensible practice, known as mulesing, is rare, but is still practiced in the United States. With so many excellent sources for lamb from sheep that were allowed to live in clean, pleasant environments with dignity until their deaths, why would anyone continue to buy factory-farmed lamb?

African Djolof Rice with Salty Vegetables and Lamb Mafé

SERVES 8 Djolof rice, a national dish of Senegal, is usually made with "broken" long-grain rice. This shattered rice is available from African and some Thai specialty stores, but you can make your own by cracking Thai jasmine rice, using a mortar and pestle or a blender (a food processor won't work), until it has the texture of coarse couscous.

3 large tomatoes, peeled

2 tablespoons tomato paste

2 large onions, one sliced into ½-inch rounds, the other roughly chopped

¼ cup palm oil (authentic) or peanut oil (healthy)

½ teaspoon cayenne

2 garlic cloves, sliced

Salt and freshly ground black pepper

1 head green cabbage, cut through the core into 8 wedges

4 large carrots, cut into 2-inch chunks

2 cups broken rice (such as jasmine rice; see headnote)

1 recipe Lamb Mafé (recipe follows)

In a mixing bowl, use a fork to mash the peeled tomatoes together with the tomato paste until lumpy but uniform in color; set aside. Brush the onion slices with some of the oil and roast, grill, sauté, or broil them until golden brown and soft, about 10 minutes. Combine the cooked onions and cayenne in a mortar or food processor; pound or puree into a paste.

In a heavy Dutch oven with a tight-fitting lid, fry the chopped onion in the remaining oil until golden. Add the garlic; cook a few seconds until the garlic is white and fragrant, then add the mashed tomatoes, onion paste, 1 cup water, and salt and pepper to taste (this dish is meant to be salty, so season generously). Bring to a simmer, and add the cabbage and carrots. Cover tightly and cook over a low flame until the carrots are very tender, stirring occasionally, about 30 minutes. Carefully transfer the carrots and cabbage to a plate; keep warm.

Add the rice to the pot, stir well, and add 3 cups water. Bring to a boil, then cover, lower flame, and simmer until all the liquid is absorbed and the rice is tender, about 20 minutes. Remove from heat and let stand, covered, 10 minutes.

Stir the rice, and serve topped with the warm vegetables and a few pieces of Lamb Mafé.

Lamb Mafé

SERVES 8 AS A MAIN COURSE, IN COMBINATION WITH AFRICAN DJOLOF RICE A traditional dish of the Wolof people of Senegal and Gambia, mafé is one of the many variations of the African groundnut stew. It is often made with lamb or mutton (as is presented here); it can also be made with fowl, fish (fresh or dried), or in a vegetarian version. The basic mafé recipe calls for meat, onion, oil, tomato paste, peanut (or peanut butter), a vegetable or two, chile pepper, salt, black pepper, and water.

Certified organic lamb is available from www.michiganorganic.org/zensheep/. You can even get organic vegetable bouillon cubes from www.villageorganics.com. See Sources for additional suppliers or organic lamb.

2 tablespoons oil

2 pounds lamb neck or shoulder, bone-in, sawed into 2-inch cubes

Salt and freshly ground black pepper

2 onions, finely chopped

2 tablespoons tomato paste, or one 4-ounce can tomato sauce

4 tomatoes, peeled and quartered

1 hot chile (such as a New Mexico chile), roughly chopped, or crushed red pepper to taste (optional)

4 cups assorted vegetables, cut into 2-inch chunks, such as cabbage, carrot, sweet cassava tuber (yuca), eggplant, potato, squash, sweet potato, and/or turnip

Beef or vegetable bouillon cube (optional)

¼ cup peanut butter (natural, unsweetened)

2 cups water, beef stock, or broth

Heat the oil in a large cooking pot or Dutch oven. Season the meat well with salt and pepper. Sauté the meat and onions together over high heat until they both start to brown, about 5 minutes. Reduce the heat to low, and sweat (cook slowly to let the meat and onions release some juices) 5 to 7 minutes.

Add the tomato paste, tomatoes, chile (if using), vegetables, ¼ cup water, and the bouillon cube (if using). Slowly sweat the stew, covered, until all ingredients are tender, about 2 hours, adding small amounts of water as necessary to prevent scorching. Stir frequently.

Reduce the heat. Stir in the peanut butter. Mix in water or stock as needed to make a smooth sauce. Serve over African Djolof Rice (page 158).

Organic Lamb and White Bean Stew on Red Rice

SERVES 8 AS A MAIN COURSE Bhutanese red rice's nutty flavor and comforting, al dente texture give it a "meaty" quality that matches perfectly with this deeply flavored stew. Unlike so many colorful ingredients that fade or look completely different when they're cooked, red rice keeps its gorgeous appearance. The substantial presence of the whole-grain rice and the intensity of the lamb stew's flavor make the rice a great main element in the meal, and the stew a perfect "sauce."

See Sources for suppliers of organic lamb. Bhutanese red rice is available from www.worldpantry.com.

1½ pounds organic lamb shoulder or leg, cut into ½-inch pieces

2 teaspoons kosher salt

Freshly ground black pepper

1 tablespoon olive oil

1 large onion, chopped

3 garlic cloves, finely chopped

4 teaspoons all-purpose flour

2 bay leaves

2 fresh rosemary sprigs, about 4 inches each

1 cup white wine

2 carrots, diced

½ cup dried black-eyed peas or small white (navy) beans, simmered until tender, or one 15-ounce can white beans, drained and rinsed

2 cups Bhutanese red rice or brown rice

½ pound collard greens, blanched and finely chopped

3 tablespoons unsalted butter (optional)

Season the lamb with salt and pepper. Heat the olive oil in a heavy-bottomed pot large enough to hold the lamb and vegetables, and sear the meat over high heat until nicely caramelized. Remove with a slotted spoon; set aside. Lower the heat to medium; add the onion, garlic, flour, bay leaves, and rosemary. Cook slowly for 10 minutes, stirring occasionally.

Add the wine; simmer 2 minutes to cook out the alcohol. Stir in the browned lamb (along with any juices that have collected). Cover the pot; simmer slowly for 1 hour. Add the carrots; cook until the meat is almost tender, about 1 hour more. Add the beans; simmer until the beans and lamb are meltingly tender, about 15 minutes. While the lamb is stewing, cook the rice according to package directions.

Stir in the collard greens and butter (if using); season to taste. Serve over plates of red rice.

Soft Wheat Pilaf with Roasted Onions, Dried Fruit, and Cumin Lamb

SERVES 4 For people who eat wheat almost every day in the form of bread, pasta, baked goods, or beer, it's amazing how few Americans have ever seen actual wheat. Spring wheat's high starch content makes it fluffier when cooked, whereas winter wheat cooks to a chewier, denser texture. Both are delicious, and either can be used in this recipe. I'm partial to the more tender spring wheat.

Organic nuts and dried fruits are available from www.truefoodsonline.com; organic wheat berries can be found at www.greenmountainmills.com. See Sources for suppliers of organic lamb.

½ cup shelled nuts, such as cashews

1 cup soft winter or spring wheat berries or other whole grain

6 cups stock or water

2 teaspoons salt, plus more to taste

4 tablespoons olive oil

1 large onion, chopped (about 2 cups)

1 pound white mushrooms, sliced

2 tablespoons chopped fresh rosemary, or 1 tablespoon dried

3 garlic cloves, finely chopped

½ cup dried fruit, such as raisins, apricots, prunes, or dried cherries, cut into bite-size pieces

Freshly ground black pepper

4 medium onions, peeled but left whole

1 teaspoon cumin seeds, toasted in a dry pan until fragrant

1 boneless lamb loin (about 1 pound)

Chopped fresh flat-leaf parsley

Heat the oven to 400°F. Toast the nuts in the oven for 10 minutes until they sizzle (watch to make sure they don't burn); set aside. Wash the wheat berries well under running water. In a medium saucepot with a tight-fitting cover, bring the stock to a boil; stir in the wheat and salt. Simmer for 1½ hours, or until the grains are tender.

In a large skillet, heat 2 tablespoons of the oil until very hot, almost smoky. Add the chopped onion and mushrooms. Cook without stirring for 5 minutes, allowing the vegetables to brown. Stir in the rosemary and garlic; cook for 5 minutes more, stirring occasionally, until the onion is very soft. Combine the wheat, dried fruit, and vegetables; season to taste with salt and pepper.

While the wheat berries are cooking, roast the onions: Toss the whole onions with 1 tablespoon of the oil and roast 1 hour, until tender. Peel the leathery outer layer. Combine the remaining tablespoon oil with the cumin seeds and rub the mixture onto the lamb loin. Season the lamb well with salt and pepper. Sear the lamb on all sides in a heavy skillet over high heat and cook to medium rare, about 8 minutes. Let the lamb rest for 10 minutes before slicing into ⅛-inch slivers.

For an attractive presentation, mold the pilaf into 4-ounce custard cups, then unmold onto serving plates. Arrange the roasted onions and lamb slivers around the pilaf; sprinkle with the nuts and parsley.

Pappardelle with Braised Lamb Shanks and Winter Vegetables

SERVES 8 This is a variation on a dish from my mentor, Jasper White, who served the stewed lamb along with grilled lamb chops. His recipe served four as an entree, but when the braised lamb alone is used as a sauce for the pasta, it's enough to serve eight dinner portions.

Www.jamisonfarm.com and www.touchstonefarm.com sell humanely raised lamb. Note: Jamison sells shanks separately, while Touchstone sells only whole lamb packages. See also Sources.

¼ cup olive oil

2 lamb shanks, cross-cut into 1-inch-thick slices as for osso buco (ask your butcher, or use a hacksaw)

Salt and freshly ground black pepper

5 garlic cloves, chopped

4 shallots, chopped

2 cups dry white wine

2 cups Brown Stock (see page 155) or broth

Juice and julienned zest of 1 orange

Juice and julienned zest of 1 lemon

2 tablespoons tomato paste

2 branches fresh rosemary

2 thick parsnips, cut into 1-inch dice

1 small rutabaga, cut into 1-inch dice

1 small celery root, cut into 1-inch dice

1 pound dried pappardelle, fettuccine, or other wide, flat pasta

2 tablespoons unsalted butter

1 cup grated Parmigiano-Reggiano cheese

¼ cup roughly chopped fresh flat-leaf parsley

Lemon wedges

Heat the oil in a Dutch oven over medium heat. Dry the pieces of meat with a towel, season them well with salt and pepper, and brown them on all sides; set them aside. Add all but 1 teaspoon of the garlic and all of the shallots to the pan; cook until golden, about 6 minutes. Splash in the wine; simmer 5 minutes. Add the stock, orange juice, lemon juice, tomato paste, rosemary, the reserved lamb shanks, and any juices they have released. Cover; simmer gently for 45 minutes.

Stir in the orange and lemon zest, parsnips, rutabaga, and celery root. Cook until both the lamb and vegetables are tender, about 20 minutes more, partially covered. Set aside to cool. When the lamb is cool enough to handle, remove the meat from the bones and add it back to the stewed vegetables. Discard the bones.

Bring a large pot of salted water to a boil. Cook the pasta until al dente. While the pasta is cooking, combine the remaining teaspoon of garlic with a few drops of olive oil in a large skillet or pot over high heat; cook a few seconds until fragrant, then add the lamb and vegetable stew; bring to a simmer. Using a slotted spoon, transfer the cooked pasta directly from its cooking pot to the skillet with the stew. Add the butter, cheese, and parsley; toss to combine. Season well with salt and pepper, and serve in heated bowls, garnished with lemon wedges.

Pork

The mainstream pork industry is plagued by a problem of accountability. The hogs are raised by "contract farmers" for the large meatpacking companies. These farmers don't own the hogs they raise, but are responsible for disposing of the livestock's wastes. When contract farmers go bankrupt, as many have in the past decade, they often abandon open-air waste lagoons that they can't afford to clean up. Thousands of these toxic disease breeding grounds dot our country, while the major meatpackers who reaped the profits from the pigs aren't held accountable.

Pigs produce three times as much waste per capita as humans. The pigs raised in North Carolina alone produce more waste than all the people in New York City, Los Angeles, Chicago, and Houston combined. Even when the system is "working," the massive reservoirs of pig waste are left to ferment for months, releasing noxious compounds into the air. When enough of their toxins have broken down, these wastes are sprayed onto fields, where their excessive nutrients leach into waterways and flow into coastal estuaries, causing massive algae blooms that deoxygenate the waters and suffocate millions of fish. When hog farming was done on a small scale, the waste problems were diffuse and manageable. But the highly concentrated (and inhumane) massive feedlots developed in the 1990s have brought on a new level of pollution. Don't support this with your bacon bucks. (See Sources for ethical suppliers.)

PORCINE HERITAGE Inbreeding for bigger, leaner muscles on hogs has been a large-scale effort since the 1950s in the United States. It seems while genetically selecting away fat, breeders were selecting in a mutation that causes skeletal muscle spasms in stressed-out pigs, leading to mushy, watery meat in up to 15 percent of the 97 million hogs slaughtered here each year. It's a symptom of monoculture practices that are widespread in modern American agriculture, and it's a warning about loss of biodiversity.

The pigs are stressed because their conditions are deplorable. While the inbreeding is problematic because of obvious vulnerability issues, it's the trigger mechanism—stress—that upsets me most. I won't go into details about why you'd probably prefer to live the life of a cockroach than that of a mainstream American hog. Suffice it to say that these animals suffer confinement and physical and mental abuse that would make you mushy and watery, too. Even though the breeding for size has effectively lowered the price of pork to unbelievable cheapness, you shouldn't jump for joy about the $1.69-per-pound pork chops at the supermarket. Better to pay $10 a pound for pork from a hog that lived with some dignity and quality of life. Of course, direct purchases from the farm are usually closer to $1.50 per pound when bought in quantity. In many cases, heritage pork sells by the half-carcass rather than in small cuts.

Companies like Lobels (www.lobels.com—okay, they're the Rolls-Royce of butchers, but they deliver anywhere in the continental United States) deal in heritage pork, from older, nearly disappeared breeds like Tamworth, Gloucestershire Old Spots, and Large Blacks. These noble swine forage fresh grass and clover in movable pens in upstate New York. In the fresh air, with room to roam, they're much less susceptible to confinement-spread diseases, so they live free of subtherapeutic antibiotics and growth hormones. See Sources for other suppliers of heritage pork.

WELCOME TO THE MACHINE Most of us, when we think of a farm, conjure images of red barns, tractors, fields of crops, and grazing farm animals. But confinement is now the norm in both large and small pig farms. While many family farms still leave pigs in the field, most confine them to barns with stalls. But the biggest shift in pork production in the last two decades has been from small farm to factory farm production. Although farms with fewer than a thousand animals still represent the largest number of producers, the National Pork Producers Council reports that the largest number and percentage of pigs come from farms that produce over 50,000 head per year. Massive confined feeding operations have replaced the familiar farms in our memories. Long rows of corrugated steel buildings with concrete floors house tens of thousands of pigs in densely crowded pens. Waste flows through channels into enormous lagoons, later to be sprayed on fields. The pigs never graze. Feed is trucked in, and waste is pumped out. The energy expenditure is enormous.

CHEAP OIL, CHEAP PORK What makes energy-intensive factory farming economically feasible is our abundant supply of cheap fossil fuels. Oil plays a much larger role in modern pork production than you might think. The inputs begin with the raising of grain for feed, which relies not only on extensive mechanized preparation of fields, planting, crop dusting, harvesting, and transport, but also huge inputs of nitrogen-based fertilizer, a petroleum product. Before the advent of factory farming, grazing pigs deposited waste directly onto the fields where they grazed, incorporating it into the earth with their hooves. Their own actions replenished the ground where pigs would again graze the following season. By taking grazing out of the equation, factory farming has increased our food production system's reliance on petroleum for feed, fertilizer, and waste disposal.

Confinement buildings rely on electricity for necessarily powerful ventilation fans, lighting, pumping, and temperature control. Pigs are highly sensitive to temperature, and have very limited internal systems to control their own body temperature. In traditional farming, pigs cool off by rolling in soil or mud, and stay warm by nuzzling in hay. Confined animal feeding operations, like the massive factory farms of North Carolina and Iowa, rely on air-conditioning units and heating systems for climate control. Again, the availability of relatively cheap fossil fuels enables factory farms to perpetuate one of the most inefficient methods of food production known, and still make enormous profits.

Until the cost of food to us, the consumers, reflects the true cost of production—including the costs of environmental degradation, reliance on Middle East oil, and disease and suffering caused by unnecessarily inhumane confinement and treatment

* Meets the Humane Farm Animal Care Program standards, which include nutritious diet without antibiotics, or hormones, animals raised with shelter, resting areas, sufficient space and the ability to engage in natural behaviors.

of pigs—most of us will continue to blithely purchase cheap pork and perpetuate these systems. We have a responsibility to future generations and to the present victims of this tragic system to seek alternatives that *do* reflect those costs. Humanely raised pork, produced in ecologically sensible ways, will always be somewhat more expensive because the costs of doing it right are factored into the market price. Nothing could be a better value.

Ethically produced pork like that raised at Flying Pigs Farm in Shushan, New York (www.flyingpigsfarm.com), is just as American in origin, and, I would argue, much more American in values than the pork from Hormel or Smithfield (the two largest producers). These industry giants are pressing for trade agreements that would open Chinese markets to U.S. competition. China is currently the world's largest producer of pork, but more than 85 percent of that comes from "backyard production." Who would really benefit from the export of industrially produced pork from the U.S. to China? By supporting good producers here, we're sustaining a system that will be needed when the day of reckoning for factory-farmed swine comes.

Mushroom-Olive Spelt with Wrinkly Green Beans, Tomato Fondu, and Roasted Pork Tenderloin

SERVES 4 Mediterranean-flavored whole grain is the star of this diverse plate of flavors. It's accented by the concentrated flavor of slow-roasted tomato "confit" (I use the term loosely, since it technically refers to foods cooked in their own fat, while these tomatoes cook in their own juices, inside their skins, as they roast), the enhanced taste of Asian-cooked green beans, and the pure, simple pork flavor of roasted tenderloin slices.

Farro, a variant of spelt, is available from www.celtic-seasalt.com. To get organic mushrooms, visit www.organicmushrooms.com. See Sources for suppliers of organic and humanely raised pork.

MUSHROOM-OLIVE SPELT

1 cup spelt or other whole wheat grain, soaked 1 hour or overnight, drained

5 tablespoons extra virgin olive oil

1 pound assorted mushrooms, such as shiitake, oyster, cremini, and enoki, cut into bite-size pieces

Salt

¼ cup pitted black olives, such as oil-cured, kalamata, or Niçoise

Zest and juice of 1 lemon

¼ cup chopped fresh chives

2 shallots, finely chopped (about ¼ cup)

WRINKLY GREEN BEANS

¼ cup peanut or vegetable oil

1 pound green beans, stems removed

1 tablespoon soy sauce

ROASTED PORK TENDERLOIN

1 pound pork tenderloin

Salt and freshly ground black pepper

Vegetable oil

TOMATO FONDU

1 recipe Tomato Fondu (made according to step 1 of Tomato Fondu and Broccoli Rabe with Pan-fried Catfish Strips, page 242)

FOR THE SPELT:
Bring 1 quart of lightly salted water to a boil.

Cook the spelt, simmering over low heat until tender, about 45 minutes; drain. Heat 3 tablespoons of the olive oil in a skillet over high heat until it shimmers and almost smokes. Add the mushrooms; cook without stirring until nicely browned, about 5 minutes; season with salt, stir, and cook until soft, 5 minutes more. Add to the cooked spelt along with the olives, lemon zest and juice, the remaining 2 tablespoons of olive oil, the chives, and shallots. Season to taste.

FOR THE BEANS:
Heat the peanut oil in a skillet over medium-high heat until a piece of green bean sizzles when added. Add the beans; cook until they are tender, slightly brown, and their skin has a wrinkly appearance, about 10 minutes. Pour off most of the oil; add the soy sauce. Toss to coat.

FOR THE PORK:
Heat the oven to 400°F. Season the pork with salt and pepper. Sear with a small amount of oil in an ovenproof skillet over high heat until browned on all sides, then roast to medium doneness (about 10 minutes, depending on thickness). Rest at room temperature 5 minutes before slicing.

TO SERVE:
Spoon portions of spelt onto four plates. Make a small stack of green beans on top, cap with a roasted tomato, and fan slices of roasted pork in an attractive pattern around one edge of the plate.

Savory Corn and Vegetable Pudding with Caramelized Apples and Yams and Rosemary Pork

SERVES 6 AS A MAIN COURSE This custard-based corn pudding can be cut into squares and served warm over a salad for a lunch or brunch. Here it is used as a centerpiece of an early autumn dinner with a layer of savory Cheddar cheese. Both the pudding and the yams can be made the day before and reheated. Cut the pudding when cold for best presentation.

6 tablespoons unsalted butter

½ large onion, diced

2 large carrots, diced

¼ pound white mushrooms, quartered

1 pound day-old rustic sourdough or white bread, preferably unsliced, crust removed, cut into ½-inch dice

10 ears of corn, kernels cut off, cobs scraped for every last morsel (about 5 cups)

2 tablespoons chopped fresh flat-leaf parsley

2 teaspoons salt

1 teaspoon freshly ground black pepper

8 large eggs

4 cups milk

6 ounces Cheddar cheese, grated

1 recipe Caramelized Apples and Yams (page 110)

1 recipe Rosemary Pork (recipe follows)

Heat the oven to 350°F. Grease a baking dish large enough to hold all of the ingredients (a 9 x 13-inch baking pan is fine, but a deeper dish makes a better presentation).

Melt 4 tablespoons of the butter in a saucepan, and add the onion, carrots, and mushrooms. Over medium-low heat, gently stew the vegetables until they are tender, about 12 minutes.

Melt the remaining 2 tablespoons butter and drizzle over the bread cubes, toss well, and spread the cubes on a baking sheet. Toast them in the oven until lightly browned, 10 to 15 minutes, turning once.

Combine the toasted bread cubes with the stewed vegetables, corn, and parsley. Season with salt and pepper and spread in the prepared baking dish. Whisk together the eggs and milk; pour over the bread and vegetables. Leave the mixture to soak for 10 minutes, pressing down on the bread with your hands occasionally to encourage it to absorb the custard.

Distribute the cheese over the top. Bake until a knife inserted in the center comes out clean, about 1 hour. Let stand 10 minutes before cutting into portions.

Spoon the Caramelized Apples and Yams onto serving plates. Rest a 3- or 4-inch square of corn pudding on one side, and arrange slices of Rosemary Pork along one or both sides of the pudding for an attractive presentation.

Rosemary Pork

SERVES 6 AS A SIDE DISH The key to cooking meat that has great impact in small portions is to make each morsel an intense flavor and texture experience. Brining and marinating are two techniques that achieve that. This recipe combines both devices, resulting in pork that's so juicy, complex, and intense in flavor that two chops easily satisfy the meat palates of six guests as part of a hearty dinner along with the Savory Corn and Vegetable Pudding (page 174) and Caramelized Apples and Yams (page 110). Humanely raised pork is available from Maverick Ranch, www.flyingpigsfarm.com or www.maverickranch.com; organic pork is available from www.sforganic.com or check sources at www.localharvest.org.

2 tablespoons kosher salt

1 tablespoon brown sugar

3 garlic cloves, roughly chopped

1 bay leaf

2 teaspoons cracked black peppercorns

2 thick rib chops of pork (at least 1 inch thick, about 6 ounces each)

1 tablespoon finely chopped fresh rosemary

¼ cup olive oil

Make a brine by combining the salt, brown sugar, half the garlic, the bay leaf, and half the peppercorns with 4 cups cold water. Submerge the pork in this brine and allow to cure 4 hours.

Puree the rosemary and olive oil together in a blender; stir in the remaining garlic and peppercorns. Remove the chops and discard the brine. Pat the chops dry, and rub the rosemary oil into them well. Marinate at least 30 minutes.

Heat a stovetop grill, barbecue grill, or heavy-bottomed pan over medium heat. Grill or sauté the chops until the internal temperature reads 150°F on an instant-read thermometer, about 4 minutes per side. The meat should be slightly pink and very juicy. Set aside to rest for at least 10 minutes before cutting away the bone and slicing the chops thinly on a bias. Serve as an accompaniment to savory puddings, grain dishes, and pastas.

Game

When pioneers explored the western reaches of North America in the eighteenth century, they encountered a veritable Serengeti of wildlife. Sixty million buffalo blackened the hills, representing an unlimited supply of meat. Deer and antelope also played. Game birds like pigeon and quail were ubiquitous. Needless to say, these creatures suffered none of the indignities of feedlot injuries, body-changing hormone treatments, diseases related to confinement (and the corresponding antibiotic treatments required to control them), or inhumane crowding of modern human meat sources. Despite the occasional mauling by wolves, mountain lions, or birds of prey, life was good.

Food would have tasted different in those times. Meats carried pungent aromas and lusty flavors, described today as "gamey." They reflected the complex bouquet of wild grasses, shoots, nuts, and berries foraged by North American animals in their natural habitat. Those meats sustained generations of Native American peoples, but practically disappeared within a hundred years of the white man's conquest of the West. Few modern Americans ever taste the deep, complex flavors of wild game. Populations of wild deer, antelope, bison, and game birds have dwindled, and 100 million cattle are now at home on what's left of the range and in concentrated animal feeding operations (CAFOs), grazing on cultivated feed crops and manufactured feed pellets (which sometimes contain elements of their ground-up brethren).

BUFFALO/BISON Bison is back, sort of—350,000 bison roam the range in North America, though, admittedly, not exactly the same range their ancestors enjoyed. At ranches in Pennsylvania, Wisconsin, and New York in addition to Western states like Wyoming and Nebraska, bison are mostly grazed, and never see a feedlot. So they resume their role as fertilizers of the prairie, without introducing the hormones that conventional cattle manure carries. They do require more food than cattle do to produce a pound of meat. But they are not finicky about where it comes from, and will eat most any natural prairie grass or wild plants in their way.

Www.organic-buffalo.com, www.muscodabison.com, and www.eatwild.com sell organic bison meat.

YAK One up-and-coming ecofriendly ruminant is the yak. Over 2,000 yaks graze on North American soil, and they tread much more lightly upon it than either bison or cattle. They eat much less than either of their quadruped competitors (6 pounds of forage to gain 1 pound vs. 8 pounds for beef and 12 for bison), and their smaller hooves don't trample the earth as disruptively. Also, since they're nimble, and accustomed to mountain terrain, they can forage for food on steep hillsides that cattle and bison can't reach, so they're not limited to repeated grazes over the same parcel of land. They're raised from Minnesota to Washington State and Nebraska.

Yak ranchers have taken to calling the meat "wooly Himalayan beef," but the name, unapproved by the USDA, seems unlikely to stick. With the ruminant's remarkable resilience in the face of adverse weather and terrain, yak-riculture is likely to grow in the U.S. They withstand dry conditions well. This is especially important in light of the drought conditions that have plagued much of the western United States in recent years. When pasture grasses are short, yak stay robust grazing on sagebrush and other shrubs.

Fresh yak meat is available from www.yakmeat.us and www.schreinerfarms .com. Minimum orders are about $50 at most sites.

RABBIT One game meat that *does* resemble chicken in flavor and texture is rabbit. Their fast rate of reproduction is legendary, and they grow quickly. Most rabbit operations are small-scale, so more attention is paid to individuals. Since they don't grow as well in cages, most rabbits are raised in open areas, which is more humane.

Organic and humane sources are available from www.localharvest.org.

VENISON One chef I worked for used to bring in wild venison every winter as a special treat on the menu. The process was totally illegal, since the meat wasn't USDA inspected. But this man knew how to properly handle the meat. His father, an eastern farmer, was licensed to hunt deer with a bow and arrow if the animals were grazing on his crops. He bagged at least three bucks every year, and flew them (he was an amateur pilot) to a small landing strip an hour from the restaurant.

Under cover of night, my chef transported the carcasses into the restaurant's cooler. He spent the next two days butchering, marinating, grinding, and otherwise processing the venison. He made sausages with the legs, shanks, and neck meat. Tender cuts were marinated with juniper berries for roasting or grilling, and any tough cuts, like shoulder, went into venison goulashes and stews. The bones made great stock, which he used to make an extraordinary *sauce poivrade*.

It's illegal to serve truly wild game in American restaurants. We cooks all cherished the secret pleasure of that clandestine treat. Our consciences didn't bother us, as deer are plentiful in the wild. The meat was at once fruity, savory, herbal, and nutty; in a word: incomparable. I can only imagine what our lucky guests must have thought when they tasted something so utterly different from any "game" meat they'd ever been served. I've enjoyed domesticated venison many times, and it carries a much milder incarnation of the deep, complex, nuanced taste of the wild. Farm-raised venison is certainly a delicious meat, and it's universally raised in a much more humane way than conventional beef. Just keep an eye out for a hunting friend, who may offer you a taste of something wild. It's a once-in-a-lifetime experience. The next closest thing is a so-called wild harvest from Texas, from a company called Broken Arrow Ranch. (Broken Arrow sells both to restaurants and direct to consumers from their Web site, www.brokenarrowranch.com.)

Most venison sold in the United States (nearly 85 percent) comes from deer farms in New Zealand. Some of it is organic, and all of it is grass-fed. Broken Arrow coordinates the efforts of 150 different ranches with pastureland and forest, allowing the animals to roam freely, as they would in nature. Rather than capturing them and transporting them to slaughter, the animals are felled with a single shot to the head from a long-range rifle. The process is quick, and the animals are not stressed in the last moments of their lives. This is a respectful way to treat creatures that give their lives for us.

In Europe, moose are called "elk." In the United States, "elk" refers to members of the deer family that are smaller than moose, but larger than deer. Like deer, those raised for meat in the U.S. must be USDA inspected. They're raised on ranches, mostly in the Southwest. One such ranch, Grande, sells elk direct to consumers at www.uselk.com.

ANOTHER REASON TO TRY OTHER MEATS One of the main reasons I endorse branching out into diverse meats is that it breaks away from the factory farming system of beef, chicken, and pork. Goats, deer, elk, and in many cases sheep are raised on small farms, where they receive much more individual attention from the farmers themselves. That personal investment in the welfare of the animals translates into better treatment. These smaller operations are still farms, not production lines.

Chinese Yak Buns with Scallions and Rice Vinegar Dipping Sauce

SERVES 8 AS AN APPETIZER (ABOUT 24 BUNS) American ranchers only recently began experimenting with raising yaks. It's turning out to be a double blessing: The nimble, small-hoofed quadrupeds tread much more lightly upon the grasslands than cattle do, doing much less damage to the prairie as they forage hills too steep for steers to climb. And the intense taste of yak meat means smaller amounts impart greater meat flavor to dishes, which translates into less meat needed. These intensely flavored appetizers provide all the meat flavor a meal could need, so the rest of the repast can be meatless. Follow this up with a table full of other Asian dishes, such as Sesame Rice (page 60), Southeast Asian Slaw (page 109), and Vegetarian Peking Duck (page 116).

See Sources for suppliers of yak meat. Organic yeast is available from Village Organics at www.villageorganics.com.

DOUGH

One ¼-ounce packet active dry yeast

2 tablespoons Asian toasted sesame oil (plus a dash for frying, optional)

1 tablespoon sugar

1 teaspoon salt

2 to 3 cups all-purpose flour

Vegetable oil for frying

YAK FILLING

1 pound ground yak meat or ground sirloin of beef (if using beef, add ½ beef bouillon cube, diluted in 2 teaspoons water, to make up for the milder flavor)

1 tablespoon soy sauce

(continued)

½ teaspoon salt

Freshly ground black pepper

3 to 4 scallions, finely chopped

RICE VINEGAR DIPPING SAUCE

½ cup rice vinegar

½ cup light soy sauce

FOR THE DOUGH:

Place the yeast in ¼ cup of very warm water. Separately, combine the sesame oil, sugar, and salt in ¾ cup very warm water. Combine the yeast, water mixture, and flour by hand to make a stiff dough. Turn out onto a floured board and knead until smooth, elastic, and very stiff, 10 to 15 minutes. Cover loosely, put in a warm place, and let the dough rise until doubled, about 1 hour.

FOR THE FILLING:

Mix the meat with the soy sauce, salt, pepper, and scallions.

TO FORM AND COOK THE BUNS:

Divide the risen dough into quarters. Roll each quarter into a long, thin log. Cut or pinch off 1 to 1½ inches of each log. Roll each into a rectangle. Place approximately 1 tablespoon of meat filling onto each rectangle. Fold the corners inward (like the back of an envelope) and roll flat so there is no open seam. (Don't worry if a little meat is exposed.) Heat a ¼-inch layer of cooking oil in a frying pan (the oil should come almost halfway up the sides). Add a dash of sesame oil for flavor if you wish. Fry each bun until golden brown, turning once. When done, the filling should be cooked just past pink. While the buns are cooking, set the oven on "warm" or its lowest setting. Stack the cooked buns in layers on a baking sheet, with absorbent paper under each layer, to keep warm until serving. Do this even with the last batch—it helps absorb the oil.

TO SERVE:
Combine the vinegar and soy sauce. Serve the buns hot with the dipping sauce.

VARIATION:
These make excellent steamed dumplings also. One good way of doing this is to pan-fry them on one side, as in the main recipe, but rather than turning them, add ½ cup water and cover the pan immediately. Allow the buns to steam in the pan until fully cooked, about 5 minutes.

Bison and Black Bean Chili on Wehani Rice

SERVES 10 AS A MAIN COURSE Bison are raised in a much more humane way than most beef in America. Virtually all are pasture-raised, and they're not subject to the confinement, feedlots, and growth hormones prevalent with U.S. beef. The meat is leaner, and perfect for stewing. Wehani rice, an American brown rice, has a nutty flavor and an appealing chewy texture. It is grown in the Southwest and is available from www.truefoodsmarket.com.

2 ancho or pasilla chiles

1 tablespoon grapeseed oil or vegetable oil

2 pounds ground bison

1 large onion, chopped

4 garlic cloves, finely chopped

2 poblano or other fresh green chiles, chopped

2 jalapeños, chopped

1 red bell pepper, chopped

3 teaspoons kosher salt

One 28-ounce can crushed tomatoes

One 28-ounce can tomato sauce

1 tablespoon Spanish (hot) paprika

1 tablespoon ground cumin

½ cup ground New Mexico chili powder or other chili powder

2 cups dried black beans, not soaked, simmered until tender (about 2 hours), drained

1 cup chopped fresh cilantro

4 cups water or stock

2 cups Wehani rice or brown rice

2 tablespoons unsalted butter or olive oil

To make the chile puree, heat the oven to 400°F. Place the ancho chiles on a baking sheet and toast them for 5 minutes, until they are fragrant and starting to brown slightly. Soak the chiles in 2 cups hot water for 10 minutes, then puree the chiles in a blender, adding a few tablespoons of the water they were soaked in to facilitate the puree.

Heat the oil in a large Dutch oven. Brown the bison meat; add the onion, garlic, chopped poblano and jalapeño chiles, bell pepper, and 2 teaspoons of salt. Cook over moderate heat until soft and juicy, about 10 minutes.

Add the tomatoes, tomato sauce, paprika, cumin, and chili powder. Cook 1 minute, until fragrant. Add the chile puree, cooked black beans, and half the cilantro. Cover; simmer over low heat 3 hours. Season to taste.

Meanwhile, cook the rice: Bring the water to a boil and add the rice, butter, and remaining teaspoon salt. Simmer, covered, until all the water is absorbed, about 40 minutes. Spoon the chili over the rice; sprinkle with the remaining chopped cilantro.

Bison Osso Buco

SERVES 8 AS A SIDE DISH Lean bison meat is custom-made for stewing, as in this classic braise. As with all bison cookery, temperatures are lower than for beef. The extremely slow cooking of this method yields falling-off-the-bone tenderness. Not only can the dish be made ahead, it's actually better the next day. Make the gremolata (seasoned parsley topping) just before serving. Bison meat is available from www.njbison.com. See Sources for additional purveyors.

OSSO BUCO

2 bison shank crosscuts (about 3 pounds total), 1½ to 2 inches thick

Salt and freshly ground black pepper

Flour for dredging

2 tablespoons olive oil

1 small yellow onion, diced

1 carrot, diced

1 leek, white and light green parts, sliced

2 garlic cloves, minced

1 cup chopped tomatoes

2 teaspoons tomato paste

¾ cup red wine (or dry white wine)

1¾ cups beef, bison, or other dark broth, or as needed

1 teaspoon minced fresh thyme

½ teaspoon minced fresh rosemary

GREMOLATA

3 tablespoons chopped fresh flat-leaf parsley

2 anchovy fillets, minced

1 teaspoon grated lemon zest

FOR THE OSSO BUCO:
Season the shanks with salt and pepper and dredge them in the flour. Heat the oil in a large Dutch oven over medium-high heat. Sear the tops and bottoms until brown, about 8 minutes; set aside (the shanks are big, so work in batches). Pour off all but 2 tablespoons of fat from the pan. Add the onion; cook until golden brown, 5 to 6 minutes. Add the carrot; cook until it starts to brown, 3 minutes. Add the leek and garlic; cook until aromatic, 2 minutes more. Add the tomatoes and tomato paste; cook, stirring frequently, about 1 minute.

Heat the oven to 225°F. Add the wine to the pan, stirring to blend the wine with the tomato paste. Simmer until the wine is reduced by half, about 4 minutes. Return the bison to the pan and add broth to cover the shanks by two-thirds. Bring to a very low simmer over medium-low heat. Cover the pot and transfer it to the oven. Braise (gently stew) the bison shanks for 5 hours, turning the meat occasionally. Add the thyme and rosemary and braise, partially covered, until fork-tender, about 1 hour more.

Transfer the shanks to a warmed platter or plates and moisten with some of the cooking liquid. Cover and keep warm while completing the sauce. Place the pot over high heat and simmer the cooking liquid until it has a good flavor and saucelike consistency, about 10 minutes. Taste and adjust the seasoning with salt and pepper.

FOR THE GREMOLATA:
Mix together the parsley, anchovies, and lemon zest.

TO SERVE:
Spoon the sauce over the osso buco and sprinkle with gremolata.

Poultry: Why Free Range Matters

If we start with the premise that we won't all become vegetarian, the issue of how we treat other animals is a logical consideration. There's nothing inherently immoral or unethical about eating meat. That's life in the food chain. There's no greater nobility accorded the wildebeest because it's prey than the lion because it's a predator. Each does what it has to do to survive. We regret that our nourishment comes at the expense of other creatures' lives, though. That sympathy is one of the finest attributes of humanity.

We all know the bad things that animals experience in our American food production system. This is not meant to be an exposé about the technique of veal manufacture, foie gras creation, or chicken farming. These stories are frequently reported in the news. What's not reported are the sensible alternatives to supporting the cruelest practices in the meat industry.

For thousands of years, chickens and their wild fowl ancestors scampered freely around farms. It is only in modern times that the advent of an entirely caged life came about. A chicken that is born in darkness and lives in darkness for its entire life until it is slaughtered is a recent development. That these birds could live their entire existence in cages, stacked upon many other cages, beneath many other cages, never touching the ground, covered with the excrement of other chickens, is unnecessarily cruel. The pain these creatures endure as the chicken wire cuts into their feet, causing infections, is gratuitous. So are the antibiotics the birds have to eat because of those infections.

When I first heard of free-range chickens, my first thought was how funny the concept seemed—chickens in cowboy hats, swinging lassos as they ambled across the range. My second thought, after I tasted my first free-range chicken, was that it wasn't better than regular chicken. It wasn't as tender. I concluded that it was a scam, to make extra money from wealthy people for inferior chicken. It was only years later, as I came to know the difference between the lives of these birds and those of conventional chickens, that I gave the meat a second chance. It was worth it, after all, to support a system that allowed the animals to live in the open air, see the light of day, walk on the soft ground, and consume food unadulterated by chemicals and unnecessary medicines. That's when I opened my mind to discover that the free-range, organic bird yielded superior meat.

The first thing to learn is that conventional and free-range meats are not the same product with different prices. They're different meats. The next logical step is to treat them differently. My favorite part of a roast chicken had always been the thigh. It was juicier, fattier, and deeper in flavor than the plainer breast, which I often found dry. Thighs had bones that you could pick up with your hands (finger food is a favorite among cooks). Bones also impart flavor as the meat cooks, so pieces with central bones have more taste. And, since every part of a conventional chicken is usually tender enough to cut with the side of a fork, thigh meat was the most texturally pleasing and flavorful part to me. When I'd tasted that first free-range chicken, I'd automatically gone for my favorite thigh portion. As other guests waxed poetic about the juiciness and cleanness of flavor, I felt I was looking at the emperor's new clothes, and this chicken was naked. This time around, I sliced the breast. It was like slicing open a capon. Juice ran down the handle of my knife as I cut.

I learned that free-range chickens are much more like wild birds, in that their weight-bearing muscles, their legs, actually bear their weight. By contrast, conventional chickens' feet are in such discomfort, the birds spend most of their lives sitting down. Naturally, less active muscles make much softer meat. The plus side is that there's an intensity of flavor in a worked chicken thigh that far exceeds what a flaccid thigh can attain. One thigh can impart as much flavor as a whole conventional bird to a batch of chicken soup. Chicken and dumplings take on a depth of flavor that hasn't been widely tasted since the dish was invented. And the breast of free-range chicken is a special, sensual flavor and texture experience. That's all assuming you throw out the old chicken playbook, and cook with a new set of rules.

Free-range meat is lean, and that means that slower cooking times yield better results. Slow and low roasting brings about a sublime roasted free-range chicken, where it would make a conventional one soggy and overdone. Searing becomes more important when lower temperatures will give less browning. Learning to cook free range is like learning to cook chicken all over again. The same is true of other free-range, pasture-raised, and grass-fed meats.

Tsukune (Grilled Chicken Meatballs)

SERVES 8 AS AN APPETIZER One way to enjoy meat, and at the same time reduce the amount you consume, is to serve it as an appetizer prior to a meatless main course. These Japanese hors d'oeuvres convey intense meat flavor. A good main course to follow would be a stir-fry of mixed Asian greens (such as Chinese cabbage, mustard greens, watercress, and collards), sliced carrots, and mushrooms, served over Sesame Rice (page 60). Extra Soy-Marsala Dipping Sauce is an excellent flavor accent for such a dish.

The Accent seasoning is optional, but this MSG ingredient is widely used in authentic Japanese cuisine.

2 ounces fresh ginger, peeled and roughly chopped

1½ pounds boneless free-range chicken thighs, cut into medium dice

1 teaspoon sugar

½ teaspoon freshly ground white pepper

2 teaspoons cornstarch

1 teaspoon salt

Pinch of Accent seasoning (optional)

Oil for frying

Soy-Marsala Dipping Sauce (recipe follows)

In a food processor, pulse the ginger until finely chopped. Add the chicken, sugar, white pepper, cornstarch, salt, and Accent (if using). Pulse until the mixture is a rough puree.

Heat oil to a depth of 3 inches to 350°F. Form the chicken mixture into bite-size balls by squeezing through your loosely clenched fist. Drop the meatballs into the oil in batches of ten, and deep-fry until cooked through, about 1 minute. Transfer to a plate to drain.

Heat a grill or stovetop grill pan over medium-high heat. Skewer the cooked meatballs on bamboo sticks, two to a skewer. Grill the meatballs until they attain a slight char and have a grilled taste, about 1 minute per side. Serve with Soy-Marsala Dipping Sauce.

Soy-Marsala Dipping Sauce   YIELD: ½ CUP

¼ cup soy sauce

¼ cup Marsala wine

1 teaspoon sugar

1 tablespoon rice vinegar

1 tablespoon mirin (sweet Japanese cooking wine) or sweet wine

2 teaspoons cornstarch

Bring the soy sauce, Marsala, sugar, rice vinegar, and mirin to a boil in a small saucepan. Simmer 3 minutes.

Combine the cornstarch with 2 tablespoons of cold water to form a slurry. Thicken the sauce by stirring in the cornstarch slurry, bit by bit, until the sauce has a smooth consistency and coats the back of a spoon.

Spinach and Sage Gnocchi in Broth with Tiny Chicken Quenelles

SERVES 4 AS FIRST COURSE OR LIGHT MAIN COURSE In this warming dinner, a single chicken thigh goes a long way, sharing the heft of four portions with satisfying gnocchi. Serve each guest two quenelles of chicken. Organic ricotta is available from www.organicfreshmarket.com.

4 ounces baby spinach, blanched in boiling water, squeezed dry, and chopped

3 tablespoons julienne of fresh sage

1½ cups ricotta, drained

3 large egg yolks

Pinch of allspice

2 tablespoons freshly grated Parmigiano-Reggiano cheese

1 cup all-purpose flour, plus more for rolling the dough

2 tablespoons fine cornmeal

Salt and freshly ground black pepper

1 boneless free-range chicken thigh (about ¼ pound), roughly cut into 1-inch pieces

1 teaspoon cornstarch

1 scallion, chopped

1 quart chicken stock or broth, diluted with 1 quart water

Extra virgin olive oil

For the gnocchi, combine the spinach, 2 tablespoons of the sage, the ricotta, egg yolks, allspice, cheese, flour, cornmeal, and salt and pepper to taste in a mixing bowl. Work into a soft dough, adding extra flour if necessary. Roll on a lightly floured surface into a cylinder (¾-inch diameter) and cut into hazelnut-size segments.

For the quenelles, combine the chicken, cornstarch, scallion, remaining sage, ½ teaspoon salt, and pepper in a food processor. Puree until smooth. Refrigerate 15 minutes.

Bring the stock and water to a boil. Using two teaspoons, drop very small quenelles of the chicken mixture into the broth. You should have about 8 quenelles. Add the prepared gnocchi. Cook 5 minutes, taste and season the broth, and portion into four soup plates. Garnish with a drizzle of fine olive oil at the table.

Turkey Tonnato

SERVES 8 AS AN APPETIZER, 4 AS A MAIN COURSE This twist on a dish normally made with veal may seem quirky (one chef friend laughed out loud when he read the part about roasting canned tuna with vegetables), but the result is incredible (yes, even my chef friend is a convert). Organic, free-range turkey is available from www.lobels.com, www.diamondorganics.com, and www.eberlypoultry.com. Wild turkeys and heritage turkeys are available from www.dartagnan.com.

2 cups roughly chopped mixed vegetables such as celery, onions, fennel, and carrots

1 cup olive oil

One 7-ounce can albacore tuna, preferably packed in olive oil

2 anchovy fillets, chopped (optional)

3 tablespoons small capers

Juice of 1 lemon

¾ cup mayonnaise, preferably homemade (page 271)

Salt and freshly ground black pepper

1 pound thinly sliced roasted turkey breast

Sliced cornichons

Chopped fresh flat-leaf parsley

Lemon wedges

Heat the oven to 400°F. In a roasting pan, combine the vegetables and ¼ cup of the olive oil. Roast until nicely caramelized on all sides, about 20 minutes. Add the tuna, anchovies, and capers; roast 10 minutes more.

Cool the roasted ingredients slightly; transfer to the bowl of a food processor. Add the remaining olive oil and the lemon juice. Puree to a smooth paste; add the mayonnaise and pulse to incorporate. The sauce should be creamy. Season with salt and pepper to taste.

Pool the tuna sauce onto individual serving plates. Arrange the turkey slices in a single layer on the sauce, leaving some sauce peeking out from the edges. Drizzle with additional sauce and garnish with the cornichons, parsley, and lemon wedges.

Foie Gras

The debate about whether foie gras production is inhumane has gone on long enough. It is. No, they don't use nails to keep the ducks and geese in place during force-feeding anymore. But it's widely acknowledged in the scientific community that these animals live the final weeks of their lives in great discomfort, permanently gorged. California was right to ban the practice as it currently exists, and not to allow production of foie gras until such time as a humane way to fatten these animals exists. I love foie gras. Its buttery texture is one of the most pleasant culinary experiences I know. But I can no longer abide the cruelty that creates it. I've discovered other options. I feel the same way about conventionally raised chickens, that their production is as cruel as foie gras production. Free-range is the humane choice.

How many people who would miss foie gras have ever cooked duck liver that *wasn't* fattened by unnatural means? Do they know its complex and savory taste? The truth is that because foie gras earned such a reputation among food enthusiasts, it has become virtually the only way most people experience duck or goose liver. The livers of most fresh ducks come packed inside the cavity, just like the giblets bag in a chicken. Unlike a chicken liver, though, a duck liver is a portion big enough for two.

Poached duck liver tastes much like foie gras. Properly cooked, its tenderness is similar to a semisoft cheese. The main differences between regular and fattened duck livers are intensity of flavor and unctuousness. Both are culinary issues that can be addressed with culinary solutions. Pâtés and mousses blend meaty flavors with butter and cream to exquisite effect. Duck liver mousse tastes complex, has nuances of cognac and truffle, and pleases with the creamy, buttery feeling of foie gras. Its creaminess and butteriness come from cream and butter.

Soups are perfect venues for the bold flavors of duck and goose liver. Use every part of a duck to create the ultimate stage for its flavor and texture: Simmer the roasted bones to make a rich broth. Roast the breast until the skin crisps. Poach the liver in the natural broth, and serve slices of poached liver with portions of crisp roast breast bathed in shallow pools of that beautiful broth. A few young turnips provide textural counterpoint and a mysterious, earthy essence. As for the duck legs, they call out for salad, and serve as a follow-up main course. Alternatively, use them in a stir-fry or pan-fried noodle dish.

Ducks and geese are generally raised more humanely than mass-market poultry like chickens and turkeys. Even ducks raised for foie gras have arguably better lives than an American chicken. At least they roam the ground freely until their two-week fattening stage, rather than living their entire lives in stacked cages. By and large, ducks are treated more kindly than chickens in mainstream farm environments.

Will foie gras ever be ethically defensible? Probably so. From the time it was invented in ancient Egypt, through its long rise to culinary stardom in France over the last four centuries, ways have been devised to mitigate many of the most inhumane aspects of its manufacture—the confinement, the mechanical immobilizing of the birds, the manhandling of the healthy ones, and the continued manipulation of the injured. The one problem that remains is the force-feeding, which is, in effect, an exaggeration of the birds' natural practice of overeating before migration. Since the animals tend to naturally fatten their own livers seasonally, logic dictates that enlightened agriculturalists will find a way to encourage that behavior without unacceptably cruel means.

In April 2005, it was revealed in the *Chicago Tribune* that Charlie Trotter, Chicago's most renowned celebrity chef, had quietly eliminated foie gras from his menu for ethical reasons. Rumors had been flying, as diners noticed the conspicuous absence of foie gras on his luxury-foods-dominated menus over the preceding two years, but peer pressure had kept him in the closet about his ethical decision until the newspaper outed him. In California, Governor Arnold Schwarzenegger has banned production of foie gras starting in 2012, and New York, the other foie gras–producing state, is likely to do so as well.

Terrine of Duck Liver

SERVES 8 Enjoy rich, refined taste, amazingly similar to foie gras, in this elegant sliced terrine, using conventional duck livers instead of those from force-fed, fattened birds. It's the ultimate appetizer for a luxury dinner, pairing beautifully with dry Champagne or an opulent white Burgundy wine. Chill your grinder parts in the freezer, and work quickly to keep the mixture cold before cooking.

2 tablespoons unsalted butter

¼ pound chopped shallots (½ cup)

1¼ pounds duck livers, sinews removed, soaked overnight in milk

¼ cup Madeira or Tawny port

1 teaspoon salt

¼ teaspoon freshly ground white pepper

1 pound (4 sticks) unsalted butter, at room temperature

1 ounce (about 3 tablespoons) all-purpose flour

2 large eggs, beaten

1¼ cups heavy cream, reduced by half, kept warm

Cumberland Sauce (recipe follows)

Heat the oven to 300°F. Melt the 2 tablespoons butter in a small skillet. Add the shallots and cook gently until translucent, about 5 minutes; chill. Heat a pot of water until very warm (170°F). Grind together the livers, Madeira, shallots, salt, and pepper through the fine plate of a meat grinder, keeping the mixture very cold. Transfer to a food processor. Using a spoon, work the butter and flour together to form a paste (beurre manié).

Puree the liver mixture until smooth; pulse in the eggs. With the motor running, gradually work in the beurre manié. Scrape down the sides of the bowl. Add the cream and process until smooth. Strain through a fine mesh strainer.

Oil a 1-quart terrine mold or loaf pan and line it with plastic film. Have ready a roasting pan deep enough to hold the terrine. Spoon the terrine mixture into the mold and wrap the edges of the plastic film over the top.

Set the terrine inside the roasting pan, and fill with very warm water to about two-thirds of the way up the sides of the mold. Transfer to the oven, and cook until the center reads 165°F on an instant-read thermometer, about 1 hour. Chill overnight before serving, sliced, with a sweet fruit sauce, such as Cumberland Sauce, and toast points. It will keep, refrigerated, for 1 week.

Cumberland Sauce

YIELD:1¼ CUPS I like to soften the flavor of the shallots in this recipe by blanching them for a minute, then cooling them before chopping. This step is optional. This is a thick sauce that gains viscosity as it cools.

1 cup red currant jam

1 or 2 shallots, blanched in boiling water for 1 minute, chopped to yield 1 tablespoon

Juice and zest of 1 orange

Juice and zest of 1 lemon

1 teaspoon dry mustard

⅓ cup port

¼ teaspoon salt

Pinch of cayenne

Pinch of ground ginger

Melt the red currant jam in a small saucepan over low heat; add the blanched shallots and orange and lemon zests. Dissolve the mustard in the port; add to the jam mixture. Simmer 5 to 10 minutes, until slightly thickened; add the orange and lemon juices. Season with salt, cayenne, and ginger. Serve chilled with a pâté or terrine.

Roasted Quail Salad with Spiced Cashews

SERVES 4 AS A MAIN COURSE In keeping with the less-meat-is-more philosophy of this book, this dish is a main-course salad, where a single game bird, usually served as an appetizer, becomes part of a greater whole. The greens, nuts, and fruit are the basis of the meal, and the mustard-herb marinated quail is a flavor and texture element. Free-range quail are available from www.dartagnan.com.

4 boneless quail

¼ cup Dijon mustard

6 fresh thyme sprigs

4 garlic cloves, sliced

4 thin cross-section slices of lemon

1 shallot, thinly sliced

3 bay leaves, broken

2 tablespoons cracked black peppercorns

½ cup vegetable oil

Salt

8 cups dark leafy greens, such as arugula, spinach, or beet greens

¼ cup balsamic vinaigrette

1 cup spiced cashews (made according to the following recipe for Spiced Nuts)

1 large mango, cut into 1-inch cubes

Rub the quail all over with mustard; combine them in a covered dish with the thyme, garlic, lemon slices, shallot, bay leaves, pepper, and oil. Marinate 2 to 3 days.

Heat the oven to 350°F. Heat an ovenproof skillet over medium heat. Remove the quail from the marinade, season them with a little salt, and sear them breast side down. The oil from the marinade should be sufficient to cook them in. Place the pan in the oven (or, if your skillet isn't ovenproof, transfer the quail to a roasting pan); cook to medium doneness, about 10 minutes. Set on a board to rest 5 minutes.

Dress the salad greens with the vinaigrette and arrange in large individual serving dishes. Rest a quail atop each salad, and garnish with cashews and mango.

Spiced Nuts

YIELD: 6 CUPS My dear friends John Carroll and Mary Palermo send a homemade care package every year—a rare treat since many friends are timid about making food for a chef. In one of those packages they sent the most delicious spiced nuts I've ever tasted. Brazil nuts (which John and Mary don't like in this dish, but I do) are a sustainable rain forest product, collected by indigenous Amazon tribes. They're available from http://shop.deliciousorganics.com. Go to www.sunorganicfarm.com, www.karibafarms.com, and www.livingtreecommunity.com for organic nuts.

Powdered egg whites work well in this recipe; reconstitute as directed on the package. Garam masala is an Indian spice blend that is now widely available.

2 large egg whites

2 teaspoons garam masala

1½ to 2 teaspoons cayenne

2 teaspoons turmeric

2 teaspoons ground allspice

2 teaspoons salt

6 cups mixed raw nuts

(continued)

Heat the oven to 350°F. Lightly grease two baking sheets and line with parchment or wax paper. Spray with cooking spray.

In a bowl large enough to hold all the nuts, beat the egg whites briefly, until frothy. Add the garam masala, cayenne, turmeric, allspice, and salt; mix well. Let stand 5 minutes. Add the nuts and toss well, coating thoroughly.

Spread the nuts on the prepared baking sheets in a single layer; bake until light brown, about 30 minutes, turning with a spatula every 5 minutes. Cool on the pans before storing in a cool, dark place.

Fish and Seafood

The good news Is that poachers aren't ravaging the seas with total impunity anymore. National and international police are chipping away at the vast chaotic world of deep-sea fishing, cutting down on illegal overexploitation of threatened species.

Just how those species became threatened, and what the future of our sustainable, renewable fish supply will be, are things that the ethical home cook needs to know. Recent reports in scientific journals have only confirmed what many ecologists already know: Industrialized fishing has wiped out more than 70 percent of the oceans' great predators—tuna, swordfish, marlin, and shark—and is working its way down the food chain at breakneck speed. But enlightened fisheries management, partly spurred by grassroots movements like California's fisheries-protecting organization, Passionfish, has produced a few success stories. In the following pages you'll find out why wild Pacific salmon, mahi-mahi, bigeye tuna, and Arctic char have a future. Like meat, wild fish plays an important but less-than-dominant role in the menu plans of the ethical gourmet: Think tuna sushi instead of tuna steaks.

The very fact that 80 million tons of ocean life is landed annually might lead some to think that conservationists' warnings of dwindling fish populations are needlessly alarmist. After all, though the annual catch has been declining every year since the late 1980s, it's declining in mere 360,000-ton increments. But there's a second story hidden in these statistics. Not all ocean life is created equal. In a process that has been called "fishing down the food web," the large, predatory species that once formed the heart of the edible fish market have been systematically extracted from the seas, and our million-ship-strong fishing fleet is now harvesting the last immature specimens of these dwindling stocks, along with their former prey. The era of great, thousand-pound Atlantic tuna ended decades ago, but now, even the puny two-hundred-pound adolescents are rare. Swordfish and marlin of *The Old Man and the Sea* variety are as much a part of history as Ernest Hemingway himself. Fishermen are hauling in catches today that wouldn't have even been considered viable in the heady days of commercial fishing in the 1950s.

The *New York Times* dining section of February 11, 2004, titled, "From Trash to Treasure," features a recipe for skate, listed as a threatened species by the National Audubon Society,

Wildlife Conservation Society, and Environmental Defense, all nonprofit organizations. Author Mark Bittman noted that decades ago, the species was introduced to him as a "trash fish," but now he's given it a second look, and finds it culinarily intriguing. This is no simple personal evolution on his part. The fish is commonly available in mainstream fish markets. Despite the skate's long gestation period and low birth rate, it is now a far more reliable catch than Atlantic salmon, a once-popular food fish that is now listed by the U.S. Fish and Wildlife Service as an endangered species.

WHO BUYS FRESH FISH? The information in this book is going out to the very people who are most likely to make a difference in our ocean ecology: sophisticated food enthusiasts. Knowledgeable cooks are the consumers of the most highly prized, and often most threatened, fish species. Fish cookery requires real skill and culinary expertise. Most amateur cooks lack the confidence and competence to prepare exquisite fish dishes at home, so not many of them try. Fish cookery in America is mostly left to the professionals. Few consumers buy fresh fish at the market. Americans are much more likely to eat fish in restaurants, or buy processed fish products. Sure, everyone knows a reliable recipe for baked salmon, broiled scrod, or breaded flounder. And U.S. fish consumption has certainly soared over the last two decades. But fish is a costly commodity: Most $20-per-pound tuna, halibut, and Pacific cod are prepared by food aficionados and chefs.

That situation places the fate of the most threatened species—the giant tunas, Chilean sea bass, swordfish, and wild salmon—in the hands of the most educated consumers, who can use discretion and purchasing power to put pressure on the irresponsible players in the fishing industry. Conscientious restaurateurs and chefs have already proven, through targeted boycotts, that they can make a difference. Seventy percent of all seafood is consumed in restaurants.

Change can be effected in several ways. Responsible chefs, like those in the Chefs Collaborative (an organization of environmentally concerned chefs, whose Web site is www.chefscollaborative.org), can make a group decision to eschew a threatened or environmentally suspect type of fish, and consumers can send restaurateurs a message by boycotting that fish and patronizing restaurants that boycott it.

Wild Fisheries Management Success Stories

STRIPED BASS

Concerted efforts to bring species back from the brink have proven magnificently effective when everyone cooperates. Wild Atlantic striped bass is a case in point. It suffered the same fate as Atlantic salmon in the 1980s. It had been overfished to the point of near-extinction. At the last moment, it was brought under U.S. Fish and Wildlife Service protection by an act of Congress (the Atlantic Striped Bass Conservation Act of 1986). And the act was enforced for nearly a decade. By the mid-1990s, the species had rebounded to the point where a larger catch was permitted for sport fishermen (who had been the most avid hunters of the fish, and largely led to its decline). Proving that such protection truly works, the fish is now listed as a recommended food choice by most major fish and wildlife conservation organizations.

FLOUNDER

The National Marine Fisheries Service (NMFS), a branch of the Commerce Department, has announced—prematurely, say some environmentalist critics—that summer flounder management has been a success, bringing stocks back up to sustainable levels. While the agency's assessment may be overly optimistic, environmental leaders from nonprofits like the Ocean Conservancy agree that the fish are coming back. Pacific flounder (technically a sole), like most species caught on the West Coast of the United States, has fared better than its Atlantic cousins, maintaining healthy populations.

SWORDFISH

Even swordfish, recently the poster child for the excesses of the fishing industry and consumer demand, has enjoyed rebounding numbers since the Natural Resources Defense Council and SeaWeb (a branch of the Pew Oceans Trust) organized the now-famous "Give Swordfish a Break" campaign, which led twenty-seven high-profile East Coast restaurants to stop offering the fish. The current generation of swordfish is still young, and it will be a few years before the North Atlantic species is completely out of danger, but it looks like this fish will recover. Soon, numbers may justify a return to eating swordfish. But for now, environmental watchdog groups say to hold off.

SPANISH MACKEREL

Despite a scare during a frenzy of overexploitation in the 1980s, this fast-reproducing fish has benefited from careful, responsible management in the Atlantic and Gulf fishing regions of the United States. It's caught using low-impact line and trolling methods, which result in very little bycatch.

Securing Both an Ecological and a Culinary
Future There's no telling when the dwindling stocks of major culinary fish will cease to be a viable commercial catch, but people who've adjusted their cooking to more plentiful, sustainable fish will be at a distinct advantage when those commercial extinctions transpire. Not only will they not have to suffer the sudden loss of a major part of their diet (because they've weaned themselves during the years of decline), but they'll also know preparation methods for the delicious, plentiful fish of the future.

Today's forward thinkers have equipped their homes with solar panels for electricity or bought hybrid cars that drive fifty-plus miles on a gallon of gasoline. Not only are they doing their part to help the environment, but they're drastically cutting their own dependence on fuels that are becoming scarcer and more expensive—they're planning ahead. Today's cooks who adopt grilled bluefish in lieu of grilled bluefin are making a choice that will serve them well in the years to come. Cooks of sustainably farmed American tilapia and catfish are gaining market savvy about quality standards, and developing a feel for products that will be essential to fish lovers in the coming years. They're also "discovering" diverse ingredients like *loup de mer*, a French-farmed cousin of sea bass that is gaining popularity among American chefs.

But these discoveries are unlike the necessary adoption of "trash fish" after collapsing fisheries. Thanks to foresight and sadder-but-wiser government intervention, there's hope that the current generation of fish farmers will avoid the mistakes of the salmon-farming industry of the late twentieth century (discussed on pages 211–217), and will, instead, mirror the better successes of America's post–dust bowl, more responsible farmland management policies. Already, similarities are visible, as marine conservation regions are being set aside, and self-contained aquaculture systems are being pioneered. Wary of profit-motivated aquaculture entrepreneurs, coastal communities are taking active roles in shaping fishery policy as never before.

Alaskan marine conservationists are putting pressure on federal agencies to regulate the nascent black cod (sablefish) farming movement in the Pacific Northwest. If it's carefully, ecologically managed, this industry could take pressure off the grossly overexploited Patagonian toothfish (a.k.a. Chilean sea bass). The luxuriously rich, snowy white flesh of sablefish is strikingly similar to that of the disappearing Chilean fish. The industry is responding to community concerns by creating the fish farms three to nine miles offshore, where they say they're unlikely to impact wild fisheries.

Of course, wild fisheries will be impacted if sablefish aquaculture succeeds. Just as wild salmon fishermen suffered when aquaculture dropped the bottom out of salmon prices in the 1980s and 1990s, sablefish fishermen stand to lose a lot. Japan currently buys 20,000 tons annually, the lion's share of the catch. Americans barely know the fish exists. But as prices for Chilean sea bass soar, this attractive alternative will command attention. It is now, when the industry is in its infancy, that attention to responsible, sustainable practices is most imperative. British Columbia has granted forty licenses to farmers interested in raising sablefish. Currently, Alaska prohibits any kind of ocean fish farming. But in federal waters between three and two hundred miles offshore, known as the Exclusive Economic Zone (EEZ), the National Oceanic and Atmospheric Administration (NOAA) has been developing and promoting oceanic aquaculture.

NOAA says deeper ocean farming will mitigate the pollution, disease, and parasite transfer issues that have made salmon farming problematic. And they say that raising fish far from the rivers where wild species spawn avoids competition for resources associated with aquaculture operations in sensitive coastal estuaries. They say offshore aquaculture will meet growing demand for fish, while taking pressure off wild populations. If the method does what they hope, then some of aquaculture's problems will be solved. Still, farmed carnivorous fish like sablefish and halibut (also being tested) require several times their body weight in feeder fish to reach marketable size. So even if the promised benefits of deep-ocean farming materialize, these fish should take a secondary role to faster-growing wild fish like mackerel and herring in the diet of concerned environmentalists. Check out www.ecofish.com for a place to buy environmentally sustainable seafood.

Mercury Becomes an Issue

One health consideration in eating high-oil-content fish like swordfish, some mackerel species, and certain tunas is the possibility that they carry dangerously high levels of mercury. The heavy metal is released into the environment as industrial waste, often airborne from coal-fired power plants, and lands in the ocean, where plankton, small fish, and crustaceans ingest it as they feed. As they become prey to larger fish, the mercury moves up the food chain, increasing in concentration with each step (animals re-release hardly any of the mercury, which especially lodges in proteins).

So the top predators contain the highest concentrations of the poison. The fish named above, as well as sharks, are among the most likely to contain high levels of the toxin, which has been linked to birth defects, brain and kidney damage, and death. While the United States has never experienced the mass mercury poisonings that occurred in Japan and Canada from the 1950s to the 1970s, evidence suggests that chronic exposure to low levels of mercury from dietary sources may be hampering neurological development in American children, especially in cases where they were exposed to modest levels in the womb.

This health issue presents good reason to keep intake of these highly threatened large species low. In a way, concern about mercury may prove helpful to dwindling swordfish and tuna populations. Still, like any health advisory, it shouldn't be taken out of proportion. Moderate consumption of these fish has also been linked to healthy cholesterol levels in humans, because they are high in omega-3 fatty acids. So choose fish that are not endangered, like mackerel, and eat sensible amounts.

Aquaculture

The deception and disgraceful practices of the salmon-farming industry are well known: Coastal waters fouled by effluent from inhumanely raised fish densely crowded into polluted pens, anemic creatures fed chemical growth agents and dyes to give the appearance of health, escaped hybrid salmon crossbreeding with the handful of surviving wild species, diluting and corrupting their gene pool. But there's good news. While the salmon-farming industry has failed, the cultivation of clams, mussels, oysters, and scallops has succeeded, and then some. Bivalve aquaculture is actually filtering farm runoff that had led to algae blooms, cleaning coastal estuaries and bays. Tilapia and catfish (both fed a diet made up mostly of soybeans, corn, wheat, and vitamins), both clean white-fleshed fish, are ecologically sound fish-farming success stories. Caviar from cultivated American sturgeon (twenty years in the making, and just now bearing fruit) is of better quality than much of the osetra that is shamelessly poached from nearly depleted Caspian Sea stocks, and it is replacing endangered beluga on menus of top restaurants in Miami, Houston, Aspen, New York, and Los Angeles, to name a few cities.

Salmon, the most popular fresh finfish in the country, is also the biggest aquaculture problem. Some domestic and Canadian salmon farmers are taking bold steps to address systemic problems, but it's hard to separate the good from the bad, and know that what you're getting was raised right. For now, the responsible choice is wild salmon from Alaska, where great fisheries management is maintaining the right balance between the needs of man and nature.

SALMON: THE CONTROVERSY CONTINUES With more than twenty American wild salmon populations endangered or threatened in the 1980s, salmon farming seemed like the perfect way to protect the remaining stocks of wild fish. The prized wild Atlantic salmon had been fished nearly to the brink of annihilation, and habitat loss had left them with almost no place to spawn. So when the first American salmon farms opened in the Pacific Northwest and in Maine in the middle of that decade, they were hailed as the salvation of wild salmon.

Salmon farming had started in Norway in the late 1960s and in Canada in the 1970s. By 1989, worldwide production of farmed salmon, from Norway to Chile, Scotland to Vancouver, had flooded the market with fresh, delicious-tasting fish. Prices plummeted, and the wild salmon fisheries were in economic decline. They couldn't compete. It seemed that the plan had worked: Wild stocks were safe from overfishing at last.

The aquaculture system developed in Norway was copied everywhere. The model called for creation of hatcheries in coastal rivers and giant floating pens in ocean waters close to shore. The ocean pens act as marine feedlots, with net cages designed to contain the fish in close quarters and allow waste and excess feed to pass through into the open sea. Aquaculture operations routinely penned between 500,000 and 700,000 fish in an area roughly the size of four football fields.

From a culinary point of view, the product could be quite good. Unlike wild-caught salmon, farmed fish could be plucked from their habitat without a struggle. They could be transported directly from the water to market in record time, ensuring freshness. Fish could be guaranteed to have been live the morning of delivery. Manhandling and its resulting bruising were minimized. And the consistency of size was remarkable. They were bred to be mild in flavor, high in oil content, and very tender. Chefs loved the farmed fish, which combined freshness, consistency, reliable supply, and a sense of environmental stewardship (since the fish were seen as the salvation of the wild stocks). A chef I worked for at the time found a supplier who crossbred the Norwegian salmon with wild Atlantic salmon, so he got the stronger flavor of wild, and the silkier, richer mouth feel of farm raised. He said it was "better half wild than not wild at all."

Consumers celebrated too. The retail price of salmon dropped from $12 per pound to less than $6 per pound between 1986 and 1989. And the fish was fresher. Sushi, which was starting to take off as a culinary trend, relies on an uncompromisingly fresh product. Here it was, and it made the dishes affordable to the mass market. Health experts also lauded the higher omega-3 fat content of the farmed fish, saying it was good for combating cholesterol in humans. It all seemed too good to be true—and it was.

THE PERILS OF FISH FARMING In the early 1990s, scientists started raising concerns about various negative effects on the oceans and rivers. It seems that raising the fish in such closely confined conditions had allowed a minor problem in the wild to explode into a major one. Sea lice, parasites very similar to lice on land, had begun to afflict fish in the pens, which all became infested. The sea lice populations

The Marine Stewardship Council (MSC)

Conservationists waited for decades for sensible government action on overfishing and habitat destruction by the fishing industry. But governmental action has been timid and piecemeal. A unique partnership between the World Wildlife Fund, a leading conservation organization, and the Unilever Corporation, one of the world's largest buyers of frozen fish, spawned the MSC, an entity that fills the vacancy in fisheries oversight. Since 1997, the MSC has been a London-based certifier of sustainable fisheries, doing sound scientific research, and rewarding good actors with the organization's seal of approval.

Consumers can read the organization's regularly updated list of certified fisheries on its Web site, www.msc.org, and seek out those products at the market. MSC spokesperson Jessica Wenban-Smith points out that to be sure the product is a sustainable resource, consumers must look for the MSC logo. "The ecolabel is important because in all fisheries there are non-sustainably fishing outfits that compete with the sustainably managed ones. The point of the ecolabel is to provide consumers with a simple way of knowing which is which." She also points out that the Whole Foods Market is a supporter of the MSC, and often stocks MSC-labeled fish.

- Alaska wild salmon

- Burry Inlet cockles

- New Zealand hoki

- Loch Torridon nephrops (langoustine)

- Mexican Baja California red rock lobster

- South African hake

- South Georgia toothfish

- South West mackerel (handline)

- Thames herring

- West Australian rock lobster

boomed, spreading out into the ocean, where they could infect juvenile wild fish, such as wild salmon and sea trout.

Numerous studies have shown that sea lice populations explode in the areas where salmon are farmed. Since the lice cannot live for long in fresh water, the hatcheries where salmon are bred are largely unaffected. It's only when they transfer into the marine environment that they are susceptible to infection from older fish and free-swimming lice. Wild salmon, which often share coastal estuaries with salmon farms, must swim with parasites generated in the highly concentrated pens of the aquaculture operations. The biggest damage is done to smolts, the young salmon just entering the marine environment. The future of the species depends on high survival rates for these young fish. Unlike farmed salmon, the wild smolts have no one watching out for their welfare. Before the advent of salmon farming, sea lice mostly died off during the upriver spawning runs of wild salmon. As a result, lice were no threat to the baby salmon born in the spring. But the year-round, temperature-controlled environment of the fish farm keeps breeding conditions good for the lice during the wild stocks' off season. Their young now must run a more treacherous gauntlet than their forebears did.

To treat the sea lice problem threatening their stocks, fish farmers have begun to apply pesticides just as farmers use them to poison land insects. This has begun a slippery slope of poisoning the ocean pens to keep the salmon free of lice. The latest chemical trend is use of emamectin benzoate, which goes by the commercial name SLICE. Though it's not yet approved as a pesticide, fish farmers have been allowed to include it in fish feed pellets, where it's regulated not as a pesticide, but as medicine. Once eaten, SLICE enters the fish's tissues through digestion. Sea lice feeding on the affected fish are poisoned by the substance, which causes loss of nerve control. It takes about one week for the substance to pass through the fish's system. Scientists argue over the effects of SLICE on other marine species. It's been found to induce premature molting in lobsters. It's suspected of causing lobsters to lose their eggs before they're ready. Certain shrimp are so sensitive to the substance that half a drop in an Olympic-sized swimming pool is sufficient to poison them. It also endures for a long time in water, creating the risk that it could accumulate in marine sediments and harm other crustaceans. Packaging for one brand of emamectin benzoate, called Proclaim, bears the warning, "This pesticide is toxic to fish, birds, mammals, and aquatic invertebrates. Do not contaminate water when cleaning equipment or disposing of equipment wash water." SLICE does not appear to have a negative effect on farmed salmon.

If we are to solve this web of sea lice problems, salmon farms must be relocated to areas where they don't come into contact with juvenile wild salmon, trout, or other susceptible species. Pens need to be periodically left "fallow" to break the reproductive cycle of the pests, and allow natural predators time to bring populations of lice back into balance with the ecosystem. The farms must be contained in a way that poses no further threat to natural ecosystems. Even without sea lice, the industry has major problems to solve.

THE IRONY OF OVERFISHING PREY TO PREVENT OVERFISHING
PREDATORS Depletion of wild fish in the oceans was a prime reason why salmon aquaculture began. But to nourish farmed salmon during the two to three years it takes for them to reach marketable size, enormous weights of sardines, mackerel, anchovies, and herring must be ground up to make fish chow pellets. To produce one pound of farmed salmon, between two and four pounds of fish has to be harvested from the wild. The oil and meal contained in this feed is suspected of causing higher levels of PCBs, which bioaccumulate in farmed salmon. Those carcinogenic chemicals remain in the fatty tissues of animals, and are concentrated in animals that consume those fats. Wild salmon consume a much more varied diet.

Unlike farm-raised fish like catfish, which rely on mostly vegetarian feed, carnivorous salmon present a particular problem. In addition to threatening fish stocks lower on the food chain with the same overfishing that led to the salmon farms, we're competing with marine species for resources. Herring, mackerel, anchovies, and the like are essential prey for whales and other marine mammals, as well as wild salmon. Like the other giants that are most threatened with overfishing—swordfish, tuna, and cod—salmon live high on the food chain, so they make bad candidates for low-impact aquaculture.

In an often-overlooked side effect, the fish-farming industry's demand for smaller feed fish has impacted the poor of the world. Salmon farms provide luxury food for industrialized countries. They've created demand for mackerel, sardines, and herring, raising the market price of those feeder fish, which were among the only affordable sources of protein for people in developing countries. Fish is the most important source of protein in the human diet worldwide.

In the worst salmon farms, inefficiently distributed feed pellets fall through confinement-pen netting to the ocean floor, where they promote growth of oxygen-depleting bacteria. To reduce the amount of wild fish required to service the salmon-farming industry, farmers need to look at both the type of feed they use and the way they administer it. The World Wildlife Fund (WWF) points to efforts on one major Norwegian salmon farm, Villa Leppefisk, to show that solutions can be found. The operation uses fish feed that incorporates more vegetable products and less fish meal than conventional feed. It also uses a feeder that dispenses new food only when the fish have consumed what was available, reducing waste from feed that scatters on the ocean floor.

DOG EAT DOG IN THE DEEP BLUE SEA I wouldn't want to be a wild salmon, even on a good day. From conception to old age (should they reach it), these creatures are surrounded by murderous bullies. And good eats for themselves are increasingly hard for these fish to find, as habitat destruction and overfishing take their toll. Up to 25 percent of young salmon smolts end up as bycatch in Norwegian and Russian trawlers. Add to that the fact that escaped farm-raised superfish are flooding their habitats, competing for the choicest resources and spawning grounds, and you've got a primal struggle for survival.

Farmed salmon are bred to grow fast. Escapees in rivers eat voraciously, outcompeting smaller wild cousins on their way to the sea. But unlike the wild salmon, they mostly won't be back. Ill-equipped for the harshness of life in the wild, the farm-raised fish are killed off in the open ocean, leaving their home rivers empty of both wild and farmed fish. In British Columbia alone, the salmon-farming industry concedes that over a million farmed salmon escaped into the wild. Nearly half were Atlantic salmon. In addition to competing for resources, these escapees are interbreeding with wild fish, weakening their genetic makeup. Wild salmon species are threatened all over the globe, as invasive species like the farmed Atlantic salmon displace them. Canadian Pacific wild fisheries have been particularly affected by this species wipe-out, as have fisheries in Scotland. Stocks of wild fish have declined by 80 percent over the past thirty years, according to WWF data.

Fish farm waste includes fish feces, uneaten food pellets, drugs such as antibiotics, and residues from pest treatments. The Coastal Alliance for Aquaculture Reform (CAAR), a nonprofit Canadian environmental group, estimates that the waste produced by 85 net-cage salmon-farming operations in British Columbia is equivalent to raw sewage from a city of 500,000 inhabitants. Oxygen depletion from decomposing matter is sometimes so severe that it suffocates salmon in the farm above. When salmon farms are located in coastal estuaries, where marine life is most dense, drug residue concentrates in crustaceans and other bottom dwellers, compromising the food chain at an early stage.

Three possible approaches to the waste pollution problem are being discussed in the industry: exposed far-offshore open marine systems, closed circulating marine systems, and land-based saltwater systems.

Caviar

I couldn't believe it then, and I still can't. The cover of the January 1998 issue of *Saveur,* the glossiest of the glossy American epicure magazines, featured a spoonful of beluga being offered from an overflowing, glistening tin over the legend: "Caviar— Before It's Too Late." Naively, I presumed it heralded a piece about preservation measures gourmets could take to save the endangered prehistoric sturgeon species. When I read the piece, I didn't know whether to laugh or cry. The thrust was that food lovers should buy beluga caviar now, before the species goes extinct.

"A process, condition or period of deterioration or decline." That's how the American Heritage Dictionary defines decadence. No wonder the lifestyle associated with frequent consumption of sturgeon caviar is often called decadent. Concern over depletion of sturgeon stocks, documented since the late 1600s, spurred worried czars to regulate Russian harvests at the turn of the twentieth century. Some species are already extinct, and most are on the list of endangered species. So, does this mean that we're currently tasting the last spoonfuls of beluga caviar the world will know? Probably not.

One company forging new trails in the caviar business is Lafayette International Trading, Inc., an importer and distributor of caviar that sources from some unexpected places. President and managing partner Jerry Ivers and vice president Mark

Bolourchi describe a vital and bustling business fueled by innovations. "We're sourcing from an organization, Stolt Sea Farm in Sacramento, that has pioneered farm-raised production of caviar," says Bolourchi, describing the farm as a unique aquaculture operation that began as a research program in the 1970s, and has, since the late 1990s, been producing a very high quality of caviar derived from white sturgeon. Ivers interjects that this is *not* the product frequently marketed as "American sturgeon caviar," which actually comes from either the sturgeon-related paddlefish or the hackleback, a species of river sturgeon found mostly in the Mississippi and its tributaries. Instead, it's called Sterling caviar.

The white sturgeon, says Ivers, has a much finer quality of roe, producing a finer quality of caviar. Roe becomes caviar through a process of separating the eggs from the ovaries (screening) and salting. "White sturgeon caviar is comparable to the imports," he says, alluding to the three prized sturgeon species of the Caspian Sea: beluga, osetra, and sevruga. The white sturgeon, which occurs naturally in such American rivers as the Columbia, Willamette, Fraser, and Snake, was once at the top of American fisheries. Catches were 2,500 tons annually at the turn of the century, but are now down to 100 to 200 tons annually, according to *Caviar: The Resource Book* (Cultura, Moscow, 1993) by Vulf Sternin and Ian Doré, Russian caviar researchers who detail the history, science, and possibilities of caviar production.

Sternin and Doré reported that for wild white sturgeon, no caviar production is permitted, but also noted that at the time of publication, efforts in artificial propagation were under way that may lead to new caviar sources. Those efforts are now coming to fruition, in the form of Stolt Sea Farm's product—results of a $15 million joint venture between Stolt/Nielson (a large Norwegian salmon producer) and the University of California at Davis. Ten thousand pounds were produced in 2005. Bolourchi expects production to double annually for the next few years, as more of the sturgeon reach the twelve- to fourteen-year caviar-producing maturity. The Lafayette leaders expect production to soar. "Remember what happened with wine in California?" asks Bolourchi, slyly. The timing couldn't be better, with demand rising and the Caspian situation becoming dire.

Citing the toll overfishing and petroleum production are taking on the three nearly extinct Caspian sturgeon species, the author of the 1998 *Saveur* article lamented the high cost of "legal" caviar, produced under quotas set by the

Convention on the International Trade of Endangered Species (CITES), but suggested that the "adventurous" shopper might find "hidden treasures" for a quarter of the price on the black market. In addition to a buyers' guide to Caspian caviar, the author mentioned sturgeon caviars from China, California, and the Black Sea, but pointed out that she preferred Russian caviar's "associations with the past—the legends, the literature, the lavishness lacking in my own daily life." She added, "Only Caspian caviar provides such a blissful reward, and the cost, I've decided, can never be too high." I disagree. So, it seems, does the U.S. Fish and Wildlife Service.

In January 2004, the U.S. Fish and Wildlife Service (USFWS) ruled on whether to protect beluga sturgeon under the Endangered Species Act. An affirmative ruling would ban the sale of beluga caviar in the United States, which consumes 25 percent of the world's 12-ton annual legal production. (In 1896, Russia exported 414 tons.)

The USFWS finally imposed a ban on importation of beluga caviar in late 2005. The ban, which prohibits all beluga caviar imports, is in reaction to news that stocks of the nearly extinct species had declined as much as 30 percent in the previous year alone. The United States is the world's largest consumer of beluga caviar. The USFWS had "reviewed" Caspian practices for years, as the species wasted away there.

Meanwhile, Tsar Nicoulai Caviar (a California company, despite its Russian-sounding moniker) now sells California Estate osetra. Their sturgeon, raised in captivity, is the same species that produces the highly prized Caspian pearls, but represents a sustainable resource. The caviar is exceptional. Just like the Sterling caviar project, Tsar Nicoulai's road to production was a twenty-year ordeal. But the company has accomplished a stupendous feat. Its farm-raised osetra caviar is as stunningly complex, buttery, and elegant as the Caspian product. It doesn't taste exactly the same (the California sturgeon are raised in artesian well water), which is a comforting sign of its natural origins. Just as wines and coffees exhibit subtle flavor differences reflecting their home soil, the best caviar exemplifies the character traits of its *terroir*.

I've tasted creamy, tender pearls of Tsar Nicoulai's osetra side by side with Caspian osetra, and I preferred the domestic over the import. One of the most pleasing elements of great caviar is the savory mineral flavor that remains on the palate after the saltiness passes through. This California osetra has a long-lived finish that prolongs the pleasure of every bite.

Caviar producers pack some fresh for sale to gourmets, and pasteurize some for less savvy buyers. Since Caspian caviar is traded as a commodity, consumers have no way of tracing their caviar back to the producer, and have to rely on salesmen for quality assurance. In the caviar business, that's akin to putting the wolf in charge of the henhouse. Producers pasteurize caviar that is second-rate or close to spoilage, as a way of salvaging it. It commands a much lower wholesale price than the fresh product, but the savings seldom passes to the consumer. It just means that the lower-quality caviar goes to lesser stores, who often charge fresh market prices for it.

The point of this whole discussion is to illustrate the value of knowing the producer. Fresh California osetra will *always* trump pasteurized Caspian osetra. With the California product, you can be assured that it's never been pasteurized, it was packed to order, and that the process of making it was clean and inspected. That is never true of the Caspian product. Bait and switch is another tricky practice in the caviar trade.

The fact that Tennessee paddlefish roe has been widely disguised as sevruga caviar is both troubling and encouraging. For one thing, it underscores the shady nature of the imported caviar business. On the other hand, it illustrates the excellent quality of domestic sturgeon. Fisheries of some of these species are managed in responsible ways that allow for limited legal production of excellent domestic wild caviar. Hackleback sturgeon and paddlefish (a relative of sturgeon) both live in American rivers, including the Mississippi, Missouri, and Tennessee. State and federal governments closely manage limited catches in Kentucky, Tennessee, Missouri, Arkansas, and Illinois.

Osage Catfisheries of Osage Beach, Missouri (573-348-2305), farm-raise paddlefish. They produce an excellent product, which closely resembles Caspian osetra. A producer's advantage of farm-raising paddlefish is that they can be raised in the same ponds as catfish, reducing overhead. Feeding mainly on zooplankton and insect larvae, the paddlefish don't require the expensive pellets of fish food that many other aquaculture fish consume. Many of my cooking clients who are big fans of fine caviar swear by this American delicacy. Not only do they enjoy its flavor and pleasing texture, but they know they're doing the right thing for the environment, even though they're immersed in a culture that says they don't have to care. Suppliers for the environmentally friendly caviar choices discussed here can be found in Sources.

Tiny Potato Pancakes with American Sturgeon Caviar

SERVES 4 AS AN APPETIZER Unlike their Caspian cousins, American white sturgeon have not been exploited to near extinction by unscrupulous profiteers. They are a product of U.S. aquaculture innovation. The quality of their caviar is exceptional, and the product is slightly less expensive than the endangered osetra, beluga, and sevruga of Russia, Iran, and Kazakhstan.

American sturgeon caviar is available from Caviarteria (www.sterlingcaviar.com or 212-759-7410).

1 large egg, beaten

1 baking potato (such as russet), peeled and coarsely grated

1 very small onion, grated

½ teaspoon salt

1 teaspoon all-purpose flour

3 tablespoons Clarified Butter (recipe follows) or olive oil for frying

¼ cup crème fraiche or sour cream

1 ounce American sturgeon caviar

Combine the egg, potato, and onion in a bowl. Add the salt and sprinkle in the flour; toss with your hands to combine well.

Heat the clarified butter until it shimmers but does not smoke (a piece of potato should sizzle upon entry). Form 16 tiny pancakes from the batter, press to squeeze out excess water, and pan-fry over moderate heat. Cook slowly, without moving them for the first 5 minutes, then loosen with a spatula. When the potato appears mostly cooked, flip them to brown the second side.

Transfer to a plate, and garnish with tiny dollops of cream and caviar.

Clarified Butter

Clarified butter is the perfect cooking medium for crisp, golden brown pancakes due to its flavor and durability at high temperatures. To make it, melt a stick or two of butter, then let it stand until foam rises to the top and the water sinks to the bottom. Skim out the foam and ladle off the clear, golden oil.

Abalone—Farmed

Abalone (pronounced "a-ba-lone-ee") is a single-shelled mollusk with a giant central muscle, known as the *foot*. It is the foot, sometimes called abalone steak, that aficionados relish most. Raw, fresh abalone has the sweet, briny taste of a just-caught surf clam, the mild nuttiness of French Gruyère cheese, and the crunchy texture of bamboo shoots. To serve it raw, the preferred method in Japan, it's sliced across the grain and pounded into very thin medallions. The meat takes very well to marinades, and is one of the great taste-texture sensations of Asia.

Cooked, abalone's taste becomes more buttery, and its texture firmer, like that of a chuck steak. Until the advent of abalone aquaculture, live abalone was virtually impossible to find in the United States. Canned and dried products were the only options. Since these products are already cooked and cured, the taste of fresh abalone is something new to the American palate (except for those few who've tasted it in sushi bars in Japan). Cooked abalone is also a very special experience, as the meat's dense, lush feeling on the palate cannot be compared with that of any other food's. The closest textural comparison is perhaps to a Chinese black mushroom, but abalone is a thing unto itself.

Until recently, the only place Americans were likely to encounter abalone was in an urban Chinese restaurant, on a back page of an enormous menu. For years, I wondered what could justify the luxury prices—twice as expensive as lobster. The Chinese have a litany of special-occasion delicacies, like bird's nests, shark fins, and abalone, that play an important role in elaborate wedding celebrations. These specialties are expensive as much for their rarity as for their culinary character. Bird's nests are gathered at great risk from inaccessible places; shark fins are small, and they're the only part of the fish used; and rare abalone must be collected live by divers.

While sourcing of birds' nests and shark fins continue to be environmental problems, there's good news for lovers of the delicate seafood taste and firm, appealing texture of abalone. Successful abalone aquaculture systems have made the delicacy more plentiful and ecofriendly, if not necessarily more affordable. Abalones are vegetarian, feeding on kelp, a type of seaweed, rather than the ground fishmeal pellets fed to many aquaculture species. The four- to five-year process of raising the abalone is monitored by various government agencies. Abalone are available from the Abalone Farm of Cayucos, California (www.abalonefarm.com or www.usabalone.com). Closed systems (those that do not interact with the open ocean) keep the abalone safe from predators and bugs, protect the natural environment from waste, and contain any possible illnesses that might affect the farmed mollusks. Most abalone farms have a minimum order of about $80.

Abalone Carpaccio Salad

SERVES 4 AS AN APPETIZER The delicate crunch of paper-thin slices of nutty-tasting abalone is intoxicating. These sustainably raised mollusks take on marinades very well, enhancing their undertones of sweet clam and conch flavor. First, slice them as thinly as possible, then pound them gently but firmly, being careful to stop before they tear. Hard to find in most fish stores, these are mostly available shipped direct from the farm (www.abalonefarm.com and www.usabalone.com).

1 head green leaf lettuce, hand-torn into bite-size pieces

1 bunch watercress, stems trimmed to 2 inches

2 heads red Belgium endive or radicchio, cut into bite-size pieces

One 2-inch piece ginger, peeled and finely chopped

4 garlic cloves, finely chopped

2 tablespoons honey

¼ cup soy sauce

1 tablespoon rice wine vinegar

A few drops Asian toasted sesame oil

4 medium-size fresh abalone (about 1 pound in the shell)

1 tablespoon peanut or other oil

12 fresh shiitake mushrooms, thinly sliced

Salt and freshly ground black pepper

1 cup snow peas (about 2 dozen)

Lemon wedges

Wash the lettuce, watercress, and endive well; spin dry and toss together. Combine the ginger, garlic, honey, soy sauce, vinegar, and sesame oil; mix well.

Scoop the abalone from their shells, using an oyster knife or the handle of a spoon to break the muscle from the shell lining. Wash the shells well and set aside. Clean the abalone thoroughly, discarding peripheral viscera and inedible parts.

If a meat-slicing machine is available to you, use it to slice the abalone paper-thin. Each abalone should make between 4 and 6 slices. If not, slice as thin as possible by hand, then pound with a mallet or the side of a cleaver until the meat is almost transparent. Combine the slices in a bowl with 1 tablespoon of the soy mixture, and marinate for 20 minutes.

Heat the peanut oil in a small sauté pan until it shimmers but doesn't smoke. Add the mushrooms and a good sprinkling of salt and pepper. Cook until the mushrooms are softened and slightly browned. Add the snow peas and cook until crisp-tender, about 3 minutes.

Arrange the salad greens on plates. Place the hot sautéed vegetable mixture in the abalone shells, and arrange the shells atop the salads. Drape the abalone slices over the salad and dress with the remaining soy mixture. Serve immediately, garnished with lemon wedges.

Sautéed Abalone with Spicy Orange Beurre Blanc

SERVES 4 AS A MAIN COURSE When using fresh live abalone, refrigerate them overnight after removing them from the shell; this allows the meat to relax and become tender again. Then treat them as you would fresh scallops: Sear them at high heat, and undercook them to ensure tender and juicy meat. Serve with a grain pilaf or Coconut Rice (page 61). This dish also makes an excellent component of a meal with Caraway-Coriander Wilted Savoy Cabbage (page 111) or Mediterranean Vegetables (page 124) and steamed potatoes.

Use organic products whenever possible. Several organic wines are available from www.diamondorganics.com; organic vinegar from www.worldpantry.com. The Whole Foods Markets also carry organic vinegar, such as the Eden brand. Abalone is available from www.abalonefarm.com or www.usabalone.com.

Juice and zest of 1 orange

⅓ cup dry white wine

2 tablespoons white wine vinegar

3 tablespoons finely chopped shallots

¼ teaspoon kosher salt

4 cracked black peppercorns (or a few grinds black pepper)

1 tablespoon heavy cream

8 tablespoons (1 stick) cold unsalted butter, cut into pieces the size of a hazelnut

Pinch of cayenne

9 cultivated abalone steaks

Salt and freshly ground black pepper

Flour for dredging

Vegetable oil for sautéing

1 tablespoon unsalted butter, softened

In a small pan, simmer the orange juice until it is reduced to about 2 tablespoons. Add the zest, wine, vinegar, shallots, salt, and pepper. Simmer until reduced to about 2 tablespoons. Stir in the cream.

Remove the pan from the heat. Gradually whisk in the cold butter, one piece at a time, making sure to keep whisking as the butter melts into the sauce. If you need more heat, hold the pan briefly over low heat. The butter should not melt before it is incorporated, or the sauce will separate. Season the sauce with cayenne. Transfer the sauce to a small container, and set it in a warm place while you cook the abalone.

Season the abalone steaks with salt and pepper; dredge in flour. Heat a skillet over high heat; add a few drops of oil to coat the pan. Place the abalone in the skillet, and add the soft butter (which is there to aid in browning, not for lubrication). Sear without disturbing for 1 minute, until lightly browned; turn over. Cook 30 seconds. Serve with the beurre blanc sauce.

Anchovies—Wild

When oil-packed anchovies cook, they melt into a saucy paste, perfect for seasoning any dish for which they're destined. Sauté some anchovies in olive oil with chopped olives, crushed red pepper, parsley, and capers, and you have the base for the gutsy tomato sauce known as *puttanesca*. It boasts a robust seafood flavor, without the need for any additional seafood. Puttanesca, a beloved sauce for pasta, becomes an instant antipasto when spooned onto little crostini (rounds of grilled or toasted bread).

Anchovies are unabashedly fishy. Theirs is the flavor of Worcestershire sauce, Liptauer spread, and good Caesar dressings. They add layers of complexity to dishes from pizza to stew, and to the warm dip of Piedmont, Italy, bagna cauda. In Spain, they're pickled in vinegar and served as tapas, with many accompaniments. Most anchovies sold in America are packed in olive oil and sold either in tins or glass jars. Because they're salt cured, they can keep almost indefinitely, even after opening. I prefer fillets packed in jars because they taste cleaner to me, and the jars reclose for easy storage. Some recipes call for anchovy paste. Although this paste can be purchased in tubes, it's quite easy to make anchovy paste by mashing anchovy fillets with some coarse salt, using the side of a knife blade. Just keep chopping and mashing against a cutting board until the fillet achieves a paste consistency.

Don't hold your breath waiting to find fresh anchovies. They do show up in coastal fish markets occasionally. Their scales are so soft and tiny that they're completely edible. The easiest approach is to dip fresh anchovies in flour and fry them in 350°F oil. Serve them with lemon wedges and Remoulade Sauce (which often contains minced anchovy; see page 253).

Because they reproduce very fast and are still quite abundant, anchovies are a good way of incorporating fish flavor into your cooking without choosing endangered fish. If the salmon-farming industry finds ways to lower its use of anchovies in feed pellets for aquaculture salmon, then these briny little beauties will remain abundant for generations to come (though, admittedly, farmed salmon that are not fed a diet high in fish produce much less nutritious meat). They are caught in the wild, off America's West Coast, in Japanese waters, and off the coast of Africa. Anchovies in vinegar (known in Spain as *boquerones*), an excellent appetizer ingredient, are available from www.markys.com and www.tienda.com.

White Anchovy Canapés with Piquillo Peppers and Goat Cheese

SERVES 4 AS AN APPETIZER Some recipes succeed by matching power with power. In this case, the savory goat cheese, bittersweet piquillo peppers, and tart anchovies form a stunning triumvirate—a sandwich to remember. Anchovies in vinegar, or *boquerones,* are available from www.tienda.com or www.markys.com. Tienda also carries organic piquillo peppers.

½ **baguette**

2 **ounces fresh goat cheese, softened**

¼ **cup canned piquillo peppers, drained and cut into ½-inch strips**

12 **white anchovy fillets in vinegar, drained**

Extra virgin olive oil

Slice the bread into twelve ½-inch-thick rounds. Spread the slices with goat cheese.

Garnish with the strips of piquillos and anchovies. Serve drizzled with olive oil.

Pan Bagnat

SERVES 4 The ingenious secret to this robust-tasting sandwich is that it's made ahead and set to rest for a while, allowing juices and dressing to seep into the crusty bread. Once the ingredients have marinated, the bread is deliciously flavored, and the essences of the fillings have married to make a dish that's greater than the sum of its parts.

1 baguette

Olive oil

¼ cup Niçoise olives, pitted and finely chopped

12 basil leaves

1 green pepper, diced

1 small red onion, diced

2 radishes, sliced

Juice of ½ lemon

Salt and freshly ground black pepper

3 or 4 freshly cooked or canned artichoke hearts, sliced

3 large hard-boiled eggs, sliced

1 medium tomato, sliced

12 anchovy fillets, packed in vinegar or oil, drained

Split the bread open and scoop out two-thirds of the interior. Drizzle both halves with olive oil. Distribute the olives in an even layer on the bottom half of the bread, and lay the basil leaves over the olives.

Combine the pepper, onion, and radishes with the lemon juice, a few teaspoons of olive oil, and salt and pepper; mix well. Add this mixture to the sandwich, and then layer on the artichoke hearts, eggs, tomato, and anchovies.

Close the sandwich, cover, and refrigerate 1 hour before slicing and serving. The bread will have soaked in juices from the salad and become flavorful and soft.

Pickled Anchovies with Sautéed Almonds and Celery

SERVES 4 AS AN APPETIZER Whatever inspired chef Gabrielle Hamilton of New York's hip hole-in-the-wall, Prune, to combine anchovies, almonds, and celery must have been divine. The textures are consistently engaging, bite after bite, and the flavors touch on every taste our palates can perceive. And hey, celery?! When was the last time you featured that in a dish? Try it: It works.

Marcona almonds are available from www.tienda.com. Pickled anchovies, or *boquerones,* are available from www.tienda.com or www.markys.com.

2 tablespoons olive oil

1 teaspoon fresh lemon juice

Pinch of chopped fresh oregano

Salt and freshly ground black pepper

2 celery ribs, sliced ¼ inch thick

1 cup blanched almonds, such as Marcona

16 white anchovy fillets in vinegar, drained

Whisk together 1 tablespoon of the olive oil, the lemon juice, and oregano; season with salt and pepper. Toss with the celery; marinate 10 minutes.

Heat the remaining olive oil in a small skillet; add the almonds. Cook 5 minutes, until the almonds are lightly browned; season with salt. Cool to room temperature.

Arrange the celery on one side of a small plate. Place the almonds on the other side. Rest the anchovy fillets across the top, drizzling with any remaining dressing from the celery.

Arctic Char—Farmed

Like a cross between salmon and trout, Arctic char has flesh that ranges from dark red to pink, and a silvery skin with speckles along the belly. It is actually closely related to both salmon and trout, and has the pleasantly juicy character of that family. Its skin gets wonderfully crispy when grilled or sautéed.

Fillets of Arctic char have the same type of pinbones as the fish's cousins. The best way to remove these is with a clean pair of needle-nose pliers. Tweezers work too. Feel along the length of the fillet, moving a finger from head to tail to identify where the bones are. Sweep the back of a knife in the opposite direction from how the bones point out to lift the ends of the bones a little from the fillet. Then, grasp the ends of each bone with the pliers or tweezers, and yank them straight out in the direction they're growing. Once the pinbones are out, the fillet is completely boneless.

Lemony butter sauces, fruit sauces, and sweet-and-sour salsas pair beautifully with this robust-tasting fish. Like most fish, it's better to undercook it than overcook it. In the event of accidental overcooking, I've found that char makes excellent fish salads and fish cakes.

While wild Arctic char is now widely available in mainstream fish markets, farm-raised Arctic char is an industry in its infancy, so sourcing from the Internet might be the only option in some places. Seek out this fish, and ask your fish dealer to bring in farmed char. The fish live a better life than many other farmed fish, and the process is cleaner than most. They're farmed in land-based tanks and "raceways" in Iceland, Canada, and the United States. Arctic char are among the most ecofriendly and humane fish choices. They naturally school in tight groups, so the concentrated living conditions of the aquaculture system don't represent an undue stress to them. Since their cultivation takes place independently of natural ecosystems, they pose little to no risk of escaping and disrupting the balance of waterways and estuaries. Wastewater from their production is mostly filtered and recycled, minimizing pollution. Arctic char convert food to energy very efficiently, yielding a large amount of high-quality fish while requiring a minimum of feed fish. This is an important consideration, since fully one-quarter of all fish harvested from the wild today goes directly into production of fishmeal and fish oil for feeding of farmed fish. Char are available from www.gortonsfreshseafood.com.

Cajun Arctic Char

SERVES 4 Arctic char's rich meat and easily crisped skin make it a good choice for the extreme pan-searing technique known as blackening, which was all the rage in the 1980s. Redfish, a species from the Gulf of Mexico, was nearly wiped out during the Cajun food craze. Highly spiced rice dishes, such as "dirty rice," flavored with small bits of sausage, herbs, and vegetables, can be made with whole grains like brown rice or Wehani rice (a specialty whole-grain rice grown in the southwestern United States—organic Wehani is available from www.lundberg.com) as the main component of a meal. Served over such a rice, along with some Vegetable Stew (page 132), this robust fish dish makes a zesty meal for eight guests, twice as many as if the fish itself were used as the main dish.

1 teaspoon paprika

1 teaspoon freshly ground black pepper

1 teaspoon garlic powder

1 teaspoon dried thyme

1 teaspoon dried basil

½ teaspoon onion powder

½ teaspoon dried oregano

¼ teaspoon cayenne

2 pounds Arctic char fillets (cut into 8 pieces)

2 tablespoons unsalted butter, melted

Salt

1 tablespoon peanut oil

Lemon wedges

Combine the paprika, black pepper, garlic powder, thyme, basil, onion powder, oregano, and cayenne. Brush the fish with butter, season with salt, and coat well with the mixed spices.

Heat a large skillet over high heat 3 minutes. Add the oil and swirl the pan to coat. Add the fish fillets, skin side up. Sear until dark brown; the pan should smoke as the fish cooks. Turn once. The fish should be medium rare. Serve with lemon wedges.

Quick Fish Salad: Toss 1 pound skinless, boneless cooked fish (such as Arctic char), with 6 tablespoons mayonnaise and 2 teaspoons Dijon mustard. Season with 1 teaspoon Old Bay seasoning, a squeeze of lemon, and cayenne to taste.

Quick Fish Cakes: Add 1 egg per pound of boneless, skinless cooked fish fillet (such as Arctic char) and enough cracker crumbs to make the mixture easy to shape (usually about ¼ cup, depending on the moisture content of the fish). Season with ¼ cup chopped fresh flat-leaf parsley, ½ cup sautéed chopped onion, 2 teaspoons Dijon mustard, and 1 teaspoon Old Bay seasoning. Form into 6 cakes, roll in additional cracker crumbs, and fry in butter or olive oil. Serve with lemon wedges.

Black Cod (a.k.a. Sable)—Wild Alaskan, Farmed Canadian

Fans of the beleaguered Chilean sea bass take note: A luxuriously rich, snowy white fish is on its way, and it's not overexploited. Sensible fisheries management in Alaska and fledgling aquaculture programs heavily scrutinized by environmental watchdogs are translating into sustainable black cod supplies heading to the mainland.

Much like the overfished Patagonian toothfish (a.k.a. Chilean sea bass) in texture, look, and taste, black cod may be the salvation of the South American species. Legendary chefs like Nobu Matsuhisa have already "discovered" it (it's his signature dish). In fact, black cod was favored by a niche market, mostly Eastern European Jews, who called it "sablefish" for generations.

Black Sea Bass—Wild

A favorite firm, white-fleshed round fish in the Northeast, black sea bass is now recovering from overfishing pressures, thanks to sensible management. Blue Ocean Institute scores it as an acceptable choice, but expresses hope that the buying public will proceed with caution.

Bluefish—Wild

Running wild up and down the Eastern Seaboard in summer, bluefish are rebounding and are at their greatest abundance in fifteen years. They are high in omega-3 fatty acids, said to lower cholesterol in humans, and have a clean, briny flavor when exceptionally fresh. Because it is so perishable, bluefish should always be cooked the day it is bought. Very fresh bluefish fillets are almost white. The flesh darkens to a pale gray as the fish sits.

Zucchini Spaghetti with Garlicky Clams and Grilled Bluefish

SERVES 8 Long strands of zucchini mingle with rustic, square spaghetti *alla chitarra* in this summery play on pasta with clam sauce taught to me by Jasper White. (You can find this unusual pasta shape at www.agferrari.com or www.farawayfoods.com.) I use a Japanese mandoline, an inexpensive (about $25) cutting device that makes julienne easy (available from www.quickspice.com). But I've used a knife in a pinch, and hand-cut julienne are fine for this dish. Bluefish are a plentiful species local to the East Coast, but this dish would be equally delicious with kingfish or even salmon.

2 pounds small clams, such as littlenecks or Manila clams

1 cup dry white wine

3 or 4 large zucchini

1 pound spaghetti (preferably spaghetti *alla chitarra*)

¼ cup olive oil, plus more for brushing the fish

1 large Spanish onion, roughly chopped

Pinch of crushed red pepper

2 bay leaves

1 teaspoon dried oregano

6 garlic cloves, roughly chopped

2 tablespoons chopped fresh oregano or flat-leaf parsley

2 tablespoons unsalted butter

Salt and freshly ground black pepper

2 pounds bluefish fillets, cut into 8 pieces

(continued)

Submerge the clams in cold water for 30 minutes to allow them to eject any sand they contain. Drain the clams and transfer them to a large pot; add the white wine and steam them, covered, until all are open, about 5 minutes. Save about 2 dozen clams in the shells for garnish. Remove the other clams from their shells and roughly chop them. Strain the broth, transfer it to a saucepan, and simmer until it reduces to 2 cups.

Cut the zucchini lengthwise into very long julienne (use a mandoline for this, if you have one). The zucchini should resemble strands of spaghetti. Meanwhile, bring a large pot of water to a boil. Cook the pasta until al dente, drain, and toss with a few drops of olive oil.

Heat the olive oil in a large skillet or pot. Add the onion, red pepper, bay leaves, and dried oregano. Cook over medium heat until the onion is translucent, about 5 minutes. Add the garlic; cook until it turns white, about 1 minute. Add the reduced clam broth and julienne of zucchini. Raise the heat to high; cook just until the mixture simmers. Add the pasta and cook until heated through; stir in the chopped clams, fresh oregano, and butter. Season to taste with salt and black pepper.

Heat a grill or broiler. Season the bluefish fillets with salt and pepper. Brush the fish with some olive oil and cook, skin side up, over a hot grill or broiler for about 3 minutes. Turn once; cook 2 minutes more. Adjust the consistency of the zucchini-pasta mixture with water or clam broth (it should be saucy). Distribute among serving bowls or plates, and top with the bluefish. Drizzle any extra clam sauce over the fish. Garnish with the clams in the shell. Serve with rustic bread.

Catfish—Farmed

Indigenous to the southern United States, channel catfish is now farmed in ponds in the Mississippi Delta. These pond systems produce clean, white-fleshed fish with little collateral damage to the surrounding environment. Their feed is largely grain-based, with only a small amount of fishmeal and fish oil included, so their production doesn't rely heavily on harvest of wild fish.

Asian countries like Vietnam and China are now raising large amounts of catfish for sale on international markets. While domestic catfish are produced in a relatively ecofriendly way, they also have the advantage of requiring much less energy waste in transportation, since they're shipped for hundreds of miles, not thousands. Buying U.S. catfish also supports an ecologically sound food production system in our own country, improving living standards in a traditionally poor region (see www.deltapride.com).

Because it's mild, chefs marinate catfish and apply aggressive spices. Don't be shy about serving it with tomato sauce, vinaigrettes, or Mexican mole sauces. The easiest way to prepare catfish fillets is to season them with salt and pepper, dip them into coarse cornmeal, and fry them at a moderate heat until lightly browned. Served with either rustic tomato sauce or lemons and tartar sauce, this way to cook catfish is quick, delicious, and easy.

Catfish also takes well to Asian preparations, such as braising with black bean sauce. It's no accident that great Chinese catfish recipes abound. Catfish is an essential food in Asia.

Tomato Fondu and Broccoli Rabe with Pan-fried Catfish Strips

SERVES 4 Slowly roasting tomatoes until they become soft "fondu" concentrates their flavor, a great trick to know when your tomatoes are underripe. The sweetness and acidity of the tomatoes will counter the richness of the fried fish. Bittersweet broccoli rabe offers a palate-cleansing third element. Serve with steamed rice.

Farm-raised American catfish is available from www.deltapride.com.

4 large, ripe tomatoes

Kosher salt

1 bunch fresh thyme

6 tablespoons extra virgin olive oil

1 pound broccoli rabe, cut into 3-inch pieces

1 pound farm-raised American catfish fillets, cut into 1-inch-wide strips

Salt and freshly ground black pepper

1 cup each coarse cornmeal and flour, mixed together for dredging

¼ cup peanut oil

2 tablespoons chopped garlic

Pinch of crushed red pepper

Heat the oven to 400°F. Halve the tomatoes along their equator. Arrange them, cut side up, in a baking dish; sprinkle with some kosher salt. Distribute the thyme over the tomatoes; drizzle 3 tablespoons of the olive oil over them. Bake the tomatoes 1 hour, until very soft and juicy. Discard the thyme stems and slip the tomatoes out of their skins. Halve the pieces of tomato fondu.

Bring a large pot of salted water to a boil. Blanch the broccoli rabe until crisp-tender, about 4 minutes. Chill immediately in salted ice water. Drain and squeeze dry; set aside.

Season the catfish with salt and pepper, and coat well in the cornmeal mixture. Heat the peanut oil in a large skillet. Fry the catfish over medium heat in batches, about 2 minutes per side.

In a separate skillet, heat the remaining 3 tablespoons olive oil over medium-high heat. Add the garlic and red pepper, and cook until the garlic just turns light brown. Immediately add the blanched broccoli rabe. Cook until heated through. Arrange the broccoli rabe on serving plates. Surround with alternating strips of catfish and tomato fondu.

Asian-style Braised Catfish

SERVES 4 This simple, low-fat preparation is one of the many ways catfish is served in Asia. Many people are surprised by the very clean taste of today's catfish, which is harvested from environmentally sustainable enclosed fish farms, rather than the muddy channels where it was harvested decades ago.

Black bean garlic sauce is available in the Asian sections of many markets or online from www.importfoods.com, www.asianfoodgrocer.com or www.kalustyans.com.

3 scallions, cut into 2-inch lengths

1 cup sliced onions

2 tablespoons vegetable oil

1 pound catfish fillets, cut into bite-size pieces

Salt and freshly ground black pepper

3 tablespoons Chinese fermented black bean garlic sauce

1 cup water or stock

1 tablespoon cornstarch mixed with 2 tablespoons cold water

Cooked rice or rice noodles for serving

In a 12-inch skillet over high heat, sauté the scallions and onions in the vegetable oil.

Season the catfish liberally with salt and pepper. Add the fish to the pan, and cook for 5 minutes over medium heat; add the fermented black bean garlic sauce and water or stock.

Simmer a few minutes until the fish is tender, then thicken the sauce with the cornstarch mixture. When the sauce has thickened, serve the dish over rice or rice noodles.

Clams—Farmed (and Some Wild Species)

On summer trips to Fire Island, a barrier island not far from New York City, my family would rent a house on the bay side of the island, and my sister and I would dig for clams in the bay with our feet, or with an old clam rake. Not only were we digging for buried treasure, but we were discovering a taste we'd never known. We steamed open the clams, chopped the meat, mixed it with bread crumbs, and made baked stuffed clams.

Then came a season when the park rangers on Fire Island told us the clams weren't safe to eat. Pollution from pleasure boats (mostly from illegal discharge of wastes) had contaminated the bay. Since clams are filter feeders, they were the first victims. We never dug for clams in the Great South Bay again. It was my first personal experience with the effects of pollution. I've since learned that while I was digging with my feet in the mid-1970s, the Great South Bay was producing nearly 60 percent of the nation's hard clams. After that, the harvest plummeted.

Ironically, declining clam populations, caused by pollution, actually exacerbated the pollution problems. Without the filter-feeding activities of the bay's once-prolific clam inhabitants (they'd been seeded into the bay), brown algae blooms deoxygenated the waters, leading to declines in other species as well. In recent years, some clamming has been permitted in certain areas of the bay, while poaching of clams from polluted sectors has caused illness. But there's hope on the horizon for the waters and wildlife of the Great South Bay.

In November 2004, The Nature Conservancy took a giant leap forward in its project to revive the ecosystem of the bay. Their approach? Introduce 600,000 clams into the 11,500 acres of underwater land they've purchased at the bay's bottom. They are moving to jump-start the rebirth of the estuary by seeding it with sufficient numbers of filter feeders to start a breeding population. The organization has already seeded the clams and 10,000 bay scallops into their turf, and has a team on the water year-round to monitor their progress. I can almost smell tomorrow's clean clams baking now.

Aquaculture operations in New England waters have a symbiotic relationship with nearby towns. Algae blooms caused by excessive nutrients in the waters off Cape Cod threatened to turn the area into another Great South Bay. The blooms were fueled by agricultural runoff and fertilizer runoff from suburban lawns (a major pollutant—all for what? Don't get me started . . .). But the algae provides copious food for filter-feeding clams and oysters. As a result, the cultivated shellfish industry has flourished. The advent of suspended aquaculture systems, which raise mussels, clams, and scallops on strings, nets, or in racks submerged in coastal waters, means that modern shellfish farms have very little negative impact, if any, on the sea floor.

Now, clams are cleaner, plumper, and cheaper than they were decades ago. They're still safe (the National Shellfish Sanitation Program tracks the comings and goings of bivalves, and certifies clean waters where clams, oysters, and scallops can be harvested). Nothing tastes more like the sea than freshly shucked littleneck clams. Their salty, winey, sweet flavor, dynamic texture, and misty, oceanic aroma unify in each bite. The aggressive brininess of hard-shell clams pairs beautifully with spicy, bold condiments like wasabi and Tabasco. Bright, acidic sauces like lemon and vinegary mignonette also frame the flavor of clams beautifully. Tomato-based salsas (including the overused but delicious cocktail sauce) marry well with clam flavor, too.

I first encountered the perfect littleneck clam when I worked at Boston's Restaurant Jasper in the late 1980s. It came from Wellfleet, on Cape Cod, and was so fresh that its shells still had the blue tinge that they carry from the ocean, which fades within hours of harvest. Patrick Woodbury, a marine biologist, had started a littleneck aquaculture bed, where he harvested the clams to order, delivering them straight from the sea. He still does (check at www.patsclams.com).

Clams of all varieties are abundant and delicious. Geoducks (pronounced "gooey ducks") are exquisite giant cooking clams from the West Coast. Their siphon, which can grow to the size of a large banana, is blanched, peeled, and sliced for sushi. Geoducks are a recommended choice of Environmental Defense. The clam itself also makes good eating, in fritters.

Manila clams are especially tender. They seldom grow larger than a robin's egg, and they make exceptional broth when they're steamed. Chinese restaurants often serve Manila clams with fermented black bean sauce and steamed peppers. These clams are sustainably farm raised.

The most delicate of clams are steamers. Called soft-shell clams, or affectionately referred to as "piss clams" (because of their habit of squirting water from their siphon when they're disturbed), their flavor is sweet, delicate, and rich—almost buttery. They make excellent chowder, but are best simply steamed, as the name suggests, and dipped in lemony butter. To eat them, skin back the gritty coating on the siphon, and use the clean siphon as a handle to dip them in a mixture of melted butter and lemon.

Razor clams are so named because their elongated, brittle shells resemble old-fashioned straight razors. The flesh of East Coast razor clams is sweet and mild, and they are tender. Pacific razor clams are best used chopped in soups, stews, and stuffings. Mahogany clams, from both Maine and the Pacific Northwest, are handsome bivalves, with a mild flavor and small meats. Mahogany clams are not flavorful or juicy enough to eat raw or steamed, so they're best for chowders and broths.

Atlantic surf clams and ocean quahogs are wild clams harvested in ocean fisheries from Canada down through Cape Hatteras, North Carolina. They're brought up with dredges, which upend and disrupt the ocean floor, as strip mining does on land. These are not good ecological choices. Dredging for wild surf clams, quahogs, and other species indiscriminately kills bottom-dwelling plants and animals. Choose instead to buy cultured clams, which filter and purify the estuaries where they're grown.

Clams in Parsley-Tomato Broth

SERVES 4 AS A MAIN COURSE Thank clams for cleaner coastal waters and estuaries. By filtering out and feeding on excessive algae blooms caused by nitrogen fertilizer use, these cultivated mollusks mitigate some effects of agricultural runoff, becoming plump and healthy in the process.

2 pounds small clams, such as littlenecks

½ cup white wine

¼ cup olive oil

4 garlic cloves, sliced

2 anchovy fillets

1 pound plum tomatoes, chopped

¼ cup roughly chopped fresh flat-leaf parsley

Salt and freshly ground black pepper

3 tablespoons cream (optional)

Submerge the clams in a basin of cold water for 30 minutes to allow them to release any sand; drain. Transfer to a large pot; add the wine. Cover; steam over high heat until all clams are open. Discard any clams that do not open. Set the clams aside; strain the broth.

Heat the oil in a large skillet over medium heat. Add the garlic and anchovies. Cook, stirring with a wooden spoon, until the anchovies have disintegrated, about 5 minutes. Stir in the tomatoes, parsley, and reserved clam broth; simmer 10 minutes. Season to taste with salt and pepper. Add the cream (if using) and clams; cook until heated through, about 5 minutes. Serve with crusty garlic bread.

Crab—Wild (Except Soft-Shell, Which Are Better Farmed)

When I worked in Boston in the 1980s, winters would bring huge tanks of live Maine rock crabs to the fish store in my North End neighborhood at astoundingly low prices (99 cents a pound, as I recall). My fellow cooks at the restaurant came over on Sundays, when the restaurant was closed, and we'd spread newspapers on the floor and crack boiled crabs for dipping in zesty Dijonnaise sauce, washed down with cold beer.

Those Maine rock crabs, discovered by rock-star New York chefs a decade later and rechristened "peeky-toe crabs," were bycatch from the lobster trade. The name came from the pointed (picked) ends of the crabs' walking legs. They were called "picked-toe" crabs, which evolved into "peeky-toe." When the lobstermen found them, they set them aside to give to "pickers" at the docks (often the fishermen's wives), who removed the meat from the shells and sold it by the pound. There's not much meat in a rock crab, so it's a time-consuming task. Whatever they couldn't pick by the end of the day, they'd sell live to fish stores. Hence the under-a-buck-a-pound crab feasts in the North End. Now the crab is highly prized gourmet fodder.

The meat from those crabs is delicious, no doubt, but it pales in comparison to the juicy, succulent meat of the Dungeness crab of California, in my opinion. The texture is the same—a mix of long strands of sweet leg meat and pleasantly fluffy tufts of back meat under the shell—but the Dungeness crabs are plumper and bigger, with much more meat in their legs and backs. We'd crack five rock crabs to get as much meat as one Dungeness holds. We just couldn't afford the expensive imported crabs. In well-managed fisheries, like Alaska's, only male Dungeness crabs may be harvested, ensuring that these polygamous crustaceans remain a viable catch. They are caught in traps, which facilitates the free, live release of any bycatch. These crabs are one of the most ecologically sound seafood choices. They are also among the most delicious. Their juicy, sweet flesh releases easily from the shell, making them an excellent choice for recipes calling for crabmeat. (Dungeness crabs are available from www.seafoodsuperstore.com.)

Now, thanks to its star turn, "peeky-toe" crab is as expensive as its California cousin, but not any meatier than when it was "rock crab." In fact, though the flavor and texture of Maine crab is sweet and delicate, I'd still choose the more voluptuous Dungeness, all things being equal. Both are sustainable fisheries, harvesting few enough crabs to enable the population to rebound each season. But the Maine crab fishery isn't managed at this point, while the California fishery is, and it's managed well. When concerns began to arise about the harvests, catch limits were enacted, and the fishery's future was protected. The Maine crabs will probably become scarce before they're brought under responsible management. So now, when I lust for crabmeat, I look first for live Dungeness crabs.

Despite being held in high regard by many chefs and food enthusiasts, blue crab was never my favorite. It can taste sweet and rich, but seldom as clean and juicy as cold-water crabs like Dungeness and king crabs. When I've bought blue crabs live, they've usually been held in baskets, not in tanks. Maybe it's because they can live out of water for much longer than other crabs, but blue crabs have had the highest incidence of sand and mud in the gills of any kind of crab I've bought. I attribute that mostly to the fact that they don't have time in clean water to shed that sand. Their flavor, while rich and sweet, can be cloying. They weren't hard to give up when I discovered that environmental factors like habitat loss and pollution had decimated populations along the East Coast.

Unlike American snow crabs, Canadian snow crabs are harvested in a sustainable way, protecting female and undersized crabs. The meat of these crabs is not the most desirable, since it's almost always sold frozen, out of the shell. This crabmeat is best in warm stuffings or steamed dishes. Snow crab is one of the most affordable crab options (available from www.simplyseafood.com).

For the fun of cracking shells and savoring mouthfuls of scrumptious crabmeat, few crustacean treats compare with American stone crab claws, harvested from Florida waters. This quirky fishery relies on the ability of these hard-shelled crabs to regenerate their front pincers astoundingly fast. They're caught in traps, brought to the surface, and clipped of their larger claw. Then they're released back to the sea, where they go on with life, and regenerate the claw. Stone crabs produce so many eggs, and become sexually mature so quickly, that the future of the species continues to look bright, even as these crustaceans provide 2 million pounds of crab claws annually, worth an estimated $4 million. Stone crab claws are available from www.freshfloridastonecrab.com and www.beststonecrabs.com.

Slow reproductive patterns and susceptibility to weather effects may be why king crab populations rebound slowly, and decline from time to time in the Bering

Strait and Arctic regions where king crab is fished. Canadian snow crabs are caught in a sensible way, filtering out breeding females. Blue crabs, popular in the eastern United States, are quick to reproduce, but suffer from loss of habitat and pollution in their Chesapeake Bay and Gulf of Mexico estuaries. The best crab choice is Dungeness crab, a succulent and plentiful Pacific species.

Snow Crab–stuffed Cremini Mushrooms

SERVES 4 AS AN APPETIZER Snow crabs are fished from moderately well managed Canadian fisheries, and are a more sustainable choice than blue crab. Their meat is usually sold frozen, and should be thawed slowly in the refrigerator to protect its natural texture and prevent water loss.

16 cremini mushrooms (about 8 ounces)

½ pound (about 1 cup) snow crab or Jonah crab meat

1 tablespoon chopped fresh chives

¼ cup Aioli (page 271)

2 tablespoons fresh white bread crumbs or panko

Salt and freshly ground black pepper

1 teaspoon unsalted butter, melted

Heat the oven to 400°F. Brush the mushrooms clean and remove the stems. Combine the crabmeat, chives, aioli, and half the bread crumbs. Season to taste with salt and pepper.

Spoon the crab filling into the mushroom caps. Combine the remaining bread crumbs with the melted butter and sprinkle on top. Arrange in a baking dish; bake until the mushrooms soften and begin to release some juices, about 10 minutes. Serve immediately.

Stone Crab Claws with Remoulade Sauce

SERVES 4 AS A MAIN COURSE In a remarkable example of sustainable fishing, stone crabs are caught, clipped of one claw, and released to regrow the claw. This practice has been going on in southeastern U.S. waters for decades, with no apparent harm to the crabs. The meat is sweet and flaky. The claws are sold over the Web, usually cooked, either frozen or fresh. Sources include www.beststonecrabs.com and www.freshfloridastonecrab.com.

1 cup mayonnaise (preferably homemade, page 271)

1 large hard-boiled egg, finely chopped

1 small shallot, finely chopped

1 tablespoon capers, chopped

1 anchovy fillet, chopped until it becomes a paste

1 tablespoon chopped cornichons or dill pickle

1 teaspoon lemon juice

1 teaspoon chopped fresh flat-leaf parsley

Dash of hot pepper sauce or cayenne

Salt and freshly ground black pepper

3 pounds cracked stone crab claws

Lemon wedges

Combine the mayonnaise with the egg, shallot, capers, anchovy paste, cornichons, lemon juice, parsley, and hot sauce. Taste, season with salt and pepper, and refrigerate.

Bring a large pot of salted water (about 6 quarts) to a boil. Add the crab claws, bring back to the boil, and cook about 7 minutes (if using precooked claws, boil only 3 minutes to reheat). Drain. Chill the claws in salted ice water. Serve the claws with hammers or nutcrackers, lemon wedges, and individual bowls of remoulade for dipping.

Dungeness Crab Salad with Artichoke, Avocado, and Red Bell Pepper Dressing

SERVES 4 AS A MAIN COURSE Seafood and avocado go so well together that they seem to elevate each other, as the right wine lifts good dishes to greatness. Dungeness crabmeat, from a well-managed American fishery, is a recommended choice from Blue Ocean Institute, Environmental Defense, and other oceanic environmental advocacy groups. It is available from www.cityfish.com or www.f2m.com.

1 pound (about 2 cups) Dungeness or other crabmeat

1 shallot, finely minced

¼ cup homemade Mayonnaise (page 271)

½ cup artichoke hearts (about 6), packed in olive oil, drained, and cut into small pieces

1 tablespoon chopped fresh chives

Pinch of Old Bay seasoning

Salt and freshly ground black pepper

1 red bell pepper, seeded and roughly chopped

1 garlic clove, sliced

1 tablespoon white wine vinegar

2 tablespoons olive oil

2 ripe Hass avocados

Kosher salt

Lemon wedges

Make the crab salad: Combine the crabmeat, shallot, mayonnaise, artichokes, chives, and Old Bay; mix gently and season to taste with salt and pepper.

Make the dressing: Combine the chopped pepper, garlic, and enough water to barely cover them in a small saucepan. Simmer until the pepper is soft, about 10 minutes. Reserve the liquid; puree the pepper in a blender, adding the vinegar and olive oil once the mixture is smooth. Season to taste; adjust consistency with the reserved cooking liquid. Halve the avocados and remove the pits. Season the avocados with kosher salt. Use a spoon or ice cream scoop to mound the crab salad onto the halved avocados. Drizzle with dressing. Serve with lemon wedges.

Dungeness Crabs Dijonnaise

SERVES 4 My cook friends and I used to boil Maine rock crabs this way, long before they were "discovered" by celebrity chefs and dubbed "peeky-toe" crabs. Dungeness crabs, which come from a well-managed Pacific fishery, taste virtually the same, but have much more meat. My favorite way to serve them is to drain them, and spread out newspapers on the table or floor. Then I just go at them with mallets or nutcrackers. One crab may take an hour to pick clean, and the last morsel is as delicious as the first.

2 tablespoons Dijon mustard

1 large egg yolk

Juice of 1 lemon

1 cup peanut or other light oil

10 black peppercorns, cracked (about ¼ teaspoon)

Salt

4 large Dungeness crabs (about 2 pounds each)

Make the dressing: In a mixing bowl, combine the mustard, egg yolk, a few drops of water (about 1 teaspoon), and half of the lemon juice. Whisk in the oil gradually, using a large, fine wire whisk. You may have to add a few more drops of water or lemon juice to the mixture if it gets too stiff. It should have a creamy, saucy consistency. Season the dressing with the cracked pepper and salt and additional lemon juice to taste. This dressing can also be made in a food processor by combining the mustard, egg yolk, water, and lemon in the bowl and drizzling in the oil with the motor running.

Cook the crabs: Bring a large stockpot of water (at least a gallon) to a rolling boil. The pot should be big enough to hold all of the crabs. Add salt until the water has the taste of seawater. Add the crabs, bring back to the boil, and cook for 5 minutes at a rolling boil. Transfer the crabs to plates.

Serve each guest a whole crab, with lobster crackers or shears and individual dipping cups of Dijon dressing.

Crawfish—Farmed

Looking for all the world like miniature lobsters, crawfish are as cute as any crustacean can be. Maybe their charm is undermined by the local moniker used for them in Louisiana, "mud bugs." True, they live in muddy paddies and wetlands. But their meaty tails are as white and clean as any Gulf shrimp or Jonah crab. They also contain bits of luscious fat, which makes the best medium for cooking the vegetables and aromatics in crawfish dishes.

The aroma and tactile pleasure of a boiled crawfish dinner is unforgettable. Whether you dip the tails in lemony drawn butter, vinaigrette, mustardy dressing, or some other concoction, you'll be bowled over by the juiciness and savory flavor of the crawfish themselves. Like cracking crabs, enjoying a crawfish boil is a labor of love, since each morsel must be carefully extracted from its brittle shell. But eating should be about flavor as much as satiety, and so crawfish boils shall remain a fine culinary tradition among lovers of hands-on cuisine.

For everyone else, cans or frozen boxes of crawfish meat can make quick work of a crawfish bisque or stew (étouffée) recipe. Frozen crawfish retain the tender mouth feel of fresh only if cooked very lightly, but the flavor is always unique and bold.

Not only is crawfish farming mostly environmentally benign, but it's also led to an expansion of wetland habitat for wading birds. Crawfish are raised in shallow ponds, usually in conjunction with rice-farming areas. From midfall through spring, crawfish are raised and harvested. In summer months, farmers plant rice in those same ponds, with much less water. The crawfish live off crop residue and also eat small animals like insects that feed on the crop residue. Egrets, herons, ibis, and spoonbills are among the threatened wading birds that have been making a comeback as a result of the crawfish farms' habitats and feeding opportunities. Crawfish are available from www.cajungrocer.com or www.klcrawfishfarms.com, but be warned: There are sizable minimum orders from these dealers. Crawfish are also often found in supermarket frozen food sections, virtually all farmed, and all domestic.

Crawfish Boil

SERVES 8 This is a pile-on-the-table feast—a sort of Southern-style clambake. Have plenty of napkins on hand, and wear old clothes—it's good and messy.

Andouille is available from www.diamondorganics.com or from Whole Foods Markets. You can order live crawfish from www.cajungrocer.com or from www.klcrawfishfarms.com.

3 tablespoons crawfish boil or crab boil spice mixture or a cheesecloth sachet containing 4 tablespoons yellow mustard seeds, 3 tablespoons coriander seeds, 2 tablespoons whole allspice, 2 tablespoons dill seeds, 1 teaspoon whole cloves, 1 tablespoon crushed red pepper, and 8 bay leaves

2 pounds boiling potatoes, cut in half

1 pound white mushrooms, cleaned

1 pound andouille sausage (optional)

5 pounds live crawfish

4 ears corn, cut in half

2 lemons, cut in half

Place the crawfish boil spices in a gallon of salted water in a large stockpot or lobster pot (the water should be as salty as tears). Cover and bring to a boil. Add the potatoes; boil 5 minutes. Add the mushrooms and andouille (if using); boil 5 minutes more.

When the potatoes are almost tender, add the crawfish, corn, and lemons. Bring back to a boil; cook 3 or 4 minutes, until crawfish are just heated through. Drain. Line a table with newspaper and serve the crawfish boil directly on the paper. Everything in the pot is edible, so feast on mushrooms, sausage, corn, and potatoes between bites of succulent "mud bugs."

Crawfish Étouffée

SERVES 6 AS A MAIN COURSE This is one of the classic dishes of old New Orleans, served in the grand dining palaces like Commander's, Antoine's, Arnaud's, and Brennan's. Originally, it was made with wild crawfish, which were abundant in the bayou. But Louisiana rice farmers hit on an ingenious idea when they introduced crawfish to their rice paddies in the off season. The crawfish eat pests and residue from the previous year's crop and provide an additional source of income for the farm. Added benefit: Farm-raised crawfish are sweeter and less muddy than wild ones. This dish is best served over steaming plates of rice.

Crawfish tails are available from www.cajungrocer.com, but check local sources first. If you plan to buy online, go in with a friend—the minimum order and shipping can be sizable, and their packaging is somewhat excessive.

4 tablespoons (½ stick) unsalted butter

2 medium onions, roughly chopped (about 4 cups)

1 green bell pepper, roughly chopped

2 garlic cloves, finely chopped

2 tablespoons all-purpose flour

2 tablespoons crawfish fat (the yellow fat found in the crawfish heads) or margarine

1 teaspoon salt

¼ teaspoon cayenne

1 tablespoon tomato paste

1 pound cleaned crawfish tails

Juice of ½ lemon

Salt and freshly ground black pepper

1 scallion, chopped

Melt the butter in a large skillet. Add the onions, pepper, and garlic. Cook over medium heat until the vegetables are soft and juicy, about 10 minutes.

Sprinkle in the flour; cook undisturbed 30 seconds. Scrape the bottom of the pan with a wooden spoon, and cook 30 seconds more. Repeat for 3 minutes, until the roux is medium-brown. Add the crawfish fat, salt, cayenne, and tomato paste. Cook, stirring with a wooden spoon, 5 minutes. Gradually add 1 cup water. The mixture should be thick and saucy. Cover; simmer gently 20 minutes, stirring occasionally.

Stir in the crawfish tails. Cook just until the crawfish tails are warmed through, a minute or two. Season with lemon juice, salt, and pepper. Adjust the consistency with water—it should be thick and stewlike. Stir in the scallion and serve over rice.

Flounder/Sole—Wild

Once grossly overfished, summer flounder has benefited from aggressive fishery management in the Atlantic, and its numbers have come back. It's no longer considered overfished, though its status varies from year to year. That said, the trawls, pound nets, and gill nets used in harvesting summer flounder catch a great many incidental species, and are disruptive to the sea floor. The species is coming back after a long decline, but it should be taken sparingly. Pacific flounder, a sole, is a better choice than Atlantic.

Halibut—Pacific Wild

Some cooks are said to "kill the animal twice": once when the fish or meat they're using is slaughtered, and again when it's cooked. No fish is a greater victim of gross culinary negligence than the noble halibut. Since the Atlantic species of this hefty flatfish has been decimated by overfishing and habitat destruction, only the Pacific species, from well-managed fisheries off Alaska and Canada, remains to suffer this indignity. Word to the wise: Undercook this fish.

Pacific halibut is lean, and its snowy white flesh holds its juices very tenuously. Cook it just a little too far, and it turns chokingly dry. The best way I've ever had halibut prepared was poached in goose fat. The unctuous medium locked in and reinforced the satiny juiciness of the savory halibut. It reminded me of an aphorism from chef Jasper White: "The fish lived for a reason."

Halibut takes well to poaching, roasting, sautéing, and frying. Grilling masks its delicate, delicious flavor. If you want grilled fish, you might as well grill a sustainably farm-raised fish like tilapia that has a natural tendency to retain juices. Leave the halibut for the rest of us.

Less is more in garnishing and saucing halibut. I cringe when I see curried halibut or some other artifice. At Le Bernardin, a temple to fish perfection in midtown Manhattan, we poached the fish in a scallop-flavored court bouillon (flavored cooking stock), patted it dry, and drizzled it with a simple vinaigrette with a handful of tender chopped herbs. That was the whole dish. The fish's flavor spoke for itself.

One of the best-managed fisheries is shared by the United States and Canada for Pacific halibut (a.k.a. Alaskan halibut). These flatfish, related to flounders but much larger, are mostly caught for U.S. markets with bottom longlines off Alaska.

Responsible practices, such as bird-scaring devices that ward off seabirds like albatrosses and petrels, have minimized what was once a bycatch problem. Fishers own shares of the total annual catch, so they're less likely to fish competitively. These halibut should not be confused with Atlantic halibut, which are a depleted fishery. Find out where to find guaranteed sustainable Alaskan/Pacific halibut at www.ecofish.com.

Braised Halibut with Leeks and Chanterelles

SERVES 4 In fall, when chanterelle mushrooms are in season, their buttery, woodsy flavor and delicate texture match harmoniously with tender, mild Pacific halibut. Make sure to ask your fish dealer where the halibut comes from. If it's from the Atlantic, don't buy it. The species is near collapse, and he shouldn't even be selling it. If he says he doesn't know where it's from, choose another delicate white fish, such as hake or striped bass.

2 tablespoons unsalted butter

1 bunch leeks, white portion only, washed well and julienned

½ pound chanterelles or oyster mushrooms, cut into thick slices

Salt

¼ cup dry white wine or sherry

1 pound Alaskan or Pacific halibut, cut into 4 portions

Freshly ground white pepper

2 cups fish fumet or chicken stock (no salt)

8 slices French bread, toasted and rubbed with a whole garlic clove

In a 12-inch skillet or large Dutch oven with a tight-fitting lid, melt the butter. Add the leeks and chanterelles; sprinkle with a little salt. Cook until the leeks are translucent, about 5 minutes. Add the wine; simmer 3 minutes.

Season the halibut with salt and white pepper. Nestle the portions in with the vegetables, and add the fumet. Bring to a simmer. Lower to a very slow simmer; cover. Cook until the fish is rare, no more than 4 minutes. Remove the pan from the heat and let stand 5 minutes. Serve in shallow soup plates with broth and garlic toasts.

Herring, Sardines, and Smelts—Wild Kiosks in

northern European cities like Hamburg and Amsterdam sell briny, savory plates of herring with onions and beets. They also sell intense, salt-cured herring called *Matjes*. For deep fish flavor, nothing surpasses the taste of these plentiful small fish.

Abundant omega-3 fats in herring imbue them with not only luxurious, rich flavor but also health-sustaining nutrients. The bold flavor of dark-fleshed fish like herring, sardines, and anchovies is furnished by oils that have a health benefit. They draw dangerous free radicals from our bloodstream and strengthen heart function. Most of the great herring preparations are poached and pickled, keeping them exceptionally healthy, although my favorite herring dish is pickled herring in cream sauce. The silky soft texture that the skin attains through good pickling is accentuated by the smoothness of the sour cream that's added to the sauce. Finally, a refreshing crunch of paper-thin sliced onions brings a three-dimensional appeal to the sweet, slightly spicy personality of the dish. Keep some crusty dark bread around for sopping up extra juices on the plate.

Sardines are actually a number of species of smaller, herring-related fish from around the globe. Named for the island of Sardinia, where they were a major catch, fresh sardines now come mostly from Spain, Southern California, and Mexico. The fisheries in these places are well managed and well monitored, unlike the African waters, where some species have been overfished. The fish from Southern California are abundant and delicious. When you see those fresh sardines in the market, buy them. They're easy and practically foolproof to cook.

Plentiful and fast-reproducing, these delicious, healthy herring cousins swarm in gigantic schools. They represent a sustainable fishery, endorsed by the Monterey Bay Aquarium and the Oceans Alive campaign of Environmental Defense (contact them at www.oceansalive.org). Sardines populate both the Atlantic and Pacific oceans, and are considered an excellent ecological choice.

People are sometimes intimidated by small fish because of the bones. They either think filleting is a big deal, or that every bite will mean mouthfuls of inedible bones. In fact, filleting is easy, if a bit laborious, and most of the very fine bones become imperceptible after cooking. Smelts and other tiny "whitebait" fish (a New England term denoting little fish of many species that swim together) are routinely eaten whole, bones and all. Canned sardines are seldom filleted, and the bones in them are so soft they act more as a texture element than an obstacle to enjoying the fish (they're also a great source of calcium). To fillet sardines, one need only slide a sharp knife along the backbone from head to tail, flip the fish, and repeat on the other side. The hairlike pin-bones in the fillet, as I mentioned earlier, won't even be noticed once the fish is cooked (though you do have to remove them if you serve the fish raw, as in sashimi).

Smelts' delicate flavor and tender texture make them a perfect centerpiece for *fritto misto*, a mixture of lightly fried savories popular in Italian coastal towns. The bones of these tiny fish are soft, so the fish can be eaten whole. Fritto misto usually includes a variety of seafood, depending on what's most abundant; a balance of fried vegetables like zucchini, potatoes, or root vegetables; and a tart, creamy dipping sauce, like aioli, remoulade, or tartar sauce. In keeping with the goal of consuming fewer animals and more vegetables, fritto misto is easy to adapt to an all-vegetarian, or mostly vegetarian, mixture. Once you've mastered this dish, you can adapt it to whatever ingredients are abundant.

The largest fishing association in the North Sea herring fishery has entered the assessment program of the Marine Stewardship Council, a nonprofit setting standards for sustainable fisheries. Currently plentiful and breeding rapidly, herring are an excellent ecofriendly fish choice. Smelts swim near Pacific Northwest beaches during spawning times, making them easy to catch with dip nets. This method results in little if any bycatch. These delicious little fish, which grow only to about three inches, are not threatened with overfishing, partly because consumer demand is low.

Herring roe, a delicious, crunchy product, is safely, sustainably harvested from captured herring. The herring eggs settle into layers on sheets of tender kelp, making an exceptional appetizer food marketed as Komochi Kombu (literally, "spawn on kelp"). It's mostly produced in British Columbia, and can be researched at www.bcspawnonkelp.com. The herring are released back to the wild after spawning, and they return a year later to produce again. The crunchy, briny eggs adhere in a thick coating onto the kelp. The spawn-on-kelp fishery is practiced by native tribes along the British Columbia coast, as it has been for over a century. By contrast, commercial fishing operations harvesting just the roe kill the herring to get it. The sustainable spawn-on-kelp product can be sliced for sushi, or marinated and served on its own. It's available in Japanese specialty stores or from www.buygourmetfoods.com/k/kelp/Miyako-Pickled-Herring-Roe-With-Kelp-B00023NHBE.htm.

Marinated Pan-fried Sardines

SERVES 6 AS AN APPETIZER My favorite way to prepare sardines is to coat them in cornmeal, fry them in olive oil, and then marinate them with onions, white wine vinegar, raisins, and even more olive oil. They're exceptional paired with spicy greens like arugula, beet greens, or watercress.

2 large onions, sliced

1 cup extra virgin olive oil, plus more as needed

2 tablespoons capers

¼ cup raisins, soaked in hot water for 15 minutes and drained

2 tablespoons white wine vinegar

24 sardine fillets

Salt and freshly ground black pepper

1 cup fine yellow cornmeal

Sauté the onions in 2 tablespoons of the olive oil until very soft, about 10 minutes. Combine with the capers and raisins. Stir in the vinegar. Set aside.

Heat the remaining olive oil in a large skillet to about 340°F. Season the sardine fillets with salt and pepper. Dredge them in the cornmeal and pan-fry over medium-high heat, turning once; cool. Place a single layer of the onion marinade in a nonreactive casserole or other container that allows the sardines to lie flat. Alternate layers of fried sardines and marinade until all sardines are used. Add enough olive oil to the casserole to submerge the sardines (how much depends on the shape of the dish).

Serve the sardines over dark salad greens, such as beet or arugula, dressed with marinade ingredients. This keeps for up to a week in the refrigerator.

Labskaus (Herring with Beet Hash)

SERVES 4 Over the course of a summer I spent in Germany, I had the good fortune to taste herring dishes of all sorts. Among my favorites was a typical dish of Hamburg and the North Sea coastal regions that featured a sort of red flannel hash topped with rollmops (pickled herring rolls) and fried eggs. Since the hash relied too heavily on corned beef (which I have not found in grass-fed, humanely raised, or organic form), I asked Hinnerk von Bargen, a chef-instructor at the Culinary Institute of America and a native of Hamburg, to develop a less meat-dependent version. Here's the delicious dish he showed me.

3 medium beets (about 1 pound)

1½ tablespoons red wine vinegar

Salt and freshly ground black pepper

¼ teaspoon sugar

1 pound thin-skinned white potatoes, peeled

8 tablespoons unsalted butter, plus more as needed

2 medium onions, finely minced

5 salt-cured *Matjes* herring fillets, finely minced

4 large eggs

4 pickled herring fillets (not sweet), drained

Bring a pot of water to a boil. Trim the leaves and roots of the beets down to 1 inch. Simmer in water to cover until tender, about 45 minutes, then remove from the cooking liquid. When cool enough to touch, peel them. Chop three-quarters of the beets coarsely in a food processor. Slice the remaining beets and toss with the vinegar; season with salt, pepper, and the sugar. Set aside.

While the beets are cooking, bring a second pot of salted water to a boil. Cut the potatoes into chunks, simmer until very tender, and mash them; season with salt, pepper, and butter to taste. Combine with the chopped beets. Melt 4 tablespoons butter in a skillet. Gently cook the onions until very soft, about 10 minutes, and add to the potato-beet mixture. Add the minced herring and adjust seasoning as necessary. Return the hash to the pan and gently warm it.

Melt another 4 tablespoons butter in a skillet. Fry the eggs just until the whites are set. Spoon the hash onto serving plates. Serve topped with pickled herring fillets and fried eggs, garnished with the reserved beet slices.

Fritto Misto with Wild Smelts, Farm-raised Catfish, and Zucchini

SERVES 4 Around Naples, it's customary to fry whatever tiny baby fish (whitebait) come up in the net, along with assorted vegetables. The fish are completely edible, tender bones and all. Dipping bowls of garlicky aioli, other sauces like a simple tomato sauce or puttanesca, and lemon wedges accompany the "fried mix." While many of the small fish scooped from the Mediterranean are now threatened, the delicious little smelts taken from Atlantic and Pacific waters are plentiful and sustainable, as they reproduce very quickly. Strips of sustainably raised American catfish fillet fit right into this simple fisherman's dinner. Serve with a large salad.

½ pound small whole smelts

½ pound catfish fillets

½ pound zucchini

2 cups all-purpose flour

1 teaspoon kosher salt

½ teaspoon freshly ground black pepper

1 quart peanut oil for frying

Remoulade Sauce (page 253) or Aioli (page 271)

Lemon wedges

Make tiny incisions in the bellies of the smelts, shake out any viscera, rinse them, and dry with a towel. Cut the catfish into 1-inch-wide strips; pat dry. Cut the zucchini into 3 x ½ x ½-inch sticks. Whisk together the flour, salt, and pepper and put in a shallow dish or pie plate for dredging.

Heat the oil to 360°F in a 2-quart saucepan (the oil should be at least 4 inches deep). Check the temperature with a thermometer, or with a piece of zucchini (it should sizzle when added).

Working in small batches, coat the fish and zucchini with flour, and drop them carefully into the hot oil. Cook until the coating just begins to brown; transfer with a slotted spoon to a colander to drain. Allow the oil to return to 360°F between each batch. Serve with remoulade sauce or aioli and lemon wedges.

Mayonnaise   YIELD: ABOUT 1¾ CUPS

2 large egg yolks

1 tablespoon Dijon mustard

1 tablespoon fresh lemon juice

1½ cups vegetable oil

Salt and freshly ground black pepper

In a food processor, pulse together the egg yolks, 1 teaspoon warm water, the mustard, and lemon juice.

With the blade running, drizzle in the oil in a medium stream. If the mixture becomes too thick before all of the oil has been incorporated, add a drop or two of warm water to loosen the mixture, then continue with the remaining oil. Season with salt and pepper and store, refrigerated, in a covered plastic or noncorrosive metal container.

VARIATION
To make aioli, add 6 garlic cloves, chopped, along with the egg yolks. Season with coarse black pepper.

Lobster

The days when American (Maine) lobster were so abundant that New Englanders could gather them from the shores at low tide are long gone. But strict fishery management is protecting future generations of lobsters by prohibiting the catch of egg-bearing females. I've seen only two egg-bearing females in all the years I've worked in restaurants, and I've seen thousands of lobsters in that time.

Maine lobster (the name used for the American species harvested throughout New England and Canada's east coast) has two front claws, like the now-rare European lobster. The sweet, pure flavor of lobster boiled in seawater (or salted water), served with drawn butter and a squeeze of lemon, is a complete taste experience in itself. Some people don't see the point of doing anything to a lobster other than boiling it. But two points come to my mind in this issue: Lobster reaches even greater heights with the right pairings, and one lobster can bring pleasure to many more people served in other ways.

Maine lobster's opulent flavor and mouth feel make it a luxury dish as much as its price does. It pairs beautifully with rich ingredients like cream and butter, velvety sauces, and other unctuous ingredients like mayonnaise. Sometimes judicious use of an alternative approach, contrasting it with bright, lean accompaniments like fruit purees or tart broths, brings out fruity elements of the lobster's flavor.

My favorite lobster dish is a signature dish of my mentor, Jasper White, who created a pan-roasting technique that brings every iota of flavor in the entire lobster into the dish. It's a combination of sautéing, roasting, poaching, and steaming that unlocks and extracts essences from the shell, infuses them into clear, golden butter, and then uses that medium as a base for a shallot, wine, and brandy-laced sauce that's basted over the split lobster as it steams to medium-rare succulence. Since the whole procedure takes place in one pan—the initial searing of the quartered lobster in clarified butter, the intense flame-roasting of the shell side, the flaming with bourbon or brandy, the steaming in white wine, and the swirling in of whole nuggets of butter with chopped fresh chervil and chives—all of the drippings and natural juices of the lobster become part of the sauce, which blankets the finished dish. In the restaurant, we served the dish with a trio of grilled mushrooms. The recipe is on page 276. I no longer serve a whole lobster as a main course. I've found that the pleasure of the dish reaches its zenith at the halfway point in eating it, and so I serve one lobster for two people, as a first course, or as the crowning course in a multicourse "tasting" dinner.

The debate rages on about sustainability, as landings of Maine lobster rise and fall from year to year. On the one hand, a highly enforced policy of prohibiting the capture of egg-bearing females is widely considered effective in ensuring future stocks. But on the other hand, the decreasing size of the specimens caught indicates that the oldest generations (ones most likely to have already reproduced) are being fished out. On average, catches have risen since the millennium, perhaps partly due to depletion of natural predators. Because they are caught in traps or "pots," there is very little bycatch problem.

A different crustacean, called spiny lobster (also called rock lobster in some places), is not truly a lobster in the taxonomic sense (it's not of the genus *Homarus*). It has no front claws. Nonetheless, it can be used in many dishes where out-of-the-shell lobster meat is called for. Spiny lobsters aren't as sweet and buttery tasting as Maine lobsters, but they have a great flavor of their own. Ecologists are very concerned about the harvesting practices of spiny lobsters in the Caribbean, and beg consumers not to support that irresponsible fishery. Instead, choose spiny lobster from either the Southern California–Baja area or from Australia. The Marine Stewardship Council, an independent nonprofit organization that promotes responsible fishing practices, recently certified the Baja Red Rock Lobster and Western Australia Rock Lobster fisheries as sustainable. Only those rock lobsters sold bearing the MSC logo are certified sustainable.

California spiny lobsters (which can be distinguished from Maine lobsters by their lack of claws) are a relatively stable fishery. Their fishery is managed in a much more responsible way than that of their cousin, the Caribbean spiny lobster. Concerned chefs should choose only spiny/rock lobsters from the United States, Baja California, and Australia. Spiny lobster tail takes particularly well to grilling and broiling. Unlike Maine lobster, it's seldom boiled. Its taste is milder, and it benefits from spice accents like paprika, chiles, tomato, and lime. Seafood salads and stews, where supporting flavors create a bouquet, are great venues for spiny lobster.

Lobster salads can showcase lobster flavor in ways that can stretch a single lobster to serve several guests. As an hors d'oeuvre, miniature lobster salad rolls, made by cutting filled hot dog buns into bite-size pieces, bring mouthfuls of flavor to many guests: Two lobsters can make enough rolls for eight or more people. It's one way of serving a beloved flavor with a minimum of animal sacrifice.

Monterey Bay Aquarium's Seafood Watch, a service that assesses sustainability issues in seafood, advises consumers never to buy spiny lobster tails less than three inches long, as these come from immature lobsters that haven't lived long enough to reproduce.

HUMANE CONSIDERATIONS The first thing I acknowledge when people ask if cooking live lobsters is humane is that all eating of animals involves inflicting suffering. That's as true of the predation suffered by animals in the wild as it is of any slaughter method employed by man, no matter how careful. Lobsters that have been dead for any length of time before cooking deteriorate into an inedible mush. Most humans today never witness the slaughter of the animals they eat. So when they come upon one of the few cases where the animal must be killed just before cooking people sometimes consider the procedure cruel and inhumane. This is one of the many reasons some people choose to become vegetarians. But the life and death of most animals in our food system are far crueler than that of a lobster. Lobsters, more closely related to spiders than to mammals, lack a central nervous system. Sensation of danger is real for most animals, but sensation of pain is a different matter.

Consider the experiences a lobster goes through in its life. In fights with other lobsters, a lobster is likely to lose a claw or a leg many times in its life. New limbs grow back in their place. Now consider how a human would experience the wrenching off of an arm or a leg without anesthesia. Not only would the pain render the person unconscious, but without immediate medical treatment, such an injury would surely be fatal. We experience stimuli in much different ways. Livestock, which are much closer to us on the evolutionary scale, are more likely to suffer pain, even from minor injuries, than are lobsters. Experiencing fear is another matter, though.

Lobsters' eyes are little more than ornaments, as they navigate their world primarily by smell. But their awareness of heat is evident in their increased rate of activity as their environment becomes warmer. Their natural environment is barely above freezing, so keep them refrigerated until the last possible moment. Put them in the freezer for ten minutes before cooking them to lull them gently to sleep. They will struggle less, and will be mostly unaware of being handled.

David Foster Wallace contributed a well-written critique of the Maine Lobster Festival for *Gourmet* magazine in August 2004. Its main thrust was that the suffering of lobsters when they're boiled alive is undeniable. I agree. Whether that suffering exceeds the suffering of any other creature killed for food is a point he debates with himself in the piece. Our responsibility as human beings is to minimize the suffering we cause to any creature we eat, so if you choose to eat meat and fish, do so with the animals' experience in mind. Buy lobsters only the day you will cook them (so they spend as little time out of water as possible), chill them to near-freezing temperatures before killing them (so that they are sleepy, and barely conscious of being handled), and cook them quickly.

Pan-roasted Lobster with Chive-Butter Sauce and Broiled Mushrooms

SERVES 4 AS A FIRST COURSE, 2 AS A MAIN COURSE This dish, a variation on a signature dish of Boston chef Jasper White, has become central to the repertoire of every chef who's worked in White's kitchen. It extracts every iota of flavor from the lobster, drawing essential oils from the shell and briny drippings from the body into a sensuous, herb-laced butter sauce that's spooned over the tender, open-shelled lobster. It's such an opulent dish, and so easy to divide, I often serve half-lobsters as a first course for four guests, so that two lobsters bring pleasure to twice as many guests.

6 large shiitake mushrooms, stems removed

1 teaspoon olive oil

Salt

2 large lobsters (1½ to 2 pounds apiece)

2 tablespoons Clarified Butter (page 223) or peanut oil

¼ cup cognac or bourbon

¼ cup white wine

2 tablespoons chopped shallots

4 tablespoons (½ stick) unsalted butter

2 teaspoons chopped fresh chives

1 teaspoon chopped fresh tarragon or flat-leaf parsley

Heat the broiler as hot as possible. Toss the mushrooms with olive oil and a pinch of salt; transfer to a shallow pan. Broil until darkly browned, turning once. Set aside in a warm place. Leave the broiler on for the lobster.

Bring a large pot (5 quarts) of salted water to a boil. Twist off the claws and arms of the lobsters and boil them for 3 minutes. Remove the meat from the claws and arms, using either poultry shears or a nutcracker. Set the meat aside. Chop off the forward 2 inches of the lobster (the head) and discard. Shake out any viscera, including tomalley and roe, and discard. Halve the lobster body lengthwise, with a long chef's knife or cleaver, by cutting first through the tail, and then through the upper body. Remove the dark intestinal tract from the tail. Halve the pieces crosswise, so that each lobster is quartered.

Heat the clarified butter in a large ovenproof skillet until very hot. Place the lobster bodies, shell side down, in the pan. Sear 2 minutes. Turn the pieces over, using tongs, and place the pan under the broiler. Cook 2 minutes, until parts of the shell begin to blacken. Bring the pan back to the stove, carefully add the cognac (away from the flame), and ignite it. Put the pan back over high heat.

Once the flames have subsided, add the reserved claw and arm meat, wine, and shallots. Cook until the alcohol is absorbed, and the mixture is only slightly moist. Remove the pan from the heat and add the butter, chives, and tarragon. Swirl the pan as the butter melts to create an emulsified sauce. If the pan is too hot, the butter will separate, so keep agitating the pan until the sauce is smooth.

Reassemble the lobsters on serving plates, in an order that resembles the natural lobster shape, spooning the claw and arm meat into the cavity in the upper body. Serve with the roasted mushrooms.

Fingerling Potatoes and Baby Squash with Spiny Lobster

SERVES 4 In Australia, spiny lobsters (known there as rock lobsters) are harvested in one of the best-managed crustacean fisheries in the world. The Western Australia fishery has earned the seal of approval from the Marine Stewardship Council, a non-profit organization devoted to protecting the seas from irresponsible fishing practices. Unlike American (Maine) lobster, spiny lobster has no claws. It's usually sold frozen or thawed. Spiny lobsters are also harvested from Baja, California, and are also MSC-certified Caribbean. Caribbean lobster fisheries are not at all well managed, and lobsters from there should be avoided.

1 large spiny lobster or 1 pound lobster tails, thawed

1 pound French fingerling or other waxy potatoes, cut into 1-inch chunks

2 tablespoons extra virgin olive oil

3 garlic cloves, halved

½ teaspoon turmeric

¼ teaspoon cayenne

1 pound tender baby squashes, such as baby zucchini, yellow squash, and patty pan, cut into bite-size pieces

2 tablespoons chopped fresh chervil or flat-leaf parsley

Juice of ½ lemon

Sea salt or kosher salt

Bring a large pot of salted water to a boil (it should be as salty as seawater). Add the lobster; cook about 4 minutes per pound (slightly underdone). Remove from the pot, cool, and remove the shell. Once cool, cut the meat into bite-size nuggets.

Add the potatoes to the lobster cooking water; boil until tender, about 10 minutes. Transfer the potatoes to a bowl; drizzle with a few drops of olive oil.

Combine the olive oil, garlic, turmeric, and cayenne in a medium saucepan over low heat; cook until the garlic becomes soft and begins to sizzle. Add the baby squashes; cook 4 minutes, until crisp-tender. Add the lobster meat just to heat through. Toss the warm lobster mixture with the potatoes, chervil, lemon juice, and salt to taste.

Mackerel—Wild

Both dark-fleshed Atlantic mackerel and its light-fleshed cousin, Spanish mackerel (also harvested in U.S. waters, despite its name), are fish lovers' fishes. Bristling with lush oceanic savoriness, they have a delectable combination of star-quality flavor and meltingly tender texture thanks to their abundant fish oils. Atlantic mackerel is more assertive, prized by Japanese sushi chefs for its distinctive personality. Spanish mackerel's milder flavor makes it a good "introductory mackerel" for uninitiated tasters of this abundant species.

Like bluefish, mackerel needs to be uncompromisingly fresh to exhibit its stellar qualities. While you'll have a few days' leeway with white-fleshed fishes and large tunas, oily, dark-fleshed fishes lose their fresh taste extremely quickly, and can take on a strong "fishy" taste. When people say they don't like this fish, it's probably because they've experienced second-day mackerel. When fresh, its meat, though darker than cod or tilapia, isn't dark gray. It's off-white. Its color deepens as it sits.

Match power with power. Intense soy-based marinades, zesty tomato sauces, and complex Mexican moles pair beautifully with mackerel. Light, delicate butter sauces that would work perfectly with milder fish disappear on the palate next to this bold taste. Once you've tasted my favorite way to cook fresh mackerel—with a sweet-salty miso and sesame marinade—you'll become a believer, too. Mackerel is one of the few fish I feel benefits from grilling. Its bold flavor is the perfect foil for the smoky taste imparted by the grill. It also stands up to zesty barbecue sauce marinades and bastes.

Mackerel fillet easily. Their skin, cleaned of scales, is deliciously edible, and adds another silky texture to this tender fish. Many recipes call for wrapping the whole fish or fillet in foil before cooking. What they don't tell you is that this fish's skin is very delicate, and tears easily. You should grease the foil before wrapping it around skin-on mackerel. A better choice, both culinarily and environmentally, is simply to cook mackerel in a covered casserole or roaster.

When grilling mackerel, make sure the grill is seasoned to nonstick perfection, and brush the fish with oil before it goes on. Or, to ensure faultless mackerel grilling, use a specially designed grill basket for fish, which allows you to cook the fish over the grill, without it actually touching the grill itself. Since mackerel are small, usually only a pound apiece, watch carefully to avoid overcooking. Properly cooked mackerel is highly juicy. It has two kinds of meat, a lighter colored meat on the bones, and a darker, redder meat near the skin. Both are excellent to eat.

Two Atlantic species, King mackerel and Spanish mackerel, mature quickly and reproduce prolifically. Stocks are considered abundant in both species. They are a recommended choice by Environmental Defense, Monterey Bay Aquarium, and Blue Ocean Institute. King mackerel caught in the Gulf of Mexico, however, are recovering from a long period of overfishing, and are a significant bycatch of the shrimp industry there. Gulf mackerel should be avoided.

Miso-marinated Mackerel Baked in a Pouch

SERVES 4 Marinating fish in miso paste is an ancient Japanese tradition that capitalizes on both the complex flavor and preservative properties of the salty fermented soybean paste. I've found that the marinade works especially well on big-flavored, rich fish like mackerel, bluefish, and kingfish. It also works extremely well with black Alaskan cod (sablefish), a rich white-fleshed fish. This dish is an excellent accompaniment to Sesame Rice (page 60) or any Japanese short-grain rice, such as *koshi-hikari*.

½ cup white miso paste

1 tablespoon Asian toasted sesame oil

1 teaspoon sugar

2 tablespoons tamari or light soy sauce

1 tablespoon rice vinegar

4 small Atlantic or Spanish mackerel (about ½ pound apiece), gutted, scaled, heads removed

Whisk together the miso, sesame oil, sugar, tamari, and vinegar. Coat the fish with this mixture, inside and out. Wrap the fish individually in greased aluminum foil (or, alternatively, place in a baking dish with a tight-fitting cover) to seal in juices and keep it moist. Marinate, refrigerated, overnight (or for at least 4 hours).

Heat the oven to 350°F. Place the foil packets or dish on a baking sheet to catch any drips. Roast until the fish is fully cooked, about 25 minutes. Transfer to a board to allow the fish to rest for 5 minutes before serving.

Baked Mackerel Rillettes

SERVES 12 AS AN HORS D'OEUVRE Rillettes are rich spreads made by folding cooked meat or fish together with its own fat. Fish and seafood rillettes attain the same pâtélike consistency as the famed pork rillettes. They're served with accompaniments like crackers or toast points, and are intended to amuse the palate and take the edge off hunger prior to a dinner. Chef Jasper White combined fresh and smoked versions of the same fish, such as salmon, bluefish, or cod, to make exquisite rillettes. I found that the complex taste of miso-roasted fish also brought depth to the preparation.

1 recipe Miso-marinated Mackerel (preceding recipe) or other cooked mackerel

1 teaspoon Old Bay seasoning

Pinch of salt

Juice of ½ lemon

1 shallot, finely chopped

4 black peppercorns, cracked (or a pinch of coarse black pepper)

½ cup sour cream or softened butter

¼ cup mayonnaise

Prepare the mackerel as directed; chill. Peel off the skin. Starting from the cavity, pry the fillets from the backbone; discard the bone. Using tweezers or fingertips, carefully remove all small bones. It's okay to break up the fillets, since the fish will be broken up to make the rillettes. If desired, trim off the dark-colored meat along the outside of the fillets (this is fine to eat, but less attractive).

Place the boneless fillets in a mixing bowl; season with Old Bay, salt, and lemon. Add the shallot, cracked peppercorns, sour cream, and mayonnaise. Mix well with a fork, breaking up any large pieces. Taste for seasoning. Pack the mixture into a ramekin or small crock. Serve with toast points or crusty bread, cornichons, and Dijon mustard.

Mahi-mahi—Wild Atlantic

"It's not Flipper! It's not Flipper!" Geh Yah Yin, my chef-instructor in Cuisines of Asia at the Culinary Institute of America, was practically shouting at us, in reaction to a common misconception, voiced by one of us, that mahi-mahi was dolphin meat. Nuance wasn't Chef Yin's gift, so he neglected to note that "mahi," as it's called in the professional kitchen, is marketed under the name "dolphin fish" because they swim with dolphins, probably to chase the same prey. Some people say they look like dolphins too. I don't see it.

Juicy and meaty in taste, mahi is frequently paired with fruit flavors, for good reason. The crisp acidity in fruit invigorates the palate, cutting the natural richness of the fish. Even richer sauces, like the butter sauces often served with fish and seafood, are usually tinged with citrus or berry flavors when they're made for mahi. Another approach is pairing the fish with fruity red wine, either as a sauce, a marinade, or an accompaniment. I've made a red wine dressing based on a Dijon-mustard-tinged homemade mayonnaise, and served it over pan-seared mahi-mahi to fantastic effect.

Like bluefish, mahi-mahi takes well to grilling. Its skin is strong enough to be cooked directly on the grill without sticking, and the flesh is firm enough to flip without breaking. However, remember the most ecofriendly methods for grilling:

- Use a stovetop grill pan, which emits much less smoke and carbon than an outdoor grill.

- Cook on a gas grill, which emits fewer greenhouse gases than charcoal, and doesn't require felling of trees.

Mahi-mahi makes the juiciest fish salads I've tasted. Use the recipe on page 237 for a delicious salad that's perfect for hors d'oeuvres like canapés or mini fish sandwiches, or an elegant luncheon course, atop a lemony salad of lettuces and green beans.

Mahi-mahi grow quickly and breed up to four times a year, making them highly resistant to fishing pressures. Their range is large, including both the Atlantic and Pacific oceans. Responsible management is applied to the Atlantic fishery, while the Pacific fishery remains unregulated.

Those caught with hook and line cause very little bycatch, while longline-caught mahi do present a bycatch problem. Overall, mahi-mahi, a beautiful, very juicy, and increasingly prized fish, is a good environmental choice, endorsed by Blue Ocean Institute, Environmental Defense, Audubon, Wildlife Conservation Society, and Monterey Bay Aquarium's Seafood Watch. To find sources for mahi-mahi that was certifiably caught by troll and hand line (hook and line) fishing, see www.ecofish.com.

Grilled Mahi-mahi on Heirloom Tomato Chutney

SERVES 4 Mahi-mahi thrives on both coasts of the United States. Atlantic mahi-mahi is one of the few East Coast fisheries that have been managed responsibly. The chutney can be made with any tomatoes you wish. Heirlooms just give it a more interesting flavor and look.

2 tablespoons fresh lime juice

2 tablespoons olive oil

1 teaspoon finely chopped garlic

2 tablespoons minced fresh flat-leaf parsley

1 tablespoon chili powder

1 teaspoon ground cumin

1 pound mahi-mahi fillet (preferably Atlantic—ask your fishmonger where it's from), cut into 4 portions

Salt and freshly ground black pepper

1 tablespoon peanut or grapeseed oil

¼ cup roughly chopped fresh cilantro, plus 4 sprigs

1 recipe Red and Yellow Heirloom Tomato Chutney (recipe follows)

In a bowl, combine the lime juice, olive oil, garlic, parsley, chili powder, and cumin. Pour this over the fish; marinate 15 or 20 minutes.

Heat a grill or broiler as hot as possible. Wipe any excess marinade from the fish; reserve excess marinade. Season the fish with salt and pepper. Brush with peanut oil. Broil or grill the fish until medium, about 4 minutes per side, brushing once with leftover marinade. Stir the cilantro into the chutney. Serve the chutney with a fish portion on top, garnished with cilantro sprigs.

Red and Yellow Heirloom Tomato Chutney

SERVES 4 AS A SIDE DISH Abundant summer tomatoes find their perfect use in a fresh relish like this. (If you want to try growing your own, check out the heirloom tomato seeds available from www.seedsavers.org.) I like to make a bed of the chutney, and rest a slice of seared fish on top, garnished simply with cilantro sprigs and a lemon wedge.

⅓ cup sugar

Juice of 1 lemon

6 ripe red tomatoes, such as Brandywine, seeded and roughly chopped

6 ripe golden tomatoes, seeded and roughly chopped

¼ cup finely diced red onion

¼ cup roughly chopped fresh cilantro (optional)

Mix the sugar with ½ cup water in a medium saucepan. Cook over high heat until the water is evaporated and the molten sugar begins to turn golden brown. Pour in lemon juice to stop the sugar from cooking and bring it up from the bottom of the pan.

Add the tomatoes and onion. Simmer for no more than 5 minutes (this is to warm the tomatoes, not cook them). Remove from heat. Allow to cool in a colander, letting excess water drain out. Stir in the cilantro (if using).

Mussels—Farmed

Cleaner than ever before, plumper than their wild ancestors, and consistently fresh and uniform, cultivated mussels are still amazingly cheap and plentiful. American black-shelled mussels retain their good looks, buttery, briny flavor, and sweet, elegant juices to every preparation we can throw at them. Once a poor man's food, growing along seaside rocks and docks like barnacles, now anyone can cook them, since a good mussel dish requires nothing more than a closed pot and a few drops of water (even better with the addition of some wine and garlic). But mussels can also achieve greatness.

The standard method for cooking mussels, which results in an exceptional broth, is to sweat (gently cook over low heat to extract juices) aromatic vegetables like onions, shallots, and garlic in olive oil. Add plenty of mussels and a splash of wine, and cover. Raise the heat to high, and cook until the shells open. After transferring the mussels to a serving plate, most chefs reduce the broth to concentrate its flavors, then finish it with a nugget of whole butter before basting it over the mussels and serving them with crusty bread for dipping. The classic side dish for mussels in Belgium is *frites*, double-cooked fried potatoes.

Variations for steamed mussels are endless. Portuguese chefs include bay leaves and bell peppers with the aromatic vegetables, and add slices of chorizo sausage with the mussels. Mussel broth marries beautifully with the tang of tomatoes, so *moules marinière* consists of mussels steamed not in wine but in herb-laced tomato sauce. This is also delicious over pasta. Spanish paellas call for mixtures of seafood and other ingredients, but an all-mussel paella is fabulous, and ecologically sound. Mussels, like clams, actually contribute to marine environmental health by ridding the water of excess nutrients and phytoplankton. Mussel farming is one of the greatest accidental benefits mankind has ever given back to nature.

Mussel broth makes great soup. By itself, it's a nourishing, comforting dish. But it's also a great base for noodle soups that can be garnished with leafy green vegetables, mushrooms, and mussels. Extra broth from cooked mussels should always be saved as a stock for seafood risottos, stews, and sauces.

No success story trumps the adoption of widespread mussel aquaculture in America. These filter feeders strain ten to fifteen gallons of water daily, gleaning for algae, phytoplankton, bacteria, and organic matter. In the process of fattening up, they remove excessive algae blooms from coastal waters. Since fertilizer-intensive farming near waterways and wetlands introduces excessive nutrients in those waters, algae blooms have become a big problem, starving estuaries of oxygen as the algae decays. But the advent of large-scale mussel farms has changed all that. The mussels thrive on the plentiful algae, fattening up as they filter excessive organic matter from the water. The results: plump mussels and clean coastal estuaries.

Farmed mussels are cleaner, without seabed mud and grit, and safer, grown in controlled waters. While wild mussels come up tangled in "beards" of fiber they use to hold onto rocks, cultivated ones are mostly beardless (and barnacle-less). They represent most of the mussels sold in the United States. Three types of mussel are cultivated in American waters—blue mussels on the Northeast coast and in the Pacific, California mussels from Alaska to Baja, California, and Mediterranean mussels, grown in the Pacific Northwest. A small number of jumbo New Zealand green mussels are imported, mostly frozen. These are also sustainably farmed.

Tiny Mussel Salads on the Half Shell
with Asian Aioli

SERVES 4 AS AN APPETIZER, 2 AS A MAIN COURSE This recipe, inspired by Ming Tsai of Blue Ginger restaurant in Massachusetts, is a fusion of New England ingredients with the flavors of China.

1 cup Aioli (page 271)

1 tablespoon grated fresh ginger

½ teaspoon sugar

About 2 tablespoons Chinese fermented black bean sauce

1 teaspoon Asian chili sauce

1 teaspoon Asian toasted sesame oil

1 pound blue mussels, cleaned

¼ cup Chinese cooking wine *(shaoxing)* or sherry

1 cucumber, peeled and seeded

Salt and freshly ground black pepper

1 cup finely chopped green or Napa cabbage

12 fresh cilantro sprigs, chopped, plus cilantro leaves for garnish

Flavor the aioli by whisking in the ginger, sugar, black bean sauce, chili sauce, and sesame oil to taste; chill. Place the mussels and wine in a large pot with a tight-fitting lid; steam open over medium-high heat just until the shells open, about 6 minutes. Discard any mussels that do not open. When the mussels are cool enough to touch, remove them from their shells, saving half the shells for service; strain the broth. Chill the mussels and broth.

Shred the cucumber on the large side of a box grater; combine with 1 teaspoon salt and drain in a colander for 15 minutes. Press out any remaining moisture, then combine the cucumber with the cabbage and chopped cilantro to create a slaw. Season to taste.

Spoon small tufts of the cucumber slaw into the shell halves to form little beds; set a chilled mussel atop each. Whisk a few teaspoons of reserved mussel broth into the aioli; dress each mussel with the aioli and garnish with cilantro leaves. Serve on a bed of crushed ice.

Oysters—Farmed

Oysters are the most commonly farmed shellfish worldwide. Widespread cultivation of Pacific oysters in nets, trays, and racks suspended in the currents has mitigated some of the effects of excessive nutrients introduced to the ecosystem by fertilizer runoff. A good thing continues to get even better, as cultivation replenishes this beneficial species in areas that had been overexploited when harvesting of wild oysters was the norm. Japanese *kumomoto* oysters, a line of Pacific oysters, are also benefiting from the nutrient-rich environment, and they are of exceptional taste and texture.

Harvesting of wild oysters on the East Coast has decimated beds from Maine to Virginia, and only now are responsible aquaculture projects starting to stem that destructive tide. Introduction of cultivated Belon (flat European) oysters is part of that new generation of bivalves, and growers are replenishing beds in New England. Pacific oysters can be generally assumed to be sustainably produced, while consumers should ask whether Eastern oysters are wild or farmed.

Oysters take on distinct characteristics from the environment in which they grow, developing elongated shells in areas with swift currents, becoming oversized and plump when nutrients so dictate. For that reason, even though most oysters grown in U.S. waters are of three species (Pacific oyster—*Crassostrea gigas,* Eastern oyster—*Crassostrea virginica,* or European oyster—*Ostrea edulis*), they are usually marketed by the name of the place where they grew. Thus, although they're of the same species, oyster bar patrons often choose between Wellfleets, Blue Points, Malpeques, and Pemaquids, among dozens of others.

Redfish—Wild

After being decimated in the Gulf of Mexico for blackened fish dishes during the Cajun craze of the 1980s, redfish are reappearing thanks to closed-pond fish farming by the Fish Farm in Bacliff, Texas. They're raised on organic feed and have a clean taste reminiscent of striped bass. Currently the fish are available only to restaurants, but in the coming years, they will start showing up in consumer markets.

Salmon—Wild Alaskan Chinook, Chum, Coho, Pink, Sockeye, and Canned

Wild Alaskan salmon is a well-managed fishery, with strict catch quotas coming from remarkably pristine waters. Much of the fish goes into cans, making American canned salmon one of the most reliably ethical salmon choices. What's sold fresh is wonderfully sweet, full-flavored fish, often coming in vibrant natural colors. While salmon farms require huge ocean harvests to generate the synthesized feed on which their fish subsist, these wild salmon are part of the ecosystem, and source their sustenance directly from the most plentiful natural sources.

The Marine Stewardship Council certifies Alaska salmon as a "Best Environmental Choice." It was the first U.S. fishery to achieve that distinction. (Alaska pollock is now also certified.) To read about fisheries endorsed by MSC, go to www.msc.org.

The USDA is developing organic standards for domestic fish and seafood, and has certified only a handful of producers or specific products so far. Since many of the most egregious practices of the salmon-farming industry involve pesticides and feed supplements that would be banned from organic fish, these new standards might offer a glimmer of hope for consumers seeking more sustainable farmed salmon. After all, wild Alaskan and Pacific stocks will never be able to meet all of the demand for salmon.

Scallops—Farmed, Bay (Except Atlantic Calico)

Bay scallops are largely farmed, and cultivated in an ecologically sound way. In the eastern United States, some bay scallops are still caught wild, but the stocks are severely depleted, especially in the prized Nantucket and Peconic Bay areas. Bay scallops are mostly farmed in China. The suspension net system of bay scallop aquaculture is benign, and is one of the better seafood-farming systems practiced there. Bay scallops are recommended by Blue Ocean Institute and Environmental Defense, and cautiously endorsed by Monterey Bay Aquarium.

Taylor Bay Scallops, the best farm-raised scallops in the United States, are grown on Cape Cod, Massachusetts, by Rod Taylor (508-990-0591). His exquisitely sweet scallops are sustainably raised and come in the shell, usually live. They're not to be missed.

Sea Scallops

Talk about self-sabotage. . . . Fishermen balked when, in the mid-1990s, the beds off George's Bank, a prime New England fishing ground, were closed to protect overfished sea scallops. But numbers were so low that the fishery was on the verge of collapse anyway. The species was nearly depleted. When fisheries management officials announced that the moratorium had worked, and that sea scallops were rebounding, fishermen immediately demanded permits to harvest the bank. The scallop beds were reopened, and overfished again. Management must catch up with the fishing industry's demands on the fishing grounds until a sensible harvest level is reached. In 2004, the harvest was considered sustainable.

Some thought it pretentious when restaurants began indicating that their sea scallops (the largest type) were "diver scallops." That these special scallops were dug by hand from the sea floor by scuba-equipped harvesters seemed an unnecessary extravagance. In fact, though, in addition to bringing up fresher, undamaged product, the technique also protected sensitive seabeds from disruptive dredging. Conventional harvesting relies on heavy nets that are dragged along the sea floor, up-ending everything in their path.

I buy diver-caught sea scallops that I can cook with a clean conscience because their harvesting is gentle on the seabed. But I regularly check back to ocean research Web sites (such as the SeaSense database at the Seafood Choices Alliance, www.seafoodchoices.com/seasense/) to consult about their status.

Shrimp—Wild from the Gulf and SE Coasts, New England, and Canada, and Farmed from Florida

Shrimp has replaced tuna as America's favorite seafood. And as any species should know, being America's favorite isn't always a blessing. Most shrimp are caught wild, and stocks have declined. Net fishing has trapped numerous endangered turtles. American shrimpers have demonstrated admirable sensitivity, installing specialized turtle-release nets and fishing near less ecologically sensitive seabeds. North Carolina and Georgia have notable state fisheries management of shrimp, which are usually marketed as "pink shrimp."

A shrimp farm in Florida, Ocean Boy Farms, produces the only certified organic shrimp in the United States. They organically raise tilapia, and some are used in the organic shrimp feed that the company produces. The farm is environmentally responsible, discharging no water from its ponds. Instead, water filters through a biofiltration system of natural vegetation. The shrimp are sold frozen, headless, and shell-on and are almost the same price as conventional shrimp. These shrimp are widely distributed, and direct info from the company about the shrimp and where to buy them can be found at www.oceanboyfarms.com, or by calling (863) 983-9941. While the ecological approach of the company is praiseworthy, the ones I've had are small and somewhat bland. They should be marinated, and cooked very lightly.

Newfoundland northern shrimp, found in the North Atlantic, North Pacific, and Arctic oceans, are plentiful and well managed. Most of the northern shrimp sold in the United States are fished in the U.S., Canada, and Scandinavia. They're mostly caught with specialized trawls that minimize bycatch. The Environmental Defense site www.oceansalive.org lists northern shrimp as an "eco-best" choice. Find out where to buy them at www.ecofish.com.

Overall, however, shrimp are not the best choice, environmentally. Southeast Asia, which produces the bulk of farmed shrimp, is being damaged by the industry, which pollutes and displaces marine estuaries. Ocean Garden brand is a company that has also made notable efforts to minimize the environmental impact of their shrimping operations off Mexico and South America.

Spot Prawns—Wild Mainly harvested from U.S. waters, from Alaska to Southern California, spot prawns (actually not prawns, but shrimp) are a well-managed fishery. Their harvest results in less bycatch than most other shrimping

because they're caught in traps, not nets. They're an "eco-best" choice from Environmental Defense. Buy them direct from fishermen at www.westportwa.com/seafood/prawns/.

Squid—Wild

Most calamari sold in the United States is from American waters. The two main species, market squid and northern shortfin squid, reproduce quickly, within a year of birth, so they seldom suffer from overfishing. Although some bottom trawls have high bycatch, most squid are drawn to the surface with bright lights, then harvested in nets with little bycatch.

Striped Bass—Wild and Farmed

One of the greatest success stories of managed fisheries in history is the return of wild striped bass. These clean, white-fleshed fish were harvested to near commercial extinction in the 1980s, until the Fish and Wildlife Service stepped in and banned the catch. During the ban, a responsible aquaculture industry arose along the Atlantic, Pacific, and Gulf coasts, farm-raising "stripers" in closed systems that had little or no polluting effects on wild habitats. The inland pond and tank systems, a model that has also had great results with tilapia and catfish, produces exquisite, healthy fish that are highly admired by chefs. Feed, though made from wild-harvested fishmeal, is efficiently used in the closed system.

After a decade of protection, wild striped bass numbers rebounded, and the species was saved from extinction. The bass have thrived, enabling fisheries services to allow a limited catch. Most of the striped bass sold today in the United States is responsibly farmed, and the rest is drawn from sustainably managed fisheries. Striped bass is one fish that consumers with a conscience can enjoy with impunity.

Farm-raised Striped Bass Tartare with American Sturgeon Caviar

SERVES 4 AS AN APPETIZER This recipe is a marriage of two aquaculture success stories. When overfishing threatened the survival of wild striped bass, a successful, low-impact striped bass farming industry was established. It was so successful that many chefs prefer the farmed over the wild, even though the wild stocks have largely recovered and are on the market. And the severely threatened decimated stocks of sturgeon in the Caspian Sea, source of most of the world's fine caviar, led to experiments in farming sturgeon off the California coast. Those experiments, started in the 1960s, gave birth to sustainable farm-raised sturgeon caviar for the first time in history. (See Sources for caviar suppliers.)

1 pound striped bass fillets, skinned, ice-cold

1 tablespoon chopped fresh chives

½ teaspoon finely chopped cornichons

1 teaspoon finely chopped capers

3 ounces American sturgeon caviar

2 teaspoons peanut or grapeseed oil

Pinch of kosher salt

Pinch of cayenne

1 tablespoon fresh lemon juice

¼ cup Herb Vinaigrette (recipe follows) or other vinaigrette dressing

Trim any dark meat, small bones, and connective tissue from the fillets (or have your fishmonger do this). Dice the fish very finely. Combine it with chives, cornichons, capers, and a quarter of the caviar. Gently fold in the peanut oil. Refrigerate for 20 minutes.

Season the mixture with salt, cayenne, and lemon juice. Mold the tartare onto serving plates using a 3-inch ring mold or an empty tuna can. Top with spoonfuls of the remaining caviar. Dress with Herb Vinaigrette immediately before serving with toast points.

Herb Vinaigrette YIELD: 1 CUP

1 tablespoon Dijon mustard

1 shallot, finely chopped

¼ cup red wine vinegar

1 teaspoon kosher salt

Freshly ground black pepper

½ cup extra virgin olive oil

¼ cup vegetable oil, such as canola

½ cup chopped tender herbs, such as chives, chervil, tarragon, and flat-leaf parsley

In a mixing bowl, combine the mustard, shallot, vinegar, salt, and pepper. Allow to marinate a few minutes.

Whisk the vinegar mixture vigorously while gradually drizzling in the oils to form a smooth, emulsified sauce. Stir in herbs just before serving (this can be done in small batches, as the dressing is used; it will keep, refrigerated, for 5 days).

Seared Fingers of Striped Bass

SERVES 4 AS A LIGHT MAIN COURSE Striped bass, one of the success stories of fisheries management, is available farmed or wild. The farmed fish were cultivated when the wild stocks were depleted. When wild stocks rebounded, limited harvests were permitted. Both farmed and wild are sustainable. Serve this dish with a Ragoût of Fingerling Potatoes, Niçoise Olives, and Sweet Onions (page 126), or over a large salad of tender lettuces or spinach.

3 teaspoons olive oil

1½ teaspoons ground coriander

¼ teaspoon ground cumin

2 garlic cloves, crushed

Pinch of crushed red pepper

Zest and juice of ½ lemon

1 pound striped bass or tilapia fillets, cut into 8 strips

Salt and freshly ground black pepper

1 teaspoon unsalted butter (optional)

Combine 1 teaspoon of the olive oil, the coriander, cumin, garlic, red pepper, and lemon zest. Coat the fish with this mixture; marinate, refrigerated, 45 minutes.

Scrape excess marinade from the fillets; season with salt and pepper. Heat a nonstick skillet over high heat. Add the remaining 2 teaspoons olive oil (it should shimmer, but not smoke). Add the fish to the pan skin side up. Add the butter (if using) to aid in browning. Sear the fillets without moving them, until browned, about 2 minutes. Turn; cook until done, about 1 minute more. Remove from heat; splash in the lemon juice.

Sturgeon—Farmed

Inland tanks for raising white sturgeon protect coastal waters from potential pollutants generated by the system. White sturgeon are long-lived and are fed fishmeal that is sourced in the wild. But the fish are efficient feeders, and they consume less food per pound of meat they produce than other fish, like salmon. The wild species is severely threatened, but the farmed product is of high quality and is raised in a reasonably ecologically sound way. Audubon, the Wildlife Conservation Society, and the Monterey Bay Aquarium all recommend farmed white sturgeon. A reliable supplier is www.farmtomarket.com.

White sturgeon also produce eggs that are second in quality only to the Russian species for caviar. Considering the relative cleanness of the waters they're raised in, white sturgeon have a purity advantage over beluga, osetra, and sevruga sturgeon from the Caspian Sea. Sterling caviar (www.sterlingcaviar.com) is exceptional American sturgeon caviar made from white sturgeon roe. It is similar to osetra in taste and texture. The meat from white sturgeon is deliciously firm, rich, and mild.

Creamed Sturgeon Crêpes on Spiced Oats

SERVES 8 Almost all white sturgeon sold today is farm raised. Except for copious bones, there are nothing but good features to this sustainable fish.

1 recipe Crêpes (recipe follows), or your own recipe

1 pound shrimp, peeled and cleaned

2 large eggs, beaten

1½ cups heavy cream, cold

1 tablespoon chopped fresh dill, plus sprigs for garnish

Salt and freshly ground black pepper

1½ pounds farmed white sturgeon, sablefish (black cod), or tilapia fillet

1 tablespoon anise liqueur, such as Pernod

1 recipe Spiced Whole Oats (page 303)

8 teaspoons unsalted butter

Prepare the crêpes as directed and stack them, separated by sheets of wax paper; set aside. Make a paste of the shrimp by pureeing them in a food processor until smooth. Gradually pulse in the eggs and cream. Transfer the shrimp paste to a bowl, then fold in the dill. Add salt and pepper to taste. Cover and chill 1 hour. Cut the sturgeon into 8 portions; if the tail end is very thin, score it about halfway to the tip, and double it back over itself to make it thicker for even cooking. Sprinkle with anise liqueur and season with salt and pepper to taste.

Spread some shrimp paste over each crêpe, leaving a 1-inch border. Place a portion of sturgeon onto each, and roll into a cylinder.

Heat the oven to 350°F. Grease a baking sheet. Arrange the filled crêpes on the baking sheet with the loose end underneath. Bake about 20 minutes, until the edges are crispy and the fish is just cooked. Heat the oats if they are not still warm, and spoon onto warm plates. Set one crêpe on each plate of oats, and top with a teaspoon of butter. Garnish with sprigs of dill, if desired.

Crêpes

YIELD: ABOUT 8 CRÊPES Sweet or savory, filled or simply sauced, crêpes are delicate, elegant, delicious, and very easy to make. When I need to make a dessert in a hurry, I whisk together this batter, make some crêpes, and slather them with Nutella, an Italian chocolate-hazelnut spread.

½ cup all-purpose flour

3 large eggs

1 cup milk

1 tablespoon olive oil

¼ teaspoon kosher salt

Unsalted butter for the pan

Whisk together the flour and eggs until they form a smooth paste. Gradually whisk in the milk, olive oil, and salt.

Heat a 10-inch nonstick skillet over medium heat. Add some butter and spread it around the pan with a brush or the corner of a towel. Add ¼ cup of batter to the pan. Swirl the pan around in a circular pattern to evenly distribute the batter.

Cook undisturbed until the edges become visibly brown. Using a wooden or rubber spatula, lift the edge of the crêpe from the pan. Quickly flip the crêpe using your fingers or a wooden spoon. Cook 30 seconds on the second side, then slide onto a plate; keep warm while you repeat the procedure with the remaining batter. Crêpes may be made in advance and stacked one atop the other, separated by sheets of wax paper.

Spiced Whole Oats   SERVES 8

2 tablespoons olive oil

1 large onion, finely chopped

1 teaspoon ground cardamom

Salt and freshly ground black pepper

2 cups whole oats (often called oat groats)

1 cinnamon stick

2 bay leaves

8 whole cloves

8 allspice berries

Juice of 1 lemon

Heat the olive oil in a small saucepan over medium-low heat. Add the onion, cardamom, and salt and pepper to taste. Cook gently until the onion is very soft, about 10 minutes.

Combine the oats, cinnamon, bay leaves, cloves, allspice, and 1 teaspoon salt in a large pot with 5 cups water (put the spices in a sachet or tea strainer, if desired). Bring to a boil, cover, and then simmer until the oats are very tender and all the water is absorbed, about an hour. Cover and set aside to rest, undisturbed, for 15 to 20 minutes.

Season to taste with lemon juice, salt, and pepper. Remove the whole spices and fluff slightly with a fork before serving.

Tilapia—U.S. Farmed

If there's a more ethical choice in fish than American-raised tilapia, I'd like to know about it. African in origin, tilapia swim in tight formations in the wild. They are not stressed by the confined environment of the fish farm. Tilapia farms in the United States are brackish inland ponds and tanks that do not interfere with ocean ecology. In some other countries, notably in Asia and Central America, methods are more questionable. But this fast-growing fish is endorsed by virtually every environmental watchdog group, because it's a renewable, sustainable food.

Tilapia also happens to be delicious. Firm, plump white fillets release cleanly from the bone, and remain juicy even in the face of long cooking times. The fish takes well to steaming, pan-frying, and roasting. It's widely available both filleted and whole, and stays fresh longer than most other fish.

Trout—Farmed Rainbow

The oldest form of aquaculture in America is also one of the safest. Most trout available to consumers is farm raised in "raceways" in inland areas. With minimal chance of escape into the wild, and good control of feeding and wastes, rainbow trout aquaculture is far more environmentally sound than the systems used for trout's cousin, salmon.

The one drawback is that, like salmon, trout require a high-protein diet that relies on wild fish catch. Farmed rainbow trout, raised largely in the states of Idaho and North Carolina, are nonetheless a better fish choice than most, since their impact is low. They are rated as a good choice by Blue Ocean Institute, Monterey Bay Aquarium, and Audubon.

Tuna—Yellowfin, Bigeye, Albacore (Pole/Troll Caught)

No wild fish has garnered more attention from environmentalists at the dawn of the twenty-first century than tuna. Two decades earlier, tuna had been America's introduction to sashimi and other raw fish preparations (probably because its red color reminded consumers of red meat, which was universally accepted as okay to eat rare). Massive sushi consumption here and in Asia, combined with America's already-enormous demand for canned tuna (only recently surpassed by shrimp as the most popular seafood in the country), has led to the near-annihilation of some tuna species.

Tuna's fate echoes the fate of nearly all major predatory fish in the oceans (including swordfish, marlin, sharks, cod), which have been nearly wiped out in the fifty years since industrial fishing operations eclipsed small fishermen as the main harvesters of the seas. The most prized fish for sushi, especially in Japan, is, of course, the most threatened: the bluefin tuna. A few decades ago, bluefin of nearly 1,500 pounds were landed along the Atlantic seaboard. Now, 200-pound youngsters are considered a good catch. The capture methods used include longline fishing, wherein hundreds of hooks are strung on a few lines, and towed behind the fishing vessel. This method leads to an unacceptable amount of bycatch, including endangered sea turtles and marine mammals.

Purse seines, another method used for catching bluefin, is little better. All of the major environmental groups and ocean ecology organizations urge consumers to avoid bluefin tuna at all times. As we strip the oceans of the last of the breeding stock, the future looks bleak for the species. Nonetheless, bluefin tuna continues to sell briskly in domestic and Japanese sushi bars. Many consumers are unaware that some fish on restaurant menus and stocked abundantly in fish stores are among the last of their kind.

Fine Pacific tunas (ahi), including Pacific yellowfin, bigeye, and albacore, come from relatively well-managed fisheries. These species are not so threatened as the Atlantic bluefin. Albacore, particularly, is recommended by environmental organizations because of the species' fecundity and resilience to fishing pressures, as well as the sensible pole and troll methods employed for catching them.

Go to www.pelicanpackers.com for guaranteed troll-caught, dolphin-safe albacore, packed by the fishermen who caught them. Another supplier for sustainable catch is Mary Lu Seafoods at www.maryluseafoods.com; (707) 465-0284.

Penne with Albacore Tuna and Artichoke Cream

SERVES 8 Albacore, the fish sold as "solid white" canned tuna, represents the most well managed of tuna fisheries. While other species canned as "chunk light" are over-harvested, albacore is endorsed by Blue Ocean Institute, Monterey Bay Aquarium, and the National Audubon Society. Troll-caught albacore is available from marylu-seafoods.com. Italian and Spanish imports are also of great quality, but make sure it's albacore.

Fruity-tasting artichoke "cream" contains no dairy. Rather, it is a seasoned artichoke puree that is so smooth it feels creamy. It's a widely used ingredient around Rome, where I found the inspiration for this dish in trattorias and friends' homes. It is available from www.purelyorganic.com, or you can make your own.

1 pound penne

2 tablespoons olive oil

8 fresh or canned artichoke hearts, drained and quartered

Two 10-ounce cans troll-caught albacore tuna, preferably packed in olive oil, oil reserved

5 tablespoons artichoke cream, or ¼ cup artichoke hearts, pureed in a blender with a little olive oil

2 cups tomato sauce

Kosher salt

Freshly ground black pepper

½ cup roughly chopped fresh flat-leaf parsley

Bring a large pot of salted water to a boil. Cook the penne until it is al dente (has a slight resistance to the bite). Drain and toss with a few drops olive oil.

Over a high flame, heat 1 tablespoon of the olive oil in a very large skillet or pot large enough to hold all the ingredients. Sauté the artichokes 1 minute (careful: they spatter). Add the tuna with its packing oil, breaking it into fairly large pieces; cook 1 minute. Stir in half of the artichoke cream, and the tomato sauce. Simmer 1 minute.

Toss in the pasta along with 1 cup of the pasta cooking water. Cook until heated through; season with kosher salt and freshly ground black pepper. Drizzle with the remaining olive oil and serve, garnished with dollops of the remaining artichoke cream and a sprinkling of chopped parsley.

Endangered Fish to Avoid

BLUEFIN TUNA

- Dwindling numbers and puny specimens have not slowed the mining of the seas for the last survivors of this long-lived species. The money's too good. Bluefin for sushi can command upwards of $100 a pound in Japan's Tsukiji market, where the sushi-hungry nation's supply is auctioned off. Japan long ago wiped out most of its own populations of bluefin, and now relies on catch from Europe and North America. The once giant (routinely half-ton) predators are fast-swimming, migratory fish that circumnavigate the globe, so just about all fishing fleets are harvesting from the same pool. Fish of more than a couple hundred pounds are extremely rare now. This fish will likely be fished to extinction within our lifetimes.

CASPIAN CAVIAR

- Massive overfishing, wholesale poaching, pollution, and habitat destruction from the petroleum industry have made a mockery of the protections put in place for the three major species of sturgeon in the Caspian Sea—beluga, osetra, and sevruga. The Convention on International Trade in Endangered Species (CITES) has bowed to pressures from the poor caviar-producing countries (Russia, Kazakhstan, Iran) and super-wealthy luxury consumers in Western Europe and the United States, and has set allowable limits for catching these nearly extinct fish. Since the dissolution of the Soviet Union, poaching has been rampant. In 2005, the U.S. finally banned importation of beluga, the most endangered, but osetra and sevruga, also dwindling, are still imported. The outlook for sturgeon from the Caspian remains bleak.

CHILEAN SEA BASS

- As cod and other ground fisheries collapsed in Europe and North America, the fish industry resorted to marketing what had formerly been regarded as "trash fish" to make up for the loss of product. Such was the case with Patagonian toothfish, a.k.a. Chilean sea bass. This naturally oily fish was "discovered" in the early 1990s, and quickly became a trendy favorite in restaurants. Its high oil content makes it hard to overcook, and thus foolproof for the less-talented cook.

- Longline fishing for these southern Atlantic predators results in a huge by-catch, including a tremendous toll on endangered albatross, which follow fishing vessels in search of a free meal.

- Though international catch limits have been set, worldwide demand has encouraged widespread poaching. Populations are in what Environmental Defense calls "severe decline."

COD—ATLANTIC

- For centuries, cod was the most important fishery in Europe, Canada, and the United States. Fishing of the richest area, off Canada's Labrador and Newfoundland coasts, was done close to shore with traps, gill nets, and small trawlers. As industrialized fishing came to dominate the fishery in the 1950s, catch skyrocketed, and prices came down. Massive factory ships, modeled after then-successful whaling ships,

harvested once-unthinkable catches, which were processed and frozen onboard. The fishery had averaged 250,000 tons annually for a century, but by 1968, catch peaked at 800,000 tons. By the early 1990s, the cod fishery of Newfoundland collapsed completely, and the fishery had to be closed entirely. Forty thousand people lost their jobs. The cod never returned.

- Europe, which should have learned from Newfoundland's disaster, continued hauling in huge catches, until they began to dwindle too. By 2003, the journal *New Scientist* reported that the crop of Northern European cod for that year was the smallest ever. Scientists advising the European Union warn that complete collapse of that cod fishery is imminent, and that, as off Newfoundland, the cod may never return, even if a complete ban is placed on fishing.

- American cod fisheries, mostly in the Gulf of Maine and the area off Massachusetts known as George's Bank, are severely depleted, but continue to be fished. This is a classic scenario: The public sees a product at market, assumes that if it's for sale it must be plentiful, and thus enables the fishing industry to fish it into oblivion.

- Pacific cod, fished in the North Pacific from the Bering Strait down to California, and in the Yellow Sea in East Asia, are in better shape. Very similar to Atlantic cod, Pacific cod is not considered threatened. The bottom trawl devices used to catch Pacific cod are damaging the fish's habitat, so these cod are not recommended either. But given the choice, always choose Pacific cod over Atlantic.

HALIBUT—ATLANTIC

- Once extremely common, these large relatives of flounder largely disappeared along with the rest of the fourteen or so main bottom-dwelling species referred to collectively as "groundfish," which formed the core of the New England fishery. In the U.S. the fishery is officially closed, though there's still notable incidental catch. Although the catch has plummeted, the United States still imports Atlantic halibut from Canada and Scandinavia. This practice should stop immediately. Only Pacific halibut should be sold.

- Pacific halibut are well managed under the jurisdiction of the International Pacific Halibut Commission. While catches are lower than that of Atlantic halibut, this is a sustainable fishery, and Pacific halibut is a seafood choice recommended by Environmental Defense, Blue Ocean Institute, Monterey Bay Aquarium, and the National Audubon Society.

MONKFISH

- Like so many threatened fish species, monkfish, known in France as *lotte*, was once discarded by fishermen as "trash fish." But the collapse of other major fisheries, combined with demand for their livers in Asian markets, elevated monkfish to marketable status. By the 1980s, the fish's boneless tail loin had become the ultratrendy menu item in fine restaurants. The fish is never served whole, as its gnarly, oversized head is one of the more gruesome-looking mugs known to man.

- A bottom-dweller, monkfish is caught in dredges and trawls that disrupt the sea floor, undermining habitat for this species and others.

ORANGE ROUGHY

- This slow-growing fish is the most long-lived (up to 149 years) of any species. Populations have declined severely in much of its South Pacific range. Since they don't mature until they're at least twenty years old, they are particularly sensitive to overfishing.

- Bycatch from the trawl gear used to catch them includes endangered shark species. They were discovered as a commercial catch in the 1970s, and were considered overfished within less than two decades. All major environmental groups say to avoid orange roughy.

SALMON—ATLANTIC FARMED (EXCEPT ORGANIC)

- Where to begin with the problems in the salmon-farming industry? The feeding and antibiotic treatment regimens used spew pollution into surrounding waters. Escaped hybrids compete for resources with the endangered wild Atlantic salmon (which cannot be legally sold). Highly concentrated net pens are breeding grounds for para-sites and diseases that escape and affect wild fish. Huge tonnages of wild fish are constantly required to feed these voracious hybrid salmon, which utilize nutrients inefficiently. What was once thought to be an ethical alternative has supplanted overfishing as the main threat to the long-term survival of wild species. (See also page 211.)

- To add insult to injury, farmed Atlantic salmon (raised in both the Atlantic and Pacific oceans, from New Brunswick to Chile, Norway to British Columbia) has been found to contain dangerously high levels of PCBs and pesticides linked to birth defects and long-term illness in humans. The fish are also fed dyed fish food to color their flesh pink.

- Good wild salmon, from Pacific species like Chinook, chum, coho, pink, and sockeye, are harvested from well-managed fisheries. Not only are they sustainable, but their flavor is deeper, and their natural red color is more alluring.

- Though today the wild fish is certainly the right choice, I have to admit that I had developed a fondness for the pleasingly oily, consistently fresh farm-raised salmon. I look forward to a day when smart solutions to the myriad salmon aquaculture problems will enable fish farmers to produce a clean, ecofriendly product. The USDA is developing organic standards for farmed salmon, and the industry may yet prove that it can be a good environmental citizen.

SCALLOPS, CALICO

- Calico scallops are small, wild scallops harvested off the Florida coast. The fishery has nearly collapsed due to overfishing. Avoid calico scallops. Choose farmed domestic or imported (mostly from China) bay scallops instead.

SHARK

- The bogeyman of the briny deep, the shark is nearly universally feared, though sharks kill only about twelve people a year. Humans kill nearly 100 million sharks per year. Populations of species caught for food, such as mako, are so decimated that they should not be purchased.

SHRIMP—IMPORTED

- Avoid imported shrimp, whether wild caught or farmed. Foreign sources of shrimp, especially Asia, are problematic. Wild fisheries cause huge amounts of bycatch, killing endangered sea turtles and whales. And coastal farming operations, like those in China, are destroying mangrove forests and coastal wetlands. Coastal land is being damaged as it is cleared for shrimp farming. The industry is also displacing traditional fisheries.

- The Monterey Bay Aquarium reports that between three and fifteen pounds of unwanted animals are caught and discarded as bycatch for every one pound of shrimp landed in tropical shrimp trawling. This is the highest bycatch of any commercial fishery.

- Antibiotics are widely used to damp down diseases exacerbated by the concentrations of animals living in shrimp farms. European countries banned farmed shrimp imports from China, Indonesia, and Vietnam in 2002 because of concerns about antibiotic residue. No such ban was enacted in the U.S.

- Release of untreated wastes from coastal shrimp aquaculture in Asia is common, despite existing technology that could mitigate its environmental impact. Diseases have transferred from shrimp-farming operations to wild shrimp populations and continue to spread in the wild.

- Choose domestic shrimp, especially from the carefully managed fisheries along the North Carolina and Georgia coasts, and northern shrimp from New England or Canada. Pink shrimp and white shrimp are also domestic resources from responsibly managed fisheries, though the Gulf of Mexico has seen some habitat damage from the industry. They are a good second choice.

SKATE

- Slow to mature and reproducing in very small numbers, skate are an overlooked problem. They fall victim to bycatch in many other bottom fish fisheries, and have been protected only recently and only in the United States. The fish are sometimes used to produce fishmeal for aquaculture operations, but growing demand for them in upscale restaurants is also taking its toll.

SNAPPER

- Snappers are grossly overfished worldwide. They fall victim to the shrimping industry in the Gulf of Mexico, where up to 35 million of them are discarded as bycatch each year. Management of the five major species of snapper (mutton, red, silk, vermilion, and yellowtail) is nearly nonexistent.

- Mating rituals of snappers bring them together in huge numbers during the breeding season. This makes them easy prey for fishermen at the most crucial time for the species' survival.

- Some species of snapper, such as pink snapper, change gender as they mature, transitioning from female to male. This makes selective fishing for larger specimens especially detrimental.

SWORDFISH

- Chefs finally did the right thing by a species. A chefs' boycott of severely depleted swordfish resulted in a decline in the overfishing that was decimating this large predatory species. But continued vigilance is needed if we hope to see the species recover. Consumers still buy swordfish in retail markets, and less responsible chefs still serve it, even though the swordfish being caught are too small to have reached reproductive size.

- Mature swordfish can weigh up to 1,200 pounds. But the average size of Atlantic swordfish being caught now is about 90 pounds, significantly less than the 150-pound weight at which females are able to reproduce. Juveniles are being harvested in an unregulated international fishery that may yet bring about the demise of the species. Pacific swordfish are also severely overfished, though reliable numbers are not available about their populations. Most major environmental groups urge diners not to consume swordfish.

Afterword: Making a Difference

Our choices can improve the food world. The popularity of good organic foods returns more and more acres to chemical-tree cultivation. Our insistence on humanely raised livestock brought eggs from cage-free hens, meats from grass-fed livestock, and free-roaming poultry into the mainstream. And our demand for fair treatment of workers in foreign countries has brought Fair Trade coffee to Starbucks and other marquee outlets.

Government policies affecting water quality, such as the loosening of arsenic regulations in the early 2000s, have been reversed. Cuts in the agribusiness subsidies are being planned by former supporters. The evidence is clear: Governments and industries respond to consumer decisions. Drink more organic milk and more will be produced. (Choose Organic Valley Brand over Horizon, when given the choice—they're more responsible players on humane treatment of animals and support for small farmers.) Take a sensible, results-based approach to scientific developments, and agricultural scientists can find alternatives to pesticides and chemical fertilizers.

We're living at a time when consciousness of the effects of our purchasing decisions is catching up with the unprecedented diversity of foods available to us. We're presented with more food choices than any previous generation. With that privilege comes the responsibility to make our choices ethically, for ourselves and for future generations.

The Ethical Gourmet's Ten Commandments

1. Turn the menu upside down, so meat is an accompaniment, not the center-piece.

2. Choose local foods over imported organic, organic foods over conventional.

3. Support responsible development of genetically modified foodstuffs to reduce pesticide abuse and deforestation.

4. Choose fish from closed aquaculture systems, farmed shellfish, and fast-reproducing wild fish from managed fisheries.

5. Drink tap, not bottled, water.

6. Dine at restaurants that serve a moral menu.

7. Look for humane, sustainable, and ethical logos on packaged goods, such as Certified Humane Raised & Handled, Rainforest Alliance, Fair Trade, and the Marine Stewardship Council. Carry the Blue Ocean Institute seafood guide in your wallet.

8. Buy from companies with responsible environmental policies and invest in socially responsible funds.

9. Vote for candidates who are committed to ending agricultural subsidies and a laissez-faire approach to regulation in the meat and dairy industries. Lobby those who aren't.

10. Cook wholesome food at home more often.

Dining Out: Places That Serve a Moral Menu

From simple organic cafés and modest eateries to white-tablecloth fine dining rooms serving humanely raised grass-fed meats, choices for diners with a conscience are easier to find than ever. You can find cuisine with an ethical sensibility anywhere in the country by looking at the database on www.localharvest.org. Their portal features maps for locating the right stuff at the click of a mouse. Using the site's clickable map, zero in on where you wish to dine. Listings appear for restaurants that use locally raised ingredients, organics, and humanely produced products.

Even before New York's top fish restaurants agreed to ban threatened swordfish, pressure from conservation-minded consumers had ended the restaurant world's attack on overharvested Gulf redfish, which were practically wiped out during the Cajun cuisine craze of the 1980s. North Pond Restaurant in Chicago, Water Grill in Los Angeles, Restaurant Nora in Washington, D.C., Café Marquesa in Key West, The Herbfarm near Seattle, Peristyle in New Orleans, and Luxia in New York are just a few of the fine dining rooms around the nation that base menu decisions on sustainability, low environmental impact, organic status, and humane treatment of animals. On the lower end of the spectrum, the Better Burger chain in New York sells only vegetarian burgers, free-range turkey burgers, and organic, grass-fed beef burgers. As the list snowballs, chefs and consumers can look to resources such as the Web sites www.seafoodchoices.com and www.chefscollaborative.org to confirm that the places where *they're* ordering their caviar, French rack of lamb, and chervil-scented ratatouille are part of the solution, not part of the problem.

The LocalHarvest site also lists thousands of farmers, food co-ops, greenmarkets, and stores where ethical products are sold. Before traveling, zoom in on your destination and print out listings for the best sources for ethical cuisine there. Many of the restaurants and markets are destinations in themselves.

Antiquity Oaks

I've struggled with the veal issue many times. Brown stock made from veal bones is simply superior to brown stock made from other bones. Its gelatinous body and delicate flavor make the best demiglace sauces. But the treatment of mainstream veal calves is unacceptable, so I found an alternative: Antiquity Oaks, a farm in Cornell, Illinois (815-358-2450), raises nonconfinement veal, pastured chickens, and free-range turkeys. Though not certified organic, they use organic feed whenever available and grow heirloom vegetables without chemical pesticides and fertilizers. They're just one of many such sources in LocalHarvest's database. The demiglace (reduced brown stock) I've made with bones from humanely raised veal has been exquisite.

Blue Hill at Stone Barns

Restaurants that grow their own food are rarer than pop stars who write their own songs. But they're there. One perfect example is Blue Hill at Stone Barns, a three-star (from the *New York Times*) gourmet destination in Pocantico, New York (914-366-9600), http://bluehillstonebarns.com/bhsb .html), forty-five minutes from downtown Manhattan. As self-sufficient as a restaurant can be, the white-tablecloth dining room serves dishes made from ingredients grown on adjacent farmland, all part of the Stone Barns Center for Food and Agriculture. It's a model of local sourcing and humane treatment of animals. At the farm, Stone Barns' farmers raise both commercial and historic breeds of livestock, including Berkshire pigs, Bourbon Red and Gina White turkeys, Cotswold and Hampshire sheep, and Cornish/White Rock chickens. Vegetables grow year-round in the center's half-acre greenhouse, and in summer on its organic gardens and pastures.

Composting and recycling play important roles in the center's mission. Scraps and food waste go right back to the earth in which new ingredients are grown. There are even odor-free composting Clivus toilets that yield directly usable plant fertilizer. To those who say that such a system is impractical on a large scale, the Stone Barns people say they're making it practical on the scale they have. Menu prices at the restaurant and café are high because they represent the true cost of producing food in a sustainable way, something ethical consumers should get used to.

Restaurant Nora

Restaurant Nora (202-462-5143), the first certified organic restaurant in the country (the second is California's Ukiah Brewing Co., certified in 2005), is the culinary ethicist's destination restaurant in Washington, D.C. Located in a nineteenth-century carriage house, it's one of the most acclaimed restaurants inside the Beltway. Ninety-five percent of ingredients used at the restaurant come from certified organic producers. Chef-owner Nora Pouillon devotes as much effort to promoting sustainable cuisine as she does producing it, playing a founding role in Chef's Collaborative 2000, a nutritional organization committed to environmentally sustainable living, and consulting with responsible food marketers like Fresh Fields/Whole Foods and Walnut Acres and environmental groups like the Natural Resources Defense Council (NRDC). She was instrumental in the "Give Swordfish a Break" campaign, started in 1998 to relieve fishing pressures on threatened swordfish. She called her chef colleagues all over the country and engaged many of them in a project to remove that fish from their menus. As a result of the joint effort by SeaWeb and NRDC, North Atlantic swordfish have recovered to 94 percent of levels required for the species' likely survival, according to reports from the International Commission for the Conservation of Atlantic Tunas. Numbers are still too low to justify commercial fishing. The campaign drew chefs' attention to the plight of wild fishes in an unprecedented way, and represented the first major effort to involve the culinary community in saving wild species. Hundreds of top chefs participated, and U.S. policies were enacted in 2000 to protect the species. She also puts her philosophy into practice at Asia Nora (202-797-4860).

Chez Panisse
Since 1971, Alice Waters has crafted exceptional locally produced organic and ethical ingredients into great-tasting food at her restaurant, Chez Panisse, in Berkeley, California (510-548-5525). She and her staff have established a network of over sixty farmers, foragers, fishermen, and ranchers to supply the restaurant with products that meet her own high standards of sustainability. The Chez Panisse model has inspired many of today's responsible chefs to break from the older American system of ingredients sourcing, which relied on a small number of purveyors to supply all provisions. Though the older system was simpler, it laid accountability for responsible sourcing on the purveyors, not the chefs and restaurateurs. Waters's approach, bringing chefs as close to the food production sites as possible, benefits the farmers and fishermen as much as it does the restaurant and the consumer, by cutting out middlemen and highlighting the achievements of good players.

rm
As chef at Oceana restaurant in New York, Rick Moonen took Chilean sea bass off his menu when it was his best-selling item. He'd become a leading spokesman for responsible sourcing of "the last wild product": fish. He carries that sensibility with him as he sources only sustainable fish (some wild, some farmed) for his restaurant, rm, at Mandalay Place in Las Vegas. He took Atlantic salmon off his menu also because, as he points out, some farms do it right, but there are too many irresponsible players. Without micromanagement, you can't be sure that what you're getting is always produced in an environmentally sound way.

Other Notable Restaurants

- On the West Coast, Oliveto restaurant in Oakland, California (510-547-5356), is one of many that serve free-range pork from the ethically aware Niman Ranch.

- So does the Flea Street Café in Menlo Park (650-854-1226) and Lucques in Los Angeles (323-655-6277). Places where chefs buy direct from farmers are providing a triple service: oversight of production methods, reduction of transportation pollution between middlemen, and support for the farmers themselves.

- The Herbfarm in Woodinville, Washington (425-485-5300), is legendary for its pasture-raised lamb dishes and nine-course, ecologically sound tasting menu.

- Seattle's Flying Fish (206-728-8595) has partnered with the local Whistling Train Farm for year-round organic produce. Chef Christine Keff refuses to sell Chilean sea bass and farmed Atlantic salmon. Instead, she features wild fish from well-managed fisheries like pole-caught albacore tuna and king salmon, and responsibly farmed fish like striped bass.

Chefs Collaborative

More than a thousand members of the food community participate in a network dedicated to promoting sustainable cuisine through support of local, sustainable, and artisanal cooking. Since 1993, the organization has made education its primary goal. Since many in the community were unaware or ill-informed about the serious ecological threats and inhumane practices of the food industry, the Chefs Collaborative has played a crucial role in raising awareness of the very problems I address here.

The regularly updated Chefs Collaborative restaurant guide lists member restaurants who've agreed to the ethical principles discussed here, and who try to put them into action on their menus. See the entire listing of Chefs Collaborative member restaurants at www.chefscollaborative.org.

For the latest on new alternatives for ethical foods, equipment, and lifestyle, check out the publications of the organization Lifestyles of Health and Sustainability (www.lohas.com) and the Green Guide Institute (www.thegreenguide.com).

Sources

Note: Entries in this listing are loosely arranged into categories that naturally overlap in many cases. Sources may not appear in all applicable categories, so be sure to check the most obvious cateogry (such as "Lamb") but also related listings (such as "Grass-fed and Pasture-raised Meat" and "Organic Meats").

Beverages

Wine
Appellation Wine & Spirits (212-741-9474)

www.astorwines.com (organic wines)

www.ecowine.com (organic wines)

www.freywine.com (organic wines)

Coffee
www.adamsorganiccoffees.com

www.cafecanopy.com

www.CafeLaSemeuse.com

www.cafemam.com

www.deansbeans.com

www.elanorganic.com

www.greenmountaincoffee.com

www.groundsforchange.com

www.jimsorganiccoffee.com

www.kalanicoffee.com

www.mountainviewcoffee.com

www.saltspringcoffee.com

www.urthcaffe.com

Groceries

Fair Trade Products
Certifier
www.transfairusa.org

www.ifat.org

Listings
www.globalexchange.org

www.fairtradefederation.com

Chocolate
www.dagobachocolate.com

www.newmansownorganics.com

Coffee
www.cafecanopy.com

www.CafeLaSemeuse.com

www.cafemam.com

www.mountainviewcoffee.com

Humane and Organic Dairy
www.certifiedhumane.com

www.organicfreshmarket.com (ricotta cheese)

Organic Groceries
www.arrowheadmills.com (grains, flours, nut butters)

www.beanbag.net (beans)

www.celtic-seasalt.com (grains, mustard)

www.dagobachocolate.com (541-664-9030)

www.diamondorganics.com (dried fruits, grains, tea, coffee, herbs, oils, etc.)

www.edenfoods.com (Asian ingredients)

www.garlicgourmet.com (garlic)

www.greatgrainsmilling.com (grains)

www.greenmountainmills.com (grains)

www.lotusfoods.com (exotic rice)

www.newmansownorganics.com

www.organic-planet.com (dried fruits)

www.publix.com (supermarket carries organic shrimp)

www.purelyorganic.com (artichoke cream)

www.seedsavers.org (heirloom seeds)

www.sunorganicfarm.com (grains)

www.thegarlicstore.com (garlic)

www.truefoodsonline.com or www.truefoodsmarket.com (Brazil nuts, wild rice)

www.villageorganics.com (Thai ingredients, coconut milk, vinegar)

www.wholesomesweeteners.com (sugar)

www.woodprairie.com (nuts)

www.worldofrice.com (exotic rice)

www.yatatex.com (Japanese rice)

Rain Forest–Friendly Products
www.transfairusa.org

www.rainforest-alliance.org

www.dagobachocolate.com (541-664-9030) (chocolate)

www.cafemam.com (coffee)

www.cafecanopy.com (coffee)

www.chiquita.com (Rainforest Alliance–certified bananas)

Specialty and Ethnic Groceries
http://shop.deliciousorganics.com (Brazil nuts)

www.agferrari.com (spaghetti *alla chitarra*)

www.asianfoodgrocer.com

www.cybercucina.com (Italian)

www.edenfoods.com (Asian ingredients, Japanese)

www.ethnicgrocer.com (foods of all nations)

www.farawayfoods.com (spaghetti *alla chitarra*)

www.goya.com (Spanish and Latino)

www.harvestsensations.com (fresh fava beans in season)

www.importfoods.com

www.kalustyans.com (Middle Eastern, Indian, grains, spices, specialty flours)

www.karibafarms.com (nuts)

www.kitchenmarket.com (Mexican, Southeast Asian)

www.livingtreecommunity.com (nuts)

www.mexgrocer.com (Mexican)

www.mustaphas.com (Moroccan, preserved lemon)

www.oceanmist.com/cardone.htm (info on fresh cardoons, artichokes)

www.orientalpantry.com (Asian foods)

www.pointshop.com (Mediterranean)

www.sunorganicfarm.com (nuts)

www.villageorganics.com (Thai ingredients, coconut milk)

Sugar
www.lasiembra.com

www.levelground.com

www.marquisproject.com

www.wholesomesweeteners.com (organic Fair Trade American sugar)

Meat and Poultry

Beef
www.dakotabeefcompany.com

www.diamondorganics.com (beef, bison, chicken, grass-fed lamb, ham, pork, fish)

www.meadowraisedmeats.com (veal, beef, chicken, pork, lamb, etc.)

www.organicvalley.coop (beef, pork, poultry)

www.pratherranch.com

www.sunnysidefarms.com

Pork
Charis Eco-farm, Staunton, VA
(540-886-8486)

Four Winds Farm, River Falls, WI
(715-425-6037) (sells individual cuts)

Fresh Start Farms, Bend, OR
(541-317-5925)

Garden Mountain Farm, Tazwell, VA
(276-472-2511)

Lake View Farm, Halsey, OR
(541-369-2393)

www.andersonfarm.us

www.brokenarrowranch.com (wild boar)

www.colemannatural.com (800-442-8666) (beef, bison, lamb, pork, chicken)

www.diamondorganics.com (beef, bison, grass-fed lamb, pork, fish)

www.flyingpigsfarm.com (small cuts always available)

www.jolievuefarms.com

www.naturalmeat.com (beef, chicken, pork)

www.nimanranch.com (510-808-0340) (beef, pork, lamb; small cuts always available, including humanely raised hams)

www.oldmillfarm.org (pork sometimes available)

www.organicvalley.coop (beef, pork, poultry)

www.peacefulpastures.com

www.sforganic.com (organic pork)

www.texasgrassfedbeef.com

www.thegreenguide.com (212-598-4910) Contact them for a "Smart Shopper's Beef & Pork" wallet card with some suggested brands.

Lamb

www.colemannatural.com (800-442-8666) (beef, bison, lamb, pork, chicken)

www.diamondorganics.com (beef, bison, grass-fed lamb, pork, fish)

www.jamisonfarm.com (lamb)

www.meadowraisedmeats.com (veal, beef, chicken, pork, lamb, etc.)

www.michiganorganic.org/zensheep/ (lamb)

www.nimanranch.com (510-808-0340) (beef, pork, lamb)

www.touchstonefarm.org (lamb)

Chicken/Turkey

www.dartagnan.com (including heritage and wild turkeys)

www.diamondorganics.com (beef, chicken, ham, bison)

www.eberlypoultry.com

www.lobels.com

www.meadowraisedmeats.com (veal, beef, chicken, pork, lamb, etc.)

www.naturalmeat.com (beef, chicken, pork)

www.organicvalley.coop (beef, pork, poultry)

www.sforganic.com (beef, pork, chicken)

www.wisekosher.com (kosher, organic chicken and turkey)

Game Meats

Byards, Clarksville, TN (931-237-5006) (rabbit)

Snoep Winkel Farm, Branchville, NJ (973-702-2047) (rabbit and goat)

www.brokenarrowranch.com (free-range venison, antelope, wild boar)

www.dartagnan.com (organic bison, duck, small game birds, ostrich, pheasant, rabbit, etc.)

www.eatwild.com (bison)

www.muscodabison.com (bison)

www.njbison.com (bison)

www.organic-buffalo.com (bison)

www.rissmanorganicfarm.com (organic rabbit and duck)

www.schreinerfarms.com (yaks, elk, emu, antelope, and many more, live)

www.uselk.com (elk, bison, venison)

www.yakmeat.us (yak)

Humanely Raised Meats

www.dartagnan.com (game meats, duck livers)

www.diamondorganics.com (bison)

www.dubreton.com (pork)

www.jamisonfarm.com (lamb)

www.lobels.com (free-range poultry)

www.maverickranch.com (heritage pork)

www.meadowraisedmeats.com (veal, beef, chicken, pork, lamb, etc.)

www.michiganorganic.org/zensheep/ (lamb)

www.naturalmeat.com (beef, chicken, pork)

www.overthemoonfarm.com (veal and veal bones)

www.touchstonefarm.org (lamb)

Grass-fed and Pasture-raised Meats

Little Alaska Farm (Maine)
Call: Roger or Linda Fortin (207-933-3300)
or e-mail littleafarm@ctel.net

Vermont Pasture Network
www.uvm.edu/~susagctr/

www.buffalogroves.com (877-468-2833)

www.chilenobeef.com (707-765-6664)

www.conservationbeef.com (877-749-7177)

www.eatwellguide.org

www.eatwild.com

www.grassorganic.com (beef)

www.lasatergrasslandsbeef.com
(866-454-2333)

www.meadowraisedmeats.com
(607-278-5602)

www.newlivestockalliance.org

www.organicpiedmontesebeef.com (beef)

www.sforganic.com (beef)

www.westerngrasslands.com (beef)

Organic Meats
www.dakotabeefcompany.com (beef)

www.diamondorganics.com (beef, bison, chicken, grass-fed lamb, ham, pork, fish)

www.dubreton.com (pork)

www.eatwild.com (bison)

www.grassorganic.com (beef)

www.lobels.com (free-range poultry)

www.michiganorganic.org/zensheep/ (lamb)

www.muscodabison.com (bison)

www.organic-buffalo.com (bison)

www.organicpiedmontesebeef.com (beef)

www.organicvalley.coop (beef, pork, poultry)

www.pccnaturalmarkets.com (beef)

www.pratherranch.com (beef)

www.rissmanorganicfarm.com (rabbit, chicken, turkey, duck)

www.sforganic.com (beef, pork, chicken)

www.sunnysidefarms.com (beef)

www.wisekosher.com (kosher chicken and turkey)

Natural Meats
www.3br.com

www.brokenarrowranch.com (free-range venison, antelope, wild boar)

www.colemannatural.com (800-442-8666) (beef, bison, lamb, pork, chicken)

www.creekstonefarmspremiumbeef.com (beef)

www.montanarange.com (beef)

www.naturalmeat.com (beef, chicken, pork)

www.nimanranch.com (510-808-0340) (beef, pork, lamb)

www.thegreenguide.com (212-598-4910) Contact them for a "Smart Shopper's Beef & Pork" wallet card with some suggested brands.

Produce

Organic Produce
www.diamondorganics.com

www.eatwellguide.org

www.garlicgourmet.com

www.iatp.org

www.organicmushrooms.com

www.seedsavers.org (heirloom seeds)

www.thegarlicstore.com

Local Produce
www.csrees.usda.gov/qlinks/partners/state_partners.html

www.eatwellguide.org

www.foodroutes.org

www.gardenersnet.com/atoz/ces.htm

www.localharvest.org

www.sustainabletable.org

www.wegmans.com

www.wholefoodsmarket.com

Seafood

Fish and Shellfish
www.abalonefarm.com (farmed abalone)

www.bcspawnonkelp.com (herring roe)

www.beststonecrabs.com (stone crab claws)

www.buygourmetfoods.com/k/kelp/Miyako-Pickled-Herring-Roe-With-Kelp-B00023NHBE.htm (herring roe)

www.cajungrocer.com (crawfish)

www.cityfish.com (crab)

www.deltapride.com (U.S. farmed catfish)

www.farmtomarket.com (farmed white sturgeon)

www.freshfloridastonecrab.com (stone crab claws)

www.f2m.com (crab, fish, and shellfish)

www.gortonsfreshseafood.com

www.klcrawfishfarms.com (crawfish)

www.legalseafoods.com

www.markys.com (pickled anchovies)

www.maryluseafoods.com (sustainable tuna and Pacific fish) (707-465-0284)

www.oceanboyfarms.com (863-983-9941) (organic shrimp)

www.patsclams.com (farmed littleneck clams)

www.pelicanpackers.com (sustainable tuna)

www.seafoodsuperstore.com

www.simplyseafood.com (crab)

www.tienda.com (pickled anchovies)

www.usabalone.com (farmed abalone)

www.westportwa.com/seafood/prawns/ (spot prawns)

Caviar
www.caviaremptor.org

www.caviarideas.com

www.kysmokedfish.com

www.sterlingcaviar.com

www.sunbursttrout.com

www.tsarnicoulai.com

Seafood Ethical Buyer's Guides
www.blueocean.org

www.ecofish.com

www.mbayaq.org

www.msc.org

www.oceansalive.org

www.seafoodchoices.com

www.webseafood.com/sustainability/
seafoodadvisorylist.htm

Information

Certifying Agencies
www.americanhumane.org ("Free-Farmed"
certification)

www.ams.usda.gov/lsg/lsarc.htm

www.certifiedhumane.com

www.eatwellguide.org

www.farmtotable.org

Community-supported Agriculture (CSA)
www.csacenter.org

www.nal.usda.gov/afsic/csa/

Equipment
www.quickspice.com
(Japanese mandoline)

www.waterfiltercomparisons.net

Humane Certifying Agencies
www.ams.usda.gov/lsg/lsarc.htm

www.certifiedhumane.com

www.farmtotable.org

Organic Demographic Information
www.eatwellguide.org

www.iatp.org

www.lohas.com

Pesticide Rankings
www.foodnews.org

Political/Religious
www.lcv.org

www.sierraclub.org

www.whatwouldjesusdrive.org

Socially Responsible Company Listings
www.chefscollaborative.org

www.greenpages.org

www.localharvest.org

www.lohas.com

www.workingassets.com

Index

miso-marinated, baked in a pouch (substitute), 282

black-eyed peas, organic lamb stew on red rice with (substitute), 162–63

black sea bass, 238

blue crabs, 250

bluefin tuna, 305, 308

bluefish, 238
  grilled, zucchini spaghetti with garlicky clams and, 239–40
  miso-marinated, baked in a pouch (substitute), 282

Blue Hill at Stone Barns, 320–21

Blue Ocean Institute, 293, 304, 330

Blunt, Roy, 12

Bolourchi, Mark, 217–18

boquerones, 230, 231

bottled water, 26–27, 28

Brazil nuts, 201
  toasted hard red wheat pilaf with caramelized shallots, figs, and, 78–79
  wheat pilaf with cumin lamb, 80–81

bread(s)
  focaccia with cardoons, 112–13
  whole-grain health bread, 51–52
  See also sandwiches

Bright Food Shop, 56

broccoli, 103

broccoli rabe and tomato fondu with pan-fried catfish strips, 242–43

broth
  mussel, 288
  parsley-tomato, clams in, 248
  spinach and sage gnocchi in, with tiny chicken quenelles, 192–93
  See also stock

brown stock, 154, 155–56, 320

Bt (Bacillus thuringiensis), 98–99

buffalo. See bison

Burger King, 16

Bush, George W., 9, 10–11

butter, clarified, 223

buying food

buying local, 33–38, 41, 90, 91

direct from meat producers, 142–43, 327–29

ethical produce priorities, 88–92

seafood, 209, 330–31

source listings, 325–30

C

CAAR (Coastal Alliance for Aquaculture Reform), 217

cabbage, 88
  African djolof rice with salty vegetables and lamb mafé, 158–59
  caraway-coriander wilted Savoy cabbage, 111
  lamb mafé with, 160–61
  Southeast Asian slaw, 109; coco-vegetable rice with tamarind chicken skewers, 62–63
  stuffed (mushroom-tofu halupki), 120–21
  tiny mussel salads on the half shell with Asian aioli, 290–91

Café Mam, 24

Café Marquesa, 319

Cajun Arctic char, 236–37

cake, amaranth, with cinnamon banana sauce, 69

calamari, 296

calico scallops, 312

canary bean(s), 49
  and garlic soup, with saffron, 53

caramelized apples and yams, 110

caraway-coriander wilted Savoy cabbage, 111

cardamom-scented grass-fed rib steak with herb vinaigrette, 150–51

cardoons, focaccia with, 112–13

Carroll, John, 201

carrots
  African djolof rice with salty vegetables and lamb mafé, 158–59
  lamb mafé with, 160–61
  Moroccan squash tagine with couscous, 122–23
  vegetable stew on polenta, 132–33

cashews, spiced, roasted quail salad with, 200–201

© TUAN PU WANG

ABOUT THE AUTHOR

A graduate of the Culinary Institute of America (CIA), with a degree in journalism from New York University, JAY WEINSTEIN is a protégé of Jasper White and has cooked at Le Bernardin. He has written two cookbooks and his articles have appeared in the *New York Times* and *Travel & Leisure*. He is the editor of the CIA newsletter *Kitchen and Cook*, and he lives in New York City.